GROUPTHINK

GROUPTHINK

A Study in Self Delusion

CHRISTOPHER BOOKER

Edited by
Richard North

BLOOMSBURY CONTINUUM
LONDON · OXFORD · NEW YORK · NEW DELHI · SYDNEY

BLOOMSBURY CONTINUUM
Bloomsbury Publishing Plc
50 Bedford Square, London, WC1B 3DP, UK

BLOOMSBURY, BLOOMSBURY CONTINUUM and the Diana logo are trademarks of
Bloomsbury Publishing Plc

First published in Great Britain 2020

A catalogue record for this book is available from the British Library

Library of Congress Cataloguing-in-Publication data has been applied for

ISBN: HB: 978-1-4729-5905-8; TPB: 978-1-4729-7954-4; ePub: 978-1-4729-5908-9;
ePDF: 978-1-4729-5907-2

2 4 6 8 10 9 7 5 3 1

Typeset by Deanta Global Publishing Services, Chennai, India
Printed and bound in Great Britain by CPI Group (UK) Ltd, Croydon CR0 4YY

To find out more about our authors and books visit www.bloomsbury.com
and sign up for our newsletters

It is becoming more and more obvious that it is not starvation, it is not microbes, it is not cancer, but man himself who is his greatest danger: because he has no adequate protection against psychic epidemics, which are infinitely more devastating in their effect than the greatest natural catastrophes.

C. G. Jung, *Modern Man in Search of a Soul*

CONTENTS

PREFACE

> It is only by obtaining some sort of insight into the psychology of crowds that it can be understood . . . how powerless they are to hold any opinions other than those which are imposed upon them.
>
> Gustave Le Bon, *The Crowd*

As I write this in the early months of 2019, few would deny that the world around us is in many ways in a peculiarly odd and far from happy state. Wherever we look, there is scarcely a single country, society or continent which is not wracked by strains, stresses and divisions which even a decade ago would have been hard to imagine.

What, for instance, do all these familiar features of our time have in common?

1   The spectacular rise in our time of Islamic terrorism, extending its shadow over almost every continent, with its fanatical adherents so possessed by the rightness of their cause that it justifies them killing anyone who does not subscribe to it, and even themselves.
2   The rise of 'identity politics' and the peculiar social and psychological pressure to conform with a whole range of views deemed to be 'politically correct', marked out in those caught up in it by their aggressive intolerance of anyone who or anything which differs from their own beliefs.
3   The omnipresent influence of 'social media', again too often marked out by intolerant abuse of other people and their views.

4 The belief that the greatest threat facing the planet is man-made global warming, from which it can only be saved by eliminating the use of the fossil fuels on which modern civilization was built and continues to rely. Again, this is marked out by a peculiar intolerance of anyone who fails to share that belief, or of any factual evidence which seems to challenge it.

5 The conspicuous alienation of so many governments and political elites from the people they rule over, giving rise to populist movements which can be scorned or ignored.

6 The unprecedentedly divided state of American politics in the age of President Trump, again marked out by the inability of either side to tolerate the views of the other.

7 The similarly divided and chaotic state of politics in the UK following its referendum on leaving the European Union, again marked out by the inability of the multiple factions to understand or tolerate any views which differ from their own.

8 The other strains emerging across the European Union itself, resulting from the belief driving its evolution for over 70 years, that Europe's future must lie in integrating all its individual nations under a unique form of government such as the world had never seen before.

To these we could add countless other examples, from the fanatical intolerance of 'animal rights activists' to the peculiarly unquestioning bias shown on these and many other issues by most of the mainstream Western media, most conspicuously led in Britain by the BBC.

The purpose of this book is to provide the missing key to understanding much about these bewildering times that so many people have found increasingly alarming. We shall be looking at all these examples and more in the light of a remarkable thesis put forward in a book published more than 40 years ago by a professor of psychology at Yale University, Irving Janis.

Janis's field of study was the workings of collective human psychology, and specifically the way in which groups of people can behave when they are taken over by a kind of 'group mind'. Others had written books about this kind of human herd behaviour before, such as *Extraordinary Popular Delusions and the Madness of Crowds*, by a Scottish journalist, Charles MacKay, in 1841. A rather more profound work was *The Crowd*, by a Frenchman, Gustave le Bon, in 1895. But what made Janis's *The Victims of Groupthink* (1972) quite different from these was that, as a disciplined scientific study, it showed for the first time how this kind of collective behaviour operates according to certain consistent and identifiable rules.

A group of people comes to be fixated on some belief or view of the world which seems hugely important to them. They are convinced that their opinion is so self-evidently right that no sensible person could disagree with it. Most telling of all, this leads them to treat all those who differ from their beliefs with a peculiar kind of contemptuous hostility.

When I first read Janis's book, one of my first thoughts was how well it helped to explain and illuminate so much that I had been writing about through most of my professional life. Again and again, I had found myself analysing instances of how groups of people had got carried away en masse by some powerfully beguiling idea which was not properly based on reality. It had invariably turned out to be rooted in some way in a kind of collective make-believe. And in each case, they had displayed a particular form of dismissive intolerance towards anyone who did not share their mind-set.

We are never more aware of groupthink at work than when we come up against people who hold an emphatic opinion on some controversial subject, but who, when questioned on it, turn out not really to have thought it through. They have not looked seriously at the facts or the evidence. They have simply taken their opinions or beliefs on trust, ready-made, from others. But the very fact that their opinions are not based on any real understanding of why they believe what they do only allows them to believe even more insistently and intolerantly that their views are right.

These are the 'victims of groupthink' Janis was writing about all those years ago. Today they are around us more obviously than ever. We meet them socially, we hear and read them incessantly in the media, we see our politicians speaking in the clichés of groupthink all the time. The psychological condition from which they are suffering is contagious, extremely powerful and increasingly showing itself to be potentially very dangerous.

This book is about learning how to recognize the nature and power of groupthink in all its guises. But before we look at a wide range of examples, we need first to establish a more detailed picture of what Janis's analysis tells us about the rules governing the way groupthink works.

INTRODUCTION

The Rules of Groupthink

I use the term 'groupthink' as a quick and easy way to refer to a mode of thinking that people engage in when they are deeply involved in a cohesive in-group, when the members' strivings for unanimity over-ride their motivation to realistically appraise alternative courses of action.

Groupthink is a term of the same order as the words in the Newspeak vocabulary George Orwell presents in his dismaying 1984 – a vocabulary with terms such as 'doublethink' and 'crimethink'. By putting groupthink with those Orwellian words, I realise that groupthink takes on an Orwellian connotation. The invidiousness is intentional: groupthink refers to a deterioration of mental efficiency, reality testing and moral judgment.

Irving Janis, *Victims of Groupthink* (1972)

Of course, we hear people casually using the word groupthink all over the place, usually to dismiss those with whose opinions they disagree. But in consciously adapting this word from George Orwell, Janis was the first person to show that there is a consistent structure to the way the concept operates, which is why his work deserves to be recognized as such a valuable contribution to science. Nevertheless, there is an obvious reason why his book published in 1972 (revised

1

in 1982 as just *Groupthink*) is not better known than it might be. This is that Janis based his theory only on a very specific and limited set of examples.

His particular concern was with several notorious failures of US foreign policy between the 1940s and the 1960s. These included the failure of America to heed intelligence warnings of the Japanese attack on Pearl Harbor in 1941; General MacArthur's fateful decision to advance into North Korea in 1950; President Kennedy's backing for the CIA's disastrous Bay of Pigs invasion of Cuba in 1961; and President Johnson's decision in 1965 to escalate the war in Vietnam. In a later edition he added the conduct of President Nixon and his closest advisers in the Watergate scandal.

What he showed through each of his carefully researched case studies was that all these fiascos had essentially come about for the same reason. Those behind them had been driven by groupthink which failed to take proper account of all the realities of the situation they were faced with. And although Janis several times in his book made lists of the 'symptoms of groupthink', we can draw out the three which are absolutely basic to the way groupthink works, and relevant to all the other examples we are about to look at in this book.

THE THREE DEFINING RULES OF GROUPTHINK

1 That a group of people come to share a common view, opinion or belief that in some way is not based on objective reality. They may be convinced intellectually, morally, politically or even scientifically that it is right. They may be sure from all the evidence they have considered that it is so. But their belief cannot ultimately be tested in a way which could confirm it beyond doubt. It is based on a picture of the world as they imagine to be, or would like it to be. In essence, their collective view will always have in it an element of wishful thinking or make-believe.

2 That, precisely because their shared view is essentially subjective, they need to go out of their way to insist it is so

self-evidently right that a 'consensus' of all right-minded people must agree with it. Their belief has made them an 'in-group', which accepts that any evidence which contradicts it, and the views of anyone who does not agree with it, can be disregarded.

3 The most revealing consequence of this. To reinforce their 'in-group' conviction that they are right, they need to treat the views of anyone who questions it as wholly unacceptable. They are incapable of engaging in any serious dialogue or debate with those who disagree with them. Those outside the bubble must be marginalized and ignored, although, if necessary, their views must be mercilessly caricatured to make them seem ridiculous. If this is not enough, they must be attacked in the most violently contemptuous terms, usually with the aid of some scornfully dismissive label, and somehow morally discredited. The thing which most characterizes any form of groupthink is that dissent cannot be tolerated.

Janis showed how consistently and fatally these rules operated in each of his examples. Those caught up in the 'consensus' rigorously excluded anyone putting forward evidence which might raise doubts about their view. Such people were aggressively shut out from the discussion. And in each case, the refusal to consider any evidence or arguments which contradicted their 'consensus' eventually led to disaster.

But Janis then contrasted this with two examples of US foreign policy initiatives which provided a complete contrast: the Marshall Plan in the late 1940s and the ending of the Cuban missile crisis which had threatened a new world war in 1962. He showed how these were driven by the very opposite of groupthink. In each case, those responsible had deliberately canvassed the widest range of expert opinion, to ensure that all relevant evidence was brought to the table. They wanted to explore every possible consequence of what was being proposed. In each case the policy was outstandingly successful.

Once we recognize how these three elements make up the archetypal rules defining the workings of groupthink, we shall begin to see just how very much more widely they apply than just the narrow set of examples that were the focus of Janis's study. Indeed, they turn out to be one of the most valuable guides to collective human behaviour we have ever been given. We can see how they give us a clearer understanding of innumerable other examples of groupthink in all directions, not least in its various historical manifestations all down the ages.

GROUPTHINK IN HISTORY, POLITICS AND FICTION

One of the more obvious examples of Janis's rules in action can be seen chequering the history of most organized religions. These by definition are belief systems which, once established, have often tended to become ruthlessly intolerant of anyone who does not share them. Such outsiders are labelled as 'heretics', 'infidels' or 'unbelievers'. To protect the established orthodoxy, they must be marginalized, excluded from society, persecuted, punished or even in countless examples put to death. None of the world's great religions has been immune to this tendency, even where it appears to contradict their core beliefs: the followers of Christianity, Judaism, Hinduism and Buddhism have all at different times exhibited this tendency, as have different sects within those religions.

But no religion has remained more consistently prone to it through the centuries than Islam. And of course, there is no more extreme example in our world today than the rise of Islamic terrorist movements such as Isis or al-Qaeda, which are possessed by a form of groupthink so extreme that it turns those carried away by it into merciless killers, prepared not only to murder at random anyone they can see as 'infidels' (chiefly other Muslims), but even to commit suicide themselves in furthering their cause.

Another very obvious instance has been those totalitarian political ideologies such as Communism or Nazism, which likewise showed ruthless intolerance towards any 'subversives', 'dissidents' or anyone not in total obedience to 'the party line' (what in the Soviet Union was termed 'correct thinking'). Again, these outsiders had to be excluded from society, imprisoned, shut away in camps or physically eliminated.

In much less extreme fashion, the divisive world of politics is in fact, by its very nature, constantly prone to groupthink to a greater or lesser degree. Each political in-group has its own ideologically selective slant on the issues of the day and its own tendency to deride and caricature the views of its rivals. This becomes all the more pronounced the further any party or group moves towards the 'hard-left' or 'hard-right' ends of the political spectrum.

But politics also provide plenty of examples more akin to those analysed by Janis, where a small group of senior politicians becomes fixated on some particular policy or project doomed to end in failure because it is based on a flight from reality. One obvious instance Janis could certainly have added to his own case studies was the hubristically obsessive fashion in which George W. Bush and Tony Blair launched their invasion of Iraq in 2003. So fixated were they just on toppling Saddam Hussein that they had never given any practical thought to what might follow once their goal had been achieved. By ruthlessly over-riding any questioning of their strategy, and failing to plan for what might happen next when all the country's administrative infrastructure was destroyed, they plunged Iraq into years of bloody sectarian chaos.

But apart from politics, once we recognize the rules of groupthink, we can identify numerous other examples through the ages. Few episodes in the history of science, for instance, are more famous than the treatment accorded to Galileo for his questioning of the Church's 'consensus' that the earth was the centre of the universe and that the sun moved round it.

Around the same time, Europe was being carried away by as bizarre an example of groupthink as any: the great 'witch craze', based on the hysterical belief that tens of thousands of women and some men should be burned to death or drowned because they had become possessed by the devil. As Hugh Trevor-Roper showed in his account of this extraordinary phenomenon, which endured for more than 200 years, some of the most fanatical cheerleaders for this 'moral panic' were among the foremost intellectuals of the age.

A more recent and much more short-lived example, often described at the time as a 'witch-hunt', was the hysteria whipped up in the USA in the early 1950s by Senator Joseph McCarthy and his Senate Un-American Activities Committee, against anyone who could be demonized as a 'Communist' and therefore a traitor. There were indeed a handful of genuine traitors in America at the time, prepared to betray their country's secrets to the Soviet Union. But as a classic demagogue, McCarthy briefly came to dominate American politics by blowing this up out of any relation to the facts, to the point where he floated off into such obvious make-believe as to bring his own downfall.

In fiction, two of the best-known novels of the twentieth century, George Orwell's *Nineteen Eighty-Four* and Aldous Huxley's *Brave New World*, both centred on an imaginary totalitarian state of the future which attempted to brainwash all its citizens into a rigidly intolerant state of groupthink which obeyed all the familiar rules. It was no accident that Janis adapted his term 'groupthink' from Orwell's thinly disguised picture of life in Stalin's Soviet Union, where the sense of a 'group mind', personified in 'Big Brother', was ruthlessly reinforced by means of endlessly repeated slogans, and ritualized 'hate sessions' directed at anyone daring to dissent in any way from the Party's line.

But fiction contains no more perfect short parable of groupthink in action than Hans Christian Andersen's story 'The Emperor's New Clothes'. When the emperor parades through the streets in what he has been talked into imagining is a dazzling new suit, all his obsequious subjects rush to acclaim it as handsome beyond compare. Only the little hero of the story points out that the emperor is not wearing any clothes at all. He is stark naked. The idea that he is wearing any clothes is wholly imaginary. But by Janis's third rule, of course, those caught up in the 'consensus' make-believe angrily turn on the boy for pointing out nothing less than the truth.

Before we see how Janis's rules apply to some of the more obvious examples of groupthink at work in the world today, however, we must also add one more very important element in the way it comes to exercise its power which Janis didn't touch on, because it wasn't relevant to the specific examples on which he based his study.

THE POWER OF SECOND-HAND THINKING

> Great power is given to ideas propagated by affirmation, repetition and contagion by the circumstances that they acquire in time that mysterious force known as 'prestige'.
>
> Whatever has been a ruling power in the world, whether it be ideas or men, has in the main enforced its authority by means of that irresistible force we call prestige.
>
> Gustave Le Bon, *The Crowd*

Janis's book was really concerned only with how groupthink affected small groups of men in charge of US policy at the highest level. But the forms of groupthink which are the subject of this book are often shared by countless other people, who come to make up what Le Bon called 'the crowd'. The vast majority of these only get carried along by groupthink because they have taken it on ready-made from others. They accept as true what they have been told or read without ever seriously questioning it, which means that they don't really know why they think as they do.

Of course, we all accept much of what we believe or think we know without bothering to check the reliability of whatever source we first learned it from: such as that the Earth is 93 million miles from the Sun, or that Tokyo is the capital of Japan. We take on trust that such things are true because everyone else does, and assume that, if necessary, they can be confirmed by practical evidence. But when it comes to most examples of groupthink, another factor is at work. Although in many cases the belief system behind it begins only with a small group of people, what allows it to catch on much more widely rests on the authority that can be attributed to those who originated it.

Long before Janis came up with his theory of groupthink, similar ideas had been explored less scientifically by Le Bon. One of his shrewdest observations was the crucial part played in changing the opinions of huge numbers of people by 'prestige': the particular deference paid to those taking the lead in putting them forward. We shall see examples of how this principle operates over many different issues and causes, and in each case the power of second-hand thinking, and the crucial role played in shaping it by those who have been accorded some position of 'prestige'.

We shall be looking at instances as varied as the 'Modern Movement' in architecture, which did such immense social and aesthetic damage to Britain's cities in the Sixties; the hysteria worked up over a whole sequence of what turned out to be entirely bogus health scares in the Nineties; and how the belief in global warming was then manipulated by dodgy science into the biggest, most expensive scare the world has ever known. We shall see how the creation of the European Union was itself ultimately a product of the make-believe inseparable from groupthink. And we shall even see how Janis's rules apply to what is arguably the most fundamental scientific question of them all: how life on earth came to evolve.

But there could be no more appropriate place to begin than with a particular manifestation of groupthink as infectious and all-pervasive as any in our time: the rise in recent decades of that remarkable social and political pressure to conform to all the rigid mind-sets lumped together as 'politically correct', notably on the most sensitive issues of all, 'gender' and 'race'. Although this is much the longest case-study in the book, it will set the scene, historically and psychologically, for all that follows.

Part I

*Political Correctness –
A First Case Study*

1

The Origins of Political Correctness

HOW THE FIGHT FOR TOLERANCE LED TO THE NEW
INTOLERANCE

Why do we hate and despise each other so much these days?

Peter Hitchens, *Mail on Sunday*, 2017[1]

In Britain today it seems an army of self-appointed censors –
from internet trolls to angry students, lobby groups, town hall
officials, craven politicians and lawyers and Establishment
figures, as well as a host of other sanctimonious and often
bilious busy-bodies – have taken it upon themselves to police
what we can and cannot think and say.

A. N. Wilson, *Daily Mail*, 30 September 2017

When everybody defers to everyone else's judgment, nobody
thinks for himself. And so perhaps the most unfortunate
aspect of the trendy curriculum is that it trains students to
think with the herd, rather than to think critically. The new
curriculum may be described as the product of an echo effect,
in which different people in the Stanford community, faculty

---

[1] Peter Hitchens, 'Cyclists, drivers and joggers need brakes … on their egos,' *Mail on Sunday*,
27 August 2017.

and students alike, repeated one another's claims until so many people make the same claims that everybody believes them. Such conformity can be psychologically overpowering, but it does not promise to yield the truth or to communicate anything significant.

David Sacks and Peter Thiel, *The Diversity Myth* (1995)[2]

It might seem odd to begin this book with a chapter on political correctness. But to anyone old enough to remember the days before it crept up on us all, it is one of the oddest things to have happened in our lifetime. In fact, the evolution of political correctness over the decades is a perfect case study in the workings of groupthink. And in one way or another the mentality behind it is relevant to all the other examples we shall be looking at. By way of a prelude, we start with a handful of episodes which happened to be making news around the autumn of 2017, when I began writing this book, because they typify the strangely surreal world political correctness has led us into.

In October 2017 it was reported that, in the Leicestershire town of Loughborough, the local council had warned a market trader that, following a complaint from an anonymous member of the public, she must stop selling 'offensive' items on her stall. These turned out to be pottery mugs decorated with pictures of twelfth-century monks, the Knights Templar, who at the time of the Crusades had gone out to the Holy Land to protect Christian pilgrims going to Jerusalem from being slaughtered by the Saracens. Because these monks had murdered Muslims, claimed the complainant, any Muslim passing the trader's stall might be offended. When the stallholder ignored this warning on the grounds that it seemed ridiculous, the council withdrew her licence to trade anywhere in the town.[3]

[2]David O. Sacks and Peter A. Thiel (1995/1998), *The Diversity Myth: Multi-culturalism and Political Intolerance on Campus*. Oakland, CA: The Independent Institute.

[3]Richard Littlejohn, 'Right-on crusade that makes mugs of us all', *Daily Mail*, 13 October 2017.

In Oxford, a student committee at Balliol College prohibited the university's Christian Union from running its usual stall at the annual 'Freshers' Fair', on the grounds that Christianity 'is used in many places as an excuse for homophobia and certain forms of neo-colonialism'. Their presence would therefore 'cause further harm against the already most vulnerable and marginalised groups'.[4]

In Cardiff, at a time when official figures were showing a sharp rise in national crime and that in the previous five years the number of arrests made by the police had halved, police officers were ordered to walk around the streets in women's high heels, to raise awareness of 'domestic violence by men against women'. In Warwickshire police support officers held 'tea-and-cup-cake parties' in community centres to promote 'National Hate Crime Awareness Week', tweeting pictures of themselves with the hashtag #cakenothate.[5]

In the same week in Bristol, police officers painted their fingernails blue to highlight the problem of 'slavery in nails bars'. When this attracted caustic comments on Twitter such as, 'What about nailing some criminals?', Avon and Somerset Police issued a statement announcing that 'if anyone found these comments offensive, please report them to Twitter. If you feel that you were targeted and are the victim of a hate crime, please report this to us. We take this issue extremely seriously.'

In a Belfast cabaret club, two gay men staged a mock wedding conducted by a drag queen in angry protest against the fact the Northern Ireland was the only part of the United Kingdom where same-sex marriage was still illegal, thus denying them their right to the 'dignity' of being able to call each other 'husband'.[6]

---

[4] 'Oxford bans "harmful" Christian Union from freshers' fair', *Daily Telegraph*, 10 October 2017. It is only fair to add that, after this was reported in the national press, a full college student meeting voted to deplore their committee's decision on the grounds that it was against the rights to free speech and religious expression. In future the Christian Union could again have a stall at the fair,

[5] 'High heels to "highlight domestic violence"', *Daily Mail*, 21 October 2017.

[6] '"My love isn't second-class": the struggle for marriage equality in Northern Ireland', *Guardian*, 19 October 2017.

A few weeks later, the Church of England sent out instructions to its 4,700 primary schools that boys as young as five should be told that they were allowed to wear high heels, tiaras or tutus, and that girls should not be made to wear skirts, to avoid offending 'transgender' children who might be wishing to change sex. The new rules were designed to challenge 'homophobic, biphobic and transphobic bullying'. On the same day it was reported that a 27-year-old Christian teacher in Oxfordshire might face the sack for saying 'Well done, girls' to two young pupils, one of whom was a boy who wished to be treated as a girl.[7]

Although none of these examples were untypical, two others which had made front-page news a few weeks earlier were of rather wider significance.

The first, in August, was the sacking from Labour's parliamentary front bench of Sarah Champion, the party's chief spokeswoman on 'Women and Equality' issues. Her offence in the eyes of her fellow Labour MPs was to have written in a national newspaper that 'Britain has a real problem with Pakistani men raping and exploiting young white girls.'[8]

In fact, Champion was better qualified to speak on this particular issue than any other MP, since it had been in her constituency of Rotherham three years earlier that there had come to light one of the most disturbing scandals in modern Britain. It had been revealed that some 1,400 girls in the town, many of them under-age children in state care, had long been systematically drugged, raped and subjected to every kind of criminal abuse by gangs of men, mainly originating from the more primitive tribal areas of Pakistan-controlled Kashmir.

What made this even worse was that, although the local police, councillors and social workers had been well aware of what was going on for more than a decade, they had taken no action. They

---

[7]'Church: let little boys wear tiaras' and 'Facing the sack, teacher who accidentally called transgender boy a girl', both in the *Daily Mail*, 12 November 2017.
[8]*Sun*, 10 August 2017.

had conspired to ignore it and to hush it up because they thought that an issue so obviously involving 'race' was too sensitive to touch.

As a new MP, Champion herself had spoken out strongly about this ever since the horrifying story first emerged. Similar scandals involving mainly Pakistani men had since been widely reported in towns and cities across Britain from Rochdale to Oxford. Again, in each case the local authorities had been turning a blind eye and done nothing.

Champion was thus quite right to say that Britain did indeed have 'a real problem'. But what so incensed her fellow MPs to the point of sacking her was that, by correctly identifying those responsible for these crimes as 'Pakistanis', she had given 'offence'. Yet it had been precisely the collective desire of the authorities to pretend that this problem did not exist which had for so many years allowed these horrendous crimes to continue.

Even more significant – enough to win worldwide coverage – was the sacking of a senior software engineer at the California headquarters of the internet giant Google. James Damore's 'offence' had been to send round to some of his colleagues a thoughtful 3,500-word internal email reflecting on the reasons for the failure of the company's 'diversity' policy to increase the percentage of its employees who were female, particularly in 'high-status' posts and systems engineering.[9]

His email suggested that Google's difficulty in meeting its 'gender targets' might be explained by the fact that, biologically and psychologically, men and women tend in certain respects to be different. Men, he wrote, quoting academic evidence, are more likely than most women to be concerned with 'status', and to be ruthlessly competitive and motivated to aim at top, high-stress, leadership positions. Again, psychometric studies showed that women were, by

---

[9]James Damore, 'Google's ideological echo chamber', July 2017.

and large, less likely than men to be drawn to the particular nature of computer coding and electronic systems work.

On the other hand, he suggested, such studies had shown that many women are more naturally 'empathetic' than men, preferring to work co-operatively with other people rather than aggressively competing with them. They also tend to be more creative, and more at home with 'jobs in artistic or social areas' than with the intricacies of software coding.

Damore was anxious to stress that he was not suggesting that all men or all women were like one thing or the other. He emphasized that there was 'significant overlap' between them. He was only talking about what the evidence showed to be the more likely weighting of motivation and aptitude on both sides, by way of trying to explain why Google was in these respects failing to meet its 'diversity targets'.

But his sacking and the consequent publication of his email provoked uproar. Some, both inside the company and in the wider world, applauded and sympathized with what he had written. But for many others, his suggestion that men and women might in any way be psychologically different was so outrageous as to be definitely a sackable offence.

This was very much the line taken by Google's Indian-born chief executive Sundar Pichai, who explained in a statement that Damore had to be dismissed because he had breached the company's 'basic values', by 'advancing harmful gender stereotypes in our workplace'. 'To suggest that a group of our colleagues have traits that make them less biologically suited to that work', he wrote, 'is offensive'.

What all these stories have in common is the picture they paint of how society had become divided between two groups of people who seemed to have wholly different and incompatible views of the world. The members of one group shared a highly moralistic mind-set in respect of what was permissible for people to say, think or do. They seemed only too eager to spot anyone or anything that could be seen as having given or likely to give offence. And they invariably expressed their tight-lipped disapproval in the same kind of all-too-familiar clichés. The other group stared at the first in amazement, puzzled above all by how anyone could be so obsessively blinkered and so humourlessly intolerant. But this is not the first time in history that we have seen society divided in this way.

THE NEW PURITANISM

Few groups in the history of Britain or America have been given a worse press in later centuries than the Puritans, the members of that ideological movement combining religion with politics which played such an influential role in English and American society in the first half of the seventeenth century. Our image of Puritanism associates it with a peculiar kind of rigidly unforgiving mind-set: an overpowering sense of collective self-righteousness, and a fierce determination to sniff out and punish anyone who did not subscribe to its strict codes of belief and moral conduct.

Until comparatively recently, it would have seemed unthinkable that anything similar could reappear in our own time. But in the wave of 'political correctness' which has swept the Western world in recent years, we can see striking parallels to the fanatical intolerance of those seventeenth-century Puritans. We see the same sense of collective moral superiority, and the same readiness to take offence at anyone or anything which does not conform to its own strict articles of faith. It has indeed become our own contemporary version of what used in the old Soviet Union to be ruthlessly enforced as 'correct thinking'.[10]

---

[10]I first described the psychological similarities between political correctness and Puritanism in my book on the psychology of storytelling, *The Seven Basic Plots: why we tell stories* (Continuum, 2004). After describing the '"feminization" of men and the "masculinization" of women' as having 'become a central feature of that new ideological orthodoxy which was sweeping the Western world under the name of "political correctness"', I called this 'the new secular Puritanism', and discussed how 'the kind of intolerance once associated with the more puritanical forms of religion and the more extreme forms of socialism now reappeared to promote the "rights" of women, homosexuals, racial minorities, the disabled and any group of people who could be portrayed as being "below the line" and therefore discriminated against'.

The list of issues which have become subject to a politically correct 'party line' certainly grows ever longer. But as has been widely observed, what most have in common is the way our New Puritans like to focus their sense of outrage on behalf of any group in society that can be portrayed as the victims of some kind of oppression, prejudice, discrimination or maltreatment at the hands of others. These groups have included every kind of variation on this basic theme of 'victimhood': the oppression of women by men; of children by adults; of sexual minorities by a heterosexual majority; of ethnic minorities by 'racist' whites; of Muslims by Christians; of the disabled by able-bodied society in general; even of animals by humans. And in each case, it is this chance to combine 'virtue-signalling' sympathy for the 'victims' with a venting of outrage at their cruel, prejudiced 'oppressors' which gives this New Puritanism such a powerful moral charge.

But of all the causes this ideology has come to embrace, none have generated a more wide-ranging sense of self-righteous intolerance than those relating to two of the most fundamental social divides of all: gender and race. Here we can trace the various stages whereby this new intolerance gradually evolved out of that paradigm shift in social attitudes which took place way back in the heady years of the 1960s, eventually turning the idealistic dreams of that 'liberated' decade on their head.

STAGE ONE: BEFORE IT ALL BEGAN – THE EARLY FIFTIES

Untune that string, and hark what discord follows.

William Shakespeare, *Troilus and Cressida*, Act II, Scene iii

It is today almost impossible for anyone much under the age of 70 to imagine just how different the world was in the early 1950s.

Not since the dawn of time had anyone doubted that men and women were in many ways biologically and psychologically very different from one another. In Britain and America in those days – as in most societies through human history – it was assumed that, when the vast majority of them grew up, they would hope to pair off with someone of the opposite sex, get married, have children and remain together for the rest of their lives. There were powerful social inhibitions against any form of sex outside marriage (however much this might have taken place behind the scenes). Divorce was socially frowned on and fairly unusual. Single-parent families were almost unknown (except when a parent had died, as many men had during the war). A social stigma still attached to anyone born 'out of wedlock', who was described as 'illegitimate'. Homosexuality was generally viewed as unnatural, and sexual acts between men were a criminal offence, punishable with prison. It was similarly a criminal offence for a woman to abort an unborn child. Husbands were often described as 'the head of the family' and 'the chief breadwinner', as they entered a world of work almost wholly run and dominated by other men, from factories, offices, shipyards and coal mines to the professions, the police, the armed forces and politics.

Although many women worked before they married, once they had become mothers it was customary for most to remain at home as 'housewives', to look after their children and run the household (where, as had been true of mothers, and indeed grandmothers, down the ages, most exercised their own strong matriarchal authority). It was a general social convention for men to treat women, the 'fairer' or 'weaker' sex, protectively and with a special respect. Any attempts by men to force their sexual attentions on a woman were socially disapproved of as beyond the pale.

As Britain in the early Fifties slowly emerged from the shadows of the Second World War and post-war austerity, it was morally and socially still a staid, conservative country, where everyone was said to 'know their place' in a hierarchical class structure. Until one knew someone well enough to call them informally by their 'Christian' name, surnames were the customary form of address for adults: 'Mr Smith', 'Mrs Jones', 'Miss Brown'. The values of discipline, tradition and good manners, a sense of 'duty' and respect for authority figures, were still a core part of the social fabric, as in the respect generally paid to police officers, or to teachers, parents and other adults by the young. Mild physical punishment was still customary in families and schools. Crime figures were at an all-time low.

But when it came to matters of 'race', the first black immigrants who arrived from the West Indies in what they imagined was still a Christian Britain were startled often to be faced with the crudest 'colour prejudice' from being described as 'coloureds' or 'coons' to seeing cards in boarding-house windows reading 'No blacks'.

It was another version of that suspicion and prejudice traditionally shown to new groups of immigrants by countless societies throughout history, in this instance only exacerbated by the colour of their skin. In America, with its very much larger and already resident black population, in many of the southern states blacks were still strictly segregated from whites in a dark echo of apartheid South Africa. To a less blatant extent, this was also true of many big cities elsewhere in the USA.

But around 1955 and 1956, there were the first tremors of an impending cultural and psychological earthquake. In Britain, following America, people were just beginning to experience a new kind of material prosperity like nothing previously known. For the first time, ever more people were owning cars and fridges, or going on foreign holidays. The thrilling novelty of television was becoming a central feature in their lives, not least with the arrival in 1955 of a new TV channel featuring American-style commercials.

But of all the imports from America, there was no more telling harbinger of what was to come than the explosive arrival around 1956 of a startling new type of music. The hypnotic beat of rock 'n' roll, the 'sexy' sound and sight of Elvis Presley, were like nothing anyone had heard before. And this became the most distinctive single influence on the emergence of a self-consciously 'rebellious' teenage culture, separating the young from the adult world in a way that was quite new. Their new music, styles of dress and dancing and American slang terms such as 'hip', 'groovy' and 'cool' – even the first experimenting with drugs – opened up for the young an infinitely thrilling new dream world. Psychologically, this welded them together as an in-group, displaying that tell-tale symptom of any form of groupthink, the need to use dismissive labels for anyone who fails to share it. All adults who didn't understand it or them were scorned as being just dim, boring 'squares'.

Even more than America itself, Britain was embarking on an avalanche of social, moral and psychological change more intense and far-reaching than any in history. Over the following decade, the quiet, conservative Britain of the early Fifties was to be transformed into what seemed in many ways to be an almost unrecognizably different country.

STAGE TWO: THE 'LIBERATED' SIXTIES

When the mood of the music changes, the walls of the city shake.

Popular graffiti in the late 1960s

It was like I was out there, suspended in the air above the city. And I swore by Elvis and all the saints that this last teenage year of mine was going to be a real rave. Yes, man, come what may, this last year of the teenage dream, I was out for kicks and fantasy.

Colin MacInnes, *Absolute Beginners* (1959)

I have a dream that my four little children will one day live in a nation where they will not be judged by the color of their skin but by the content of their character.

Martin Luther King Jr, Washington, 28 August 1963

As the Western world in general entered on an unprecedented kind of 'never had it so good' prosperity, nowhere more than in Britain was that old familiar framework of moral conventions and social assumptions which had held sway until the mid-Fifties being junked wholesale. By the end of the Fifties, a new phrase heard everywhere was the need to be 'with it'. No one ever defined the nature of the 'it' with which one was meant to be, but everyone knew implicitly what it meant. There was a general sense that one should be on this escalator carrying society ever more rapidly up into an exhilarating new kind of future.

The general mood was one of heady optimism, which nothing seemed better to symbolize than the election in 1960 of the charismatic, 43-year-old John F. Kennedy as easily America's youngest-ever president, for what promised to be a new age of youthful idealism.

When in that same year Britain's Conservative Prime Minister Harold Macmillan famously spoke of a 'wind of change' blowing through Africa, he was specifically referring to the speed with which Britain was now becoming liberated from its still worldwide empire, handing its colonies over to new local black and brown rulers, as well as endorsing the general 'abhorrence' felt for the whites-only regime in apartheid South Africa. But he might have been referring not just to Africa but to almost everything else going on at the time.

So intense was the pace of change that by the end of 1962 even the formerly deferential BBC was transfixing mass audiences with its weekly late-night satire show, *That Was The Week That Was* (*TW3*), with its team of young actors mocking everything the 'Old England' and its values had stood for, including the ageing, upper-class Macmillan himself.

By 1963, as his Conservative government fell apart amid sex scandals, bewilderment and general hysteria, a new sound was becoming ever louder through the year, as Britain was swept by 'Beatlemania'. The four irrepressible lower-middle-class Beatles from Liverpool, with their contagiously cheerful and hopeful early love songs ('She Loves You', 'I Wanna Hold Your Hand'), had made them, alongside President Kennedy, the new young 'dream heroes' of the decade. By 1964 and 1965, as Britain became obsessed with the doings of rock 'n' roll singers, working-class actors, photographers' pretty model girls and trendy clothes designers,[11] even America was

---

[11]These were now receiving such obsessive coverage by the media that they had come to represent what I called in *Private Eye* at the time the 'New Aristocracy'.

gazing in awe at the new 'classless', 'irreverent' pop culture that had transformed stiff old bowler-hatted and cloth-capped London into the 'most swinging city in the world'.

So far and so fast had Britain travelled in just a few short years that it was as though it had been through a bloodless revolution. And as those traditional social and moral values of the early Fifties became a fading memory, no phrase better reflected the nature of what had replaced them than the 'permissive society' that Britain had now become, with particular reference to everything surrounding its liberated new view of sex.

Led by the young, but spreading out socially ever wider, sexual promiscuity was becoming socially accepted as never before. And this seemed to apply just as much to the behaviour of many girls and young women as it did to men, not least thanks to their being given new 'power over their bodies' by the availability since 1961 of the contraceptive pill.[12] Young women could thus join in 'the sexual revolution' as eagerly as men, as was reflected in 1965 by the speed with which they took to the new fashion for wearing sexually provocative, ever shorter 'miniskirts'.

But nowhere was this urge for liberation more publicly evident than in the relentless drive to 'push back the boundaries' in how the imagery of sex could be portrayed in books, on screen and on stage, and how openly female nudity could now be displayed in magazines and even newspapers. Ever commoner became the use of hitherto socially taboo four-letter words. And anyone daring to question all this new 'permissiveness' was scornfully labelled as just a 'bigot', a 'prude' or a 'Victorian throwback'.

If the keynote of the time was 'liberation' from old inhibitions and constrictions, so this included freedom from old forms of prejudice

---

[12]It was faintly ironic that Britain's most celebrated ever political 'sex scandal', which in June 1963 led to the resignation of the Conservative War Minister John Profumo, for denying to the House of Commons that he had slept with 19-year-old Christine Keeler, should have coincided with the 'New Morality' and the 'sexual revolution' that was at the same time proclaiming that it was fine for everyone else, apart from them, to sleep with each other.

and intolerance. It seemed quite natural that in 1967 Britain should scrap the 'cruel' and 'archaic' laws which had made it illegal for men to engage in sex with one another, and for women to have abortions (again hailed as giving them new 'power over their own bodies'). Both these moves were soon to be followed in America.

It was these same ideals of liberation, tolerance and equality which inspired the great Sixties revulsion against equally cruel and archaic racial prejudice. In America, the US civil rights movement (which also included campaigners for 'Women's Liberation') had launched its nationwide battle to give equal rights to the country's large black minority. Few events more vividly symbolized the new idealism of the time than the Rev Martin Luther King's 'I have a dream' speech in Washington in August 1963, in front of a million black and white demonstrators, in which his dream was that black people might be treated as equal with whites, and live together in 'brotherhood'.

Two months later, the assassination of President Kennedy was the most shocking event since the Second World War. But before his death he had already begun to swing America's political establishment firmly behind moves to end the scandal of segregation in the South, and racial prejudice in general, marked in 1964 by the historic Civil Rights Act, trenchantly reaffirming that core principle of the Declaration of Independence, that 'All men are created equal.'

On a much smaller scale, in Britain, when a racist who had campaigned for all black immigrants to be 'sent home to where they came from' was in 1964 elected as a Conservative MP, this was so at odds with the liberal spirit of the time that he was near-universally ostracized. In 1968 Enoch Powell, a former Conservative cabinet minister and still a front-bench spokesman for his party, made his notoriously inflammatory speech predicting that within 15 or 20 years 'the black man will have the whip hand over the white man' in Britain, and that he foresaw black immigration leading to a river of blood. As by far the most blatantly racist speech ever made by a senior British politician, this provoked a nationwide wave of revulsion. Although Powell was supported by a minority of mainly working-class white racists, he was instantly sacked by his party and became a political pariah.

This reaction was certainly a measure of how much more liberal in its views British society had become. But it was also a sign that, after all the heady excitements of the previous decade, towards the end of the Sixties the skies were darkening.

As for the great 'sexual revolution', as one later American account delicately put it, liberation 'from the sexual restraints of the Western tradition' had not produced 'a utopia of untrammelled satisfaction', and 'above all, many instances of regret'.[13] Marriages were collapsing so fast that by 1972 the divorce rate would have more than quadrupled since 1956. Although many couples were now just openly living together, far more children were now growing up without two parents. The explosion in the availability of sexual imagery had led to little more than a repetitive and spiritless wilderness of pornography, equally demeaning in different ways to both women and men.

In fact, no change of mood in the Sixties was more abrupt than that which took place in the year of 1968. Only a year before, spreading from California across the West, 1967 had been acclaimed as the 'Year of Flower Power': 'peace', 'love' and 'hippy bells', fuelled by heavy doses of marijuana and LSD. But just months later, 1968 saw an extraordinary wave of unrest sweeping across the world. In the US and Europe there were huge demonstrations against America's involvement in the Vietnam War, leading to violent clashes with riot police. The ideals and optimism of the decade had given way to the anger and disillusionment which inspired mass student 'sit-ins' in universities and street demonstrations in a score of countries, from America and Europe to Cairo and Mexico City, protesting against every kind of authority.[14]

[13] *The Diversity Myth*, op.cit., 114.
[14] 1968 was also marked by the murders in the US of Martin Luther King and President Kennedy's brother Robert by assassins opposed to their liberal views. In Czechoslovakia the 'Prague Spring' saw a striking revolt against the totalitarian rule of Soviet Communism.

A leading part in many of these protests was played by a new wave of young 'neo-Marxists', who saw the world in appealingly simple terms as essentially divided between two groups. One included those 'above the line', enjoying all the privilege and power. The other consisted of all those other groups 'below the line', whom they used their power to dominate and oppress. From now on versions of this shaping image were to provide an ever more influential underpinning to the story.

Already in America in particular it was becoming obvious that some of those who had been at the forefront of the campaigns for equality between women and men, blacks and whites, were showing a new sense of frustration. The supposed advances they had so far made, they felt, had not yet gone anything like far enough.

The euphoric revolution of the 'Swinging Sixties' was morphing into a new phase.

STAGE THREE: THE SIXTIES 'DREAM' GIVES WAY TO FRUSTRATION

> The world has lost its soul, and I my sex . . . bras are a ludicrous invention, but if you make bra-lessness a rule, you are just subjecting yourself to another repression.
>
> Germaine Greer, *The Female Eunuch* (1970)

The problem with revolutions is that, once started, they find it hard to know where to stop. Those caught up in them push ever harder in chasing their dream of a new kind of society, until their revolution ends up producing consequences very different from anything imagined when it began.

When two black US athletes startled the world in 1968 by giving defiant 'Black Power' salutes from the medal-winners' podium at the Mexico Olympic Games, they were indicating that the Sixties had not given America's black people the freedom and equality of which they had dreamed. Instead of the kind of peaceful integration into white society fought for by Martin Luther King, the Black Panther and Black Power movements saw the future lying in blacks celebrating their own separate cultural identity as 'African-Americans'. Their slogan was 'Black is Beautiful'.[15]

They were not alone. In 1969, battles with the police around the Stonewall Inn, frequented by homosexuals in New York's Greenwich Village, led to the setting up of the Gay Liberation Front, not just to campaign for more freedom from oppressive laws and prejudice than they had so far won but to celebrate their own separate identity from heterosexual society. Their slogan was 'Gay Pride'.

Campaigning alongside blacks and white liberals in the US civil rights movement had been supporters of 'Women's Lib'. But by the late Sixties its younger members were becoming fiercely restive at how little had been achieved by their original leaders such as Betty Friedan, who believed that women should continue to wear make-up and look attractive to men. By 1969 this had given rise to what became known as 'Second-Wave Feminism' (the first wave having been the successful fight earlier in the century for women's right to vote). Like the more militant blacks and gays, the younger generation of feminists saw the future in asserting their own separate identity from the men who had oppressed them for so long. Many were proud to be lesbians.[16]

In 1970, a best-selling book which became something of a bible for the new-wave feminists was *The Female Eunuch* by Germaine Greer. Although not herself a lesbian, she drew a vitriolic caricature of men as selfishly unfeeling bullies, parodies of macho masculinity, who hated women and only wanted to keep them in a state of subservience.[17]

---

[15]In the last year or two of his life, before his assassination in 1968, King had himself been moving in this direction, as he became disillusioned by the progress made with his earlier dream that blacks and whites could fully integrate and live together in brotherhood.,

[16]See Emile E. Roy (2009) in: *The personal is historical: the impact of lesbian identity on the Sonoma county women's movement and beyond.* https://pdfs.semanticscholar.org/7ef5/63482432ebccebdbc530584a67815f76e4ca.pdf Roy quotes at length Ruth Mahaney, a 'Black studies' lecturer and LGBT activist at the City College, San Francisco, who retails concerns that potential black students might be put off her classes, 'because it was just a bunch of lesbians in Women's Studies'. The fact was however that a great deal of the younger people that were participating in the women's movement at this time were indeed lesbians, including Mahaney.

[17]Greer also, with equal contempt, portrayed other men as being weak, useless wimps, who were self-centred and resentful of women in a different way.

'Women', she wrote, 'have no idea how much men hate them'. But Greer did not suggest that the answer to this might be for men therefore to learn to develop those softer, more selfless qualities traditionally viewed as 'feminine', such as empathetic feeling and caring for other people.[18] Quite apart from what Greer painted as the millions of bored, lonely mothers chained at home to screaming children, she twice singled out nurses kidded into 'feeling good because they are relieving pain', underpaid, overworked, 'tired, resentful and harried'. Women, in short, were society's real victims, 'the only true proletariat left'.

Greer didn't want to see women as 'feminine' at all. She went out of her way to show how similar women were, biologically and mentally, to the hated men. Genetically, the only tiny difference between them, she emphasised, was a single chromosome out of 48. Tests had shown that when it came to 'non-verbal cognitive abilities' such as 'abstract reasoning' and mathematical and scientific skills, 'no significant pattern of difference has emerged, except for the slight pre-eminence of the girls'. But in an interview she compared them with farm animals, castrated to make them 'docile'. They have 'been cut off from their capacity for action, it's a process that sacrifices vigour for delicacy, and it's one that's got to be changed'. This meant, she argued, that women should learn to become just as tough and assertive as men, able to compete with them on masculine terms. In other words, they must develop precisely those self-centred qualities that in men she so affected to despise.[19]

---

[18]Greer was equally caustic about the idea of 'feminine' intuition, which she dismissed as 'only a faculty for observing tiny, insignificant aspects of behaviour and forming an empirical conclusion which cannot be syllogistically examined'.

[19]Greer's belief that it was demeaning for mothers to be forced to stay 'bored' at home 'chained to their screaming children' was to become increasingly fashionable. Its corollary was that they should instead be freed to 'fulfil themselves' by going out to work, which meant that they would often then have to pay other women to look after their children. But this threw up a contradiction. Why should it be considered demeaning for a mother to look after her own children but not for another woman to do so? Presumably because this enabled the other woman to 'fulfil herself' by performing the same task as part of her work. A study presented to the World Economic Forum in 2018 showed that childcare costs in Britain were the highest in the world, absorbing up to a third of a family's income.

Although as yet these much more militant groups represented only tiny if vocal minorities, the new liberal attitudes which had become established in the Sixties continued to extend their influence ever more widely through the Seventies. The talk was no longer of 'responsibilities' but of 'rights'. Society in general became familiar with the idea of 'male chauvinism' and 'sexism'. It became increasingly fashionable, for instance, that men should play more of a role in traditionally female tasks such as cooking and housework, and be present in the delivery room for the birth of their children.[20] The word 'mankind' gave way to 'humankind', 'chairman' became just 'chair', 'spokesman' and 'spokeswoman' were replaced by 'spokesperson', actresses wished to be known as just 'actors', women should no longer be differentiated as 'Mrs' or 'Miss' but described equally as just 'Ms'. Even wives and husbands, in a society where ever more couples were now living together outside marriage, were gradually learning to refer to each other as just 'my partner'.

Similarly, society came generally to use the word 'gays' rather than 'homosexuals'(let alone such offensive terms as 'faggots', 'queers' or 'poofs'), accepting them on much more equal terms than before as part of the general community.

In Britain the state stepped in with new laws and bureaucratic bodies to enforce this new 'equality agenda'. The Equal Pay Act of 1970 made it a criminal offence for employers not to pay men and women at the same rate for the same work. The Sex Discrimination Act of 1975 was designed to combat discrimination against women in the workplace and education. The Act was to operate through a new Equal Opportunities Commission based in Manchester (which *Private Eye* promptly suggested should be renamed 'Personchester'). This was followed in 1976 by the Race Relations Act, with its own Racial Equality Commission, to end any form of discrimination against people on grounds of ethnicity or colour. These new initiatives were to work in two ways. More immediately, they were designed to

---

[20]It also became fashionable from the Sixties onwards for many young men to grow their hair down to their shoulders.

provide a legal framework whereby women and members of ethnic minorities could demand redress if they considered that they had been discriminated against by employers on grounds of race or gender.[21]

But already moves were afoot to push the equality agenda by what became known as more 'pro-active' means. This was by introducing policies of positive discrimination (or affirmative action as it was known in the US). Deliberate efforts should be made to ensure that many more jobs and senior positions should go to women and members of ethnic minorities rather than to white males. This 'reverse discrimination' policy was to have the disturbing consequence of candidates being preferred for jobs not on their suitability but simply because they met the required 'diversity' criteria. In too many cases it would emerge in practice that they were less fitted for the work than the white males to whom they had been preferred.

As it happened in fact, around this time one group of non-white immigrants to Britain were now making such remarkable progress that they were bringing about a hugely beneficial change to Britain's economic and social life. These were the 27,000 East African Asians of Indian descent expelled from Uganda in 1972 (where, despite being only 1 per cent of the population, their businesses earned a fifth of the country's income). When many of these Indian families soon opened corner shops, their entrepreneurial skills, hard work and willingness to keep their businesses open until late at night quickly revolutionized Britain's hitherto sleepy retail trade.[22] But the dramatic success story of these African-Asian immigrants had

---

[21]This was to lead in some cases to very odd consequences, as when a six-months-pregnant woman went to an industrial tribunal to complain that she had been discriminated against because she had been turned down for a job which involved heavy lifting, even though she admitted that this would have been physically too much for her.

[22]As early as 1985, only 13 years after their arrival, the Inland Revenue announced that the commonest name of people whose yearly incomes had for the first time exceeded £1 million was no longer 'Smith' but 'Patel': all East African Asians.

required no help from new laws or the need to meet 'diversity' targets.[23]

This was equally true of another even more striking victory for the 'new equality': the choice in 1975 of a woman to lead the Conservative Party and her election in 1979 as Britain's first female prime minister.[24]

Already dubbed in the Soviet Union as 'the Iron Lady', and soon being described as 'the only man in the Cabinet', Margaret Thatcher might have seemed to be just what Greer had been calling for: a woman capable of out-competing men on their own terms. No one, however, could have been more scornfully opposed to her than the militant feminists. This tough-minded, right-wing lady who was 'not for turning' was not at all the kind of new woman they had in mind.

Indeed, it was in the following decade, the Eighties, when Mrs Thatcher and her strong-minded conservative ally President Ronald Reagan became the two most forceful leaders in the Western world, that all these different causes finally came to be melded together in

---

[23]The distinguished black US academic Dr Thomas Sowell, in a comprehensive study of 'affirmative action' policies around the world, showed that, both economically and educationally, black Americans had made a much more dramatic advance in the 20 years before the civil rights legislation of the 1960s than they did in the years that followed. In 1940, 87 per cent of black families had incomes below the official poverty line. By 1960 this had dropped to 47 per cent, largely due to America's growing post-war prosperity and the move of three million blacks from the South to northern states, to escape segregation laws and poor black schooling. 'Vast numbers of blacks', as Stowell comments, had 'lifted themselves out of poverty "by their own bootstraps", as the saying goes'. In the 1970s, under the federal government's new 'affirmative action programs', this percentage only dropped further from 30 per cent to 29 per cent.

As shown by another study cited by Sowell, the chief beneficiaries of affirmative action were the top 20 per cent of black income earners, whose share rose between the 1960s and 1992 at the same rate as their white counterparts. But the income of the lowest 20 per cent of blacks actually fell, at twice the rate of their white counterparts. See Stowell (2004), *Affirmative Action Around the World*. Yale: Nota Bene.

[24]Mrs Thatcher was in fact one of only 19 women MPs in the 1979 House of Commons (3 per cent), and there were still no MPs from ethnic minorities. In the US, it was already being viewed as shocking that only one Senator out of 100 was a woman.

the all-embracing ideology that was to become known as 'political correctness'.

STAGE FOUR: ENTER THE NIGHTMARE WORLD OF 'DIVERSITY' AND 'MULTI-CULTURALISM'

> The notion of political correctness has ignited controversy across the land. And although the movement arises from the laudable desire to sweep away the debris of racism and sexism and hatred, it replaces old prejudices with new ones. It declares certain topics off-limits, certain expression off-limits, even certain gestures off-limits.
>
> Speech by President George H. W. Bush, University of
> Michigan, May 1991

It was back in the early Seventies that the term 'politically correct' had first come to be used in its contemporary sense, by American New Left feminists. In 1970 a contributor to an anthology called *The Black Woman* wrote that 'a man cannot be a [male] chauvinist and politically correct.'[25] It later came to be used sarcastically, as when some 'sexist' or 'racist' comment could be derided, in a parody of a Red Guard in Mao Zedong's still recent Chinese 'Cultural Revolution', as 'not very politically correct, Comrade!'

But it was not until the Eighties that the term became more widely used in the sense now familiar. This was, firstly, because it was in those years that the pressure to hold 'politically correct' views dramatically moved up several notches, particularly in American universities. But it also then came to be used derisively by those opposed to it,

---

[25]In a useful history of the term 'Political Correctness' on Wikipedia, its first use is traced back to a US Supreme Court judgment in 1792, and it was used in this literal sense through the nineteenth century. In 1934 the *New York Times* wrote that Nazi Germany was only issuing reporting permits to 'pure Aryans whose opinions are politically correct' (at much the same time that Stalin's Soviet Union was enforcing its idea of 'correct thinking'). But it was not until the Seventies that it first came to be used in the contemporary sense.

notably after Allan Bloom in 1987 attacked it in his best-selling book *The Closing of the American Mind.*

In fact, if one had to pick one moment when 'political correctness' began to emerge in the more extreme and all-embracing form later to become so familiar, it might have been in January that same year, when around 500 students and faculty members of Stanford University in California gathered to hear a speech by the leading black civil rights campaigner, the Rev Jesse Jackson. Even Jackson was taken aback when, after hearing him, the crowd surged angrily across the campus to present a list of demands to a meeting of the university Senate, repeatedly chanting, 'Hey, hey, ho, ho, Western Culture's got to go.'

As chronicled five years later in a remarkable book, *The Diversity Myth: Multiculturalism and Political Intolerance on Campus* by two Stanford students of the time,[26] this was the start of a wave of hysteria that was to sweep through one of America's most respected universities like a cross between a psychic epidemic and an extraordinary *coup d'état*, with overtones of that 'Cultural Revolution' in China.

The specific target of the Stanford students and more radical faculty members was a course open to all students, designed to introduce them to the history, ideas and literary classics of 'Western Culture'. Everything about the picture this gave of the world, the protesters had come to believe, was wrong and deeply offensive, particularly on all issues relating to gender, race and class.

For centuries, their new narrative ran, the patriarchal, white, elitist, capitalist, Western world had oppressed women, racial and sexual minorities and the lower ranks of society. This was reflected in the course's set books, all written by 'dead white males' such as Plato and Shakespeare. The concerns and views of women, black Americans and other racial and cultural groups were simply shut out of the picture.

---

[26] *The Diversity Myth*, op.cit. After studying law at Stanford, Peter Thiel later became famous for having launched PayPal in 1999 and becoming the first outside investor in Facebook. This with his other activities made him one of the richest men in America.

In the name of the new buzzwords of 'diversity' and 'multi-culturalism' all this elitist, sexist, racist, Euro-centricity had to be thrown into the Marxists' 'dustbin of history'.[27] Over the following months, led by student activists and faculty members (many of whom had been 'radicalized' in the neo-Marxist student protests of the late Sixties) – and enthusiastically supported by the university's president, Donald Kennedy – a new course was concocted to replace 'Western Culture', to be called just 'Culture, Ideas and Values'. Out went any idea of 'universalism', or that the great authors of the past might have been concerned with trying to convey truths applicable to all mankind. The new guiding principle was 'relativism': that the students should simply 'experience' many different viewpoints, through a hotch-potch of texts old and more often new, many of which had been chosen because of their particular focus on issues of gender, race and class. Students could still read Plato, but this was placed next to texts on the 'dreamtime' beliefs of Australian Aborigines. Shakespeare's *The Tempest* had to be read alongside a modern version, *A Tempest*, written by a black French politician from Martinique. This turned Shakespeare's original on its head, with Prospero cast as its oppressive white colonialist villain and Caliban as the play's black hero, battling to throw off his master's racist tyranny, to win independence for the island under himself as its new ruler.

New courses were introduced, such as Gender Studies and Feminist Studies, to be run by specially recruited feminist staff, with such texts on their reading lists as *Feminist Frameworks: Alternative Theoretical Accounts of the Relations Between Men and Women,* which argued that

Women's struggles must be directed immediately against male domination. In order to do this, women must forsake heterosexuality, which divides women from each other and ties them to their oppressors. Women's bodies are social constructs.

[27] The phrase 'ash-heap of history' originated with Friedrich Engels, but was later adapted by Leon Trotsky and other Soviet Communists as 'the dustbin of history'.

Nothing about women is natural. Women are made not born . . .
[in the] new society, there will be only persons. Men and women
will have disappeared [if] feminism is the theory, lesbianism is the
practice.[28]

The idea that any supposed difference between women and men
was merely a 'social construct' (even their bodies) prefigured a
belief that was to become much more widely familiar in politically
correct discussions about 'gender', even though this might appear
to contradict the simultaneous insistence that women must stick
together and have nothing to do with men.

Equally promoted by the new ideology were 'gay rights', with
the university providing funds for a 'Gay Pride' statue, showing
men and women caressing partners of the same sex; a Lesbian, Gay
and Bisexual Community Center to stage 'coming out' days for
both sexes; and a university 'Gay and Lesbian Awareness Week' to
'combat homophobia'. Homosexual male couples were given places
in the university's residence for married couples, many of them with
children.

But no issue was looked on as more sensitive than 'race', and the
need to promote the 'unique perspectives' of black writers, Mexicans
and other 'ethnic minorities', even where this expected students to
analyse the words of a black rap song, to attend 'Rallies Against
Racism' and to demonstrate in support of a local strike by oppressed
Mexican farm workers.

As fully supported by the university establishment under
President Kennedy, nothing more characterised Stanford's new
'multi-culturalism' than the way it engendered a general climate
of intimidation and fear, lest one might be accused of any of its
three greatest crimes: 'sexism', 'homophobia' and 'racism', however
imaginary the supposed offence might turn out to be. In one notable
episode, for instance, a student was heard referring behind closed

[28]Edited by Alison Jagger and Paula Rothenberg. New York: McGraw-Hill, 1984.

doors in his room to their unpopular and stridently homosexual Residential Assistant as a 'faggot'. When this came to the ears of the man, he promptly expelled the student from university housing. But he justified this by alleging that the student's use of the offending word was not only 'homophobic' but also 'racist', to make it seem even more outrageous. The following evening seven students held a silent candlelit vigil to defend the non-racist offender's First Amendment right to free speech, which attracted a much larger and noisy counter-demonstration by the Black Students' Union and other students, some of whom threatened to beat up the silent protesters. But they were praised by President Kennedy in the campus newspaper for having shown 'exceptional restraint' in controlling their justified anger.

By now the student's original remark had been blown up into a campus-wide furore about 'racism'. This was confirmed by Kennedy, when he not only publicly denounced the protesters but put them 'on probation' for having shown such 'racial' insensitivity. Yet neither they nor the original offender had been 'racist' in any way.

A much greater irony was the finding of several studies that there was in fact virtually no racial prejudice among the generally liberal-minded students at Stanford. When black students were questioned about this, they were unable to come up with any specific instances of how they themselves had experienced racial prejudice. The activists had to fall back on nothing more than the charge that Stanford was 'institutionally racist', and that white students must be guilty of 'unconscious racism' simply because they were in a majority.

More telling still, however, was the evidence of black students that they were under continual pressure from black militants not to mix any longer with their white friends, because this was a betrayal of their separate black identity. As with the feminists who wanted women not to have anything to do with men, the essence of the new multi-culturalist creed was that each group must display solidarity only with its own kind, separate from those 'others' (except that, ironically, they were all meant to be politically correct together).

An appropriate footnote to the nightmare which gripped Stanford under Kennedy's presidency was what ultimately befell this arch-opponent of 'elitism' himself. In Washington in April 1991, the chairman of a Congressional committee announced the findings of an inquiry into how Stanford under Kennedy had mis-spent vast sums of federal funding given to the university for research. Millions of dollars had been diverted to benefiting the lifestyle of Stanford's own administrative elite, not least Kennedy's own, ranging from the lavish refurbishment of his official residence, including $600,000 to make it earthquake-proof, to $4,000 to pay for the reception when he married his second wife. So devastating were these revelations of how Stanford had become subject to the kind of corruption more familiar in the ruling elite of a Third World country that, despite Kennedy's desperate efforts to cling on to his job, six months later he was finally forced to resign.

We have looked at the Stanford story at some length, partly because its 'multi-cultural model' was to be copied in other US universities, but more because it prefigured so much of the 'politically correct' ideology that was to become more generally prevalent in America, Britain and elsewhere in the decades to come. It could not have better illustrated Janis's rules of groupthink: the rise of a rigid belief system not connected to reality, the intense pressure to insist that its make-believe was supported by a consensus of all right-thinking people, and consequently the extreme intolerance displayed towards anyone even wrongly suspected of failing to conform with it.

But we must now consider the rather different version of 'multi-culturalism' that in the same years was gaining ground in Britain, with particular reference to the ever-growing communities of Muslim immigrants settling in many of Britain's cities.

Where white people and Muslims lived intermingled, they often managed to integrate quite harmoniously, as individual people and families. But many Muslims, particularly those from the poorer and more backward areas of Kashmir and northern Pakistan, preferred to live together with their own kind, taking over whole areas of a city where, under the British version of multi-culturalism, they were allowed by the authorities to live without outside interference, according to their own 'cultural traditions' and laws.

This produced a glaring anomaly. Whereas mainstream British society now accepted that male 'sexism' was quite unacceptable, the 'cultural traditions' of this particular brand of Islam took a very different view. Many of the women in these Muslim 'no-go areas', often imported under arranged marriages and unable to speak English, were treated by their menfolk as very far from equal, hidden away behind *niqabs* and *burqas* and often physically ill-treated.

To the strict Islamic code, the freedom given to Western women to dress in a sexually provocative manner, and to behave accordingly, was anathema. But so fearful were the authorities, including the police, that they might be accused of 'racism', provoking a communal backlash, that they turned a blind eye to what was going on in these Muslim ghettos. It was one thing for politically correct local councils to discontinue their own customary displays of Christmas trees and festive lights for fear of offending Muslims and other non-Christian 'ethnic minorities' (who had never objected to these Western traditions, which they quite enjoyed). It was quite another to intervene in a self-segregated Muslim district, although what went on there might often be contrary to British law.

By the end of the Nineties, as we saw at the beginning of this chapter, this was already giving rise to what would only many years later come to be revealed as one of the most extraordinary scandals in modern Britain: the subjection of thousands of young white girls, many of them under-age, to rape, drug abuse and every other kind of ill-treatment, by gangs of chiefly Pakistani men.

To the rapists, these unhappy Western children, many of them in state care, with their prematurely sexualized dress, no moral inhibitions and desperate for anyone to love them, were, to quote the title of a report when all this finally came to light, 'Easy Meat'.[29] But

---

[29]Peter McLoughlin (2014), *'Easy Meat' Multiculturalism, Islam and Child Sex Slavery*, Law and Freedom Foundation, https://www.mensenhandelweb.nl/system/files/documents/08%20 feb%202016/Easy-Meat-Multiculturalism-Islam-and-Child-Sex-Slavery-05-03-2014.pdf The title turned out to be prescient. When six Pakistani men were put on trial in December 2019, for sex abuse, the court was told that a girl had been 'passed around like a piece of meat' while

what more than anything turned it into a real horror story was the way all those in authority, whose professional responsibility should have been to protect these girls and to stop this vicious criminality dead in its tracks, were led by the make-believe of 'multi-culturalism' into knowingly allowing it to continue for years on end. The desire of the public authorities not to risk a serious backlash from the Muslim community had trumped their duty to halt an example of both 'sexism' and child abuse as outrageous as could be imagined. The further the pressure to be seen as politically correct intensified, the more contradictions it threw up.

Another such contradiction only appeared many years later, when between 2012 and 2014 it progressively came to light that this particular 'multi-cultural' horror story affected not only Rotherham but a whole string of other British towns and cities: Rochdale, Oxford, Derby, Newcastle, Dewsbury, Telford and more. In every case it emerged that the public authorities had long known of what was going on and done nothing. But what was also revealing was the response to this colossal scandal of the feminists. While normally they were only too quick to express outrage at any evidence of women being sexually abused by men, over this example, more horrendous than any, they remained conspicuously silent.

STAGE FIVE: THE TWENTY-FIRST CENTURY: COLLIDING WITH REALITY

> A 'Stop the Hate' initiative has been launched on Wednesday December 4 as part of a concerted effort to find new ways to tackle hate crime in Essex. The launch was marked by a conference in Chelmsford, hosted by Chief Constable Stephen Kavanagh, which brought together 220 delegates from a range of partner organisations involved in the field.

being sold for sex with men. BBC website: 'Telford sex abuse trial: Girl "passed around like meat"', 2 December 2019, https://www.bbc.co.uk/news/uk-england-shropshire-50633181

The theme of the conference was 'Report it to Sort it' and the emphasis was on encouraging people to tell police if they have been a victim of hate crime, whether it be based on race, religion, sexual orientation, transgender identity or disability.

Essex Police News

Drag queens are being brought into taxpayer-funded nursery schools to teach children about sexual diversity. The Drag Queen Story Time organization, based in Bristol, was formed to teach children about 'LGBT tolerance'. Nursery bosses say the sessions will help children to 'see people who defy rigid gender restrictions' and grow up to combat hate crime. They want to target two- and three-year-olds, to influence them early.

Daily Mail, 12 November 2019

A recent email via the Young Vic inviting directors to apply for a play called *Dead and Breathing* says, 'Because of the nature of the production, applications who identify as BAME [Black, Asian and Ethnic minority], trans or gender queer will be guaranteed an interview. Please state this clearly in your application.' Imagine an advertisement which stipulated that the 'nature of the production' would guarantee 'a straight, white man' an interview. It would be against the law.

Charles Moore's Notebook, *Spectator*, 25 November 2017

The politics of identity is anathema to the smooth running of any organization, serving only to foster a culture of division, grievance, permanent unrest and opportunism.

Richard Littlejohn, 'And if you thought WPCs in burqas were ridiculous . . ', *Daily Mail*, 14 August 2009

We have come to the place where, as I said, we see the wretched people who have lost the good of the intellect . . .

Dante, *Inferno*, First Canto

In this section, we look at what all this 50-year-long story had been leading up to, as the multiple contradictions implicit in political correctness collided with reality and each other in all directions.

By the start of the twenty-first century, as the 'PC' belief system steadily extended its range and tightened its grip, it exhibited certain chief components.

One was the increasingly influential role played by the more extreme campaigning groups in pushing forward their own particular agenda. The second was the markedly increasing readiness of politicians and public and corporate bodies in general, very much including universities, to fall over backwards to accept those agendas.

Another was the effect all this was having on the rest of society. The majority of those not directly involved were being made ever more conscious of what it was no longer advisable to say, think or do, for fear of giving 'offence'. Those who could not go along with it, even if privately they might joke about how absurd it was becoming, were having to learn to be careful to keep their dissenting opinions to themselves.

Later we shall be looking at how around this time politically correct ideology was now taking in ever more issues, ranging from support for the more extreme 'animal rights' activists, as in their campaign to ban fox-hunting, to opposing capitalism and the need to 'save the planet' from global warming. But here we stay with the two issues which have been the chief theme of this chapter: 'gender' and 'race'. In the rest of this section, we look at these under four general headings.

1. Gender (i): Gay Rights and Same-sex Marriage

One of the most striking successes of the advancing tide of political correctness on both sides of the Atlantic in these years was the campaign to extend 'gay rights'.

Such figures as exist suggest that the actual percentage of 'gays' in Western society was not more than 2 per cent.[30] But for the more

---

[30]According to the UK Office for National Statistics, the percentage of the adult population identifying itself in 2016 as gay, lesbian or bisexual (LGBT) was 2 per cent, the great majority being gay men.

militant members of the 'gay community' – as opposed to its more reserved majority who just wished to be accepted as normal members of society – it had become important to stage 'Gay Pride' marches and demonstrations, to flaunt their collective 'gender identity' as openly and aggressively as possible, by way of asserting their opposition to any kind of 'homophobia'. In Britain, as in America and other countries, it seemed a final victory for gay 'equality' when in 2004 the right was won to form 'civil partnerships', putting gay couples legally on equal terms with heterosexual couples joined in a 'civil marriage'.

But for the more extreme campaigners this was not enough. The next year, when David Cameron became leader of the Conservative Party, he was determined to dispel its reputation for being, in the words of his colleague Theresa May, 'the nasty party'. Just before the 2010 general election, militant gay pressure groups had talked Mrs May herself into signing an official Conservative pamphlet on 'lesbian, gay, bisexual and transgender issues' which argued for fully-fledged 'same-sex marriage'. This was not in the party's manifesto, and Cameron himself had said he was opposed to it. But now he was Prime Minister, May became his Home Secretary, and for three years she and her Lib Dem coalition colleague Lynn Featherstone, as Minister for Women and Equality, worked determinedly behind the scenes to get that little-known but powerful body the Council of Europe (allied to the European Court of Human Rights) to put gay marriage at the top of its agenda.

By 27 March 2013 all was in place, At a confidential meeting of the Council, chaired and led by Featherstone and from which the public and press were excluded, representatives of its 47 member countries agreed that by June that year they would put same-sex marriage into law, which several countries, led by Britain and France, duly did.[31]

What makes this relevant in terms of the power of groupthink is that ten years earlier virtually no one had ever mentioned the idea

[31]For a fuller account of the steps which led to Britain adopting same-sex marriage, see Christopher Booker, 'Gay marriage: the French connection', *Sunday Telegraph*, 9 February 2013.

of same-sex marriage (although it had first been suggested in an American magazine article by a gay journalist, Andrew Sullivan, as far back as 1989[32]). In Parliament 133 Conservatives and others had voted against it. But no sooner had it passed into law than, socially and politically, it became wholly unacceptable to say anything against 'gay marriage'.

In America, in April 2014, the CEO of the software company Mozilla, Brendan Eich, was forced to resign after it came to light that, some years earlier, he had given $1,000 dollars to a group campaigning for an amendment to California's constitution to make same-sex marriage in the state illegal. A well-known conservative columnist, Charles Krauthammer, pointed out that even Andrew Sullivan himself had protested that Eich being forced to resign was 'disgusting', citing this as yet another example of 'a new kind of intolerance entering into the culture . . . this is the culture of the left not being satisfied with making an argument or even prevailing in an argument, but in destroying personally and marginalizing people who oppose it.' It showed, he said, 'a level of totalitarian intolerance' that should be 'unacceptable'. And just how far this had now gone was exemplified in a case which made international headlines the following year from Northern Ireland.

Two 'born-again' Christian bakers were found guilty of a criminal offence under the Equality Act (Sexual Orientation Regulations) 2006 for having refused the request of a local gay activist to ice a cake for him, decorated with two cartoon characters from the children's television series *Sesame Street* and the words 'Support Gay Marriage'.[33] Not only did the bakers thus earn themselves a criminal record by standing up for a principle the Prime Minister himself had supported only five years earlier; they were also ordered by the Court

---

[32]*Here Comes The Groom, A (Conservative) Case For Gay Marriage*, 28 August 1989, *New Republic*, https://newrepublic.com/article/79054/here-comes-the-groom

[33]The request followed shortly after the Northern Ireland Assembly had vetoed the legalisation of same-sex marriage in the province due to the opposition of the ultra-Protestant Democratic Unionist Party.

of Appeal, the second-highest court in the land, to pay the activist £500 in compensation for the 'discrimination' he had suffered.[34]

What made all this still odder, however, was that in 2002, even before the legalizing of civil partnerships, the Blair government had put through a new Adoption Act making it legal for same-sex couples to adopt children. By 2017, 10 per cent of all children sent for adoption in England and Wales were being given to same-sex partners, a much higher proportion of all couples than their actual numbers represented. In terms of political correctness, there could be nothing wrong with this. Indeed, it was widely welcomed. But inevitably there were others who questioned whether, above all for the sake of the child, it might be based on a misreading of human psychology, biology and natural instinct.

Although no statistics of adoption breakdowns were ever published to confirm this, such doubts might have been reinforced by a case which made national headlines in 2017, when a 31-year-old man 'married' to a 36-year old partner whom he called his 'husband' was found guilty of murdering an 18-month baby, Elsie, adopted by the couple only eight months previously.

Not long after the little girl came to live with the two men in September 2015, at the age of ten months, she began displaying serious injuries. Repeatedly she was seen by doctors and health visitors, and the couple's home was visited by social workers 15 times, who saw ever-growing evidence of injuries which in normal circumstances would have been more than sufficient for the child to be taken back into care. But not once did any of them take any action.

Finally, in May 2016, while as usual in the care of the 31-year-old partner, Matt Scully-Hicks, the child had to be rushed to hospital suffering from so many multiple injuries that a doctor giving evidence in court said it was as if she had been the victim of 'a car crash'.

---

[34]However, this was later overturned by the Supreme Court, quashing the £500 damages awarded. See: *Guardian* 10 October 2018, https://www.theguardian.com/uk-news/2018/oct/10/uk-supreme-court-backs-bakery-that-refused-to-make-gay-wedding-cake

Four days later Elsie died in hospital. Scully-Hicks was arrested, later tried and in November 2017 convicted of murder. The court had seen medical records and tweets from Scully-Hicks to his 'husband' which showed not only an almost unbroken series of incidents when the child had been injured, but also frequent occasions when he had clearly shown himself incapable of knowing how to care for the child and had simply lost his temper. In one text he had described the baby as 'Satan in a babygrow'.[35]

Of course, there had been similar cases before involving heterosexual couples, where a child had died after serial ill-treatment to which its own mother had been party.[36] That of 'Baby P' had become a major national scandal when the facts came to light in 2008, not least because again the authorities had failed to intervene, despite being aware for months that the boy was suffering horrendous injuries. But in Elsie's case the failings of the authorities had been even worse, because it was they themselves who had chosen to put the baby into the charge of the murderer in the first place. They had not made any proper assessment of his ability to fulfil a function for which in no way was he instinctively or psychologically fitted – simply because the ideological make-believe of the time had completely blinded them to basic human realities.[37]

[35]'He called her "Satan in a babygrow"', *Daily Mail*, 7 November 2017.

[36]However, American research has shown that young children who reside in households with unrelated adults are at exceptionally high risk for inflicted-injury death. Most perpetrators are male, and most are residents of the decedent child's household at the time of injury. Children residing in households with unrelated adults were nearly 50 times as likely to die of inflicted injuries than children residing with two biological parents. See: Patricia G. Schnitzer and Bernard G. Ewigman, 'Child Deaths Resulting From Inflicted Injuries: Household Risk Factors and Perpetrator Characteristics', *Pediatrics*, November 2005

[37]In 2006 in South Africa, which had legalized same-sex adoption the same year as Britain, a lesbian couple were found guilty of murder after one of them had beaten their adopted four-year-old son to death. An employee of the couple testified that the crime had been committed when the dominant partner had become increasingly angry at the boy's refusal to call her 'Daddy'. She was sentenced to 25 years in prison and her partner to 22 years for being a 'passive participant' in his murder. See *Mail and Guardian*, 23 March 2006, https://mg.co.za/article/2006-03-23-lesbian-couple-found-guilty-of-boys-murder.

2. 'Hate Crime', Race and the 'Snowflake' Students

A telling term which had become increasingly familiar in the same early years of the new century was 'hate crime'. This had originated in America in the Eighties, directed particularly at crimes against what had now become generally known in politically correct terminology as 'African-Americans'. The idea was that the seriousness of such offences was aggravated by evidence that they had been racially motivated.

By the early twenty-first century, the FBI was publishing an annual 'Hate Crimes Statistics' report, and the list of minority groups who could be the victims of a 'hate crime' was steadily widening. In 2009 President Barack Obama and the US Congress passed a Hate Crimes Prevention Act. This included 'actual or perceived' crimes on grounds of 'gender, gender identity, sexual orientation and disability'. By 2011 these statistics were showing that 46.9 per cent of hate crimes were motivated by race and 20.8 per cent by 'sexual orientation'.

Although America now had its first black president, after half a century of fighting for equal rights and black advancement, it was noticeable that in some respects relations between the races were actually becoming worse than they had been for years. This was evidenced in the repeated incidents where trigger-happy white police were shooting black men for what appeared to be the most spurious reasons, or blacks had died violently in police custody. In 2013 this had led to the launching of the vociferous 'Black Lives Matter' movement.

Although by now the concept of 'hate-crime' was catching on in Britain, the most shocking single example of a blatantly racist crime had already been making national headlines since the early Nineties. This was the case of Stephen Lawrence, an 18-year-old boy from a black family living in south London, who in 1993 had been stabbed to death on the street by a gang of five white teenagers. Even though the police had been given the identity of those responsible within three days of the murder, their suspicious failure to pursue the case properly or to secure any convictions gradually developed into a serious scandal.

One reason for this was that relations between the police and what were now known as 'Afro-Caribbeans' had long been severely strained, particularly with disaffected young second- and third-generation male descendants of the original immigrants from the British West Indies. Without the multi-cultural protection accorded to Muslim communities, they had no alien 'cultural traditions' to justify them being given kid-glove treatment by the authorities. A disproportionate number of these young blacks were poorly educated at inadequate state schools and unemployed. Many took or dealt in drugs, and were regularly subjected to aggressive 'stop-and-search' interventions by the police. Their sense of alienation from society had in 1981 led them into violent rioting and battles between young blacks and the police in Brixton in south London and other English cities. These were to recur later, as on the Broadwater estate in north London in 1985, where a lone white policeman was hacked to death in front of a jeering black mob.

This had no connection with the many respectable, law-abiding, happily integrated black families, such as that of Stephen Lawrence (who was studying for his A Levels when he was murdered).[38] But it certainly helped to shape the attitude of many policemen to the black community in general, and when in 1999 a retired High Court judge, Sir William Macpherson, carried out one of what were to be several inquiries into the police handling of the Lawrence case, he provocatively, but not wholly without justification, condemned the police as being 'institutionally racist'.

In fact, Macpherson went further, defining a 'race crime' as any 'incident perceived to be racist', not only by the victim but by '*any other person*' (my italics). In the Stephen Lawrence case, there was no doubt that his murder was indeed racially motivated (more than

---

[38]It was not least thanks to the determination of Stephen's capable and articulate mother Doreen that the case continued to arouse prominent public concern for many years, until finally in 2012 two of the original suspects were convicted and imprisoned. In that same year Mrs Lawrence was chosen to assist in carrying the Olympic flag at the opening ceremony of the London Olympics, and in 2013 she became a Labour member of the House of Lords as Baroness Lawrence,

one of the gang had later been found guilty of other violent racial attacks). But Macpherson was suggesting that if anyone at all chose to 'perceive' an action as 'racist', then it must automatically be classified as such.

In 2003, when a new Criminal Justice Act defined the categories of crime aggravated by 'hostility' to a victim on the grounds of their membership of a minority group, these included race, religion, sexual orientation (or 'presumed sexual orientation') and disability (or 'presumed disability'). And it was not long before any such offences were being lumped together as just 'hate crimes'.

By now, following Macpherson's charge that they were 'institutionally racist', the police were generally going to the other extreme. At a time when they were notoriously becoming more reluctant to investigate burglaries, shoplifting or other more familiar types of lawbreaking, they were becoming only too eager to look out for instances of 'hate crime', to the point where, by 2013, the Crime Survey for England and Wales was reporting that the previous year the number of 'hate crimes' had topped 278,000.

Although police records officially only registered 43,748 of these as hate crimes, by 2017 this figure had risen to 80,393, of which 78 per cent were race hate crimes, 11 per cent involved sexual orientation, 7 per cent involved religion and another 7 per cent disability. The remaining 1,248, or 2.1 per cent, were now classified as 'transgender hate crimes'. In line with Macpherson, these comprised crimes that were 'perceived' as such not only by the victim but also by 'any other person'. And on 21 August 2017 new guidance from the Crown Prosecution Service advised that 'online hate crimes' should now be treated just as seriously as offences committed 'in person'. This was particularly directed at the use of the internet to incite terrorism or engage in the sexual 'grooming' of children.

But in recent years little had done more than the internet to contribute to a much wider sensitivity, on both sides of the Atlantic, to what it was now socially acceptable to say or even be suspected of thinking. First, through 'trolling' on website comment threads, then dramatically more so with the advent of social media such as Facebook and Twitter, this had given a powerful new platform for individuals or co-ordinated groups holding politically correct opinions to broadcast their views to others. Partly it enabled them to indulge in what came to be known as 'virtue-signalling'. This was the desire to flag up their view on any particular subject to demonstrate that they sided with those who were morally 'virtuous'.[39] But even more, it allowed them, often anonymously, to vent personal abuse at anyone expressing opinions which in their view should not be allowed. It was this new aid to the contagious effect of politically correct groupthink which contributed to the emergence of what was, psychologically, one of the most remarkable products of the entire story, which had begun way back in those days of 'toleration' and 'equality' in the 1960s.

This was the movement, particularly centred on university campuses in America and Britain (foreshadowed by what had happened to Stanford in the late Eighties), to create what became known as 'safe spaces', where students could be guaranteed protection from anything which contradicted their rigid views on all the issues of the politically correct lexicon.[40]

By the time the 'safe space' movement began to sweep the universities around 2015, the list of issues on which students wanted such protection had broadened out from race and gender to anything from support for capitalism to 'climate change denial'. Under what they called their 'No platforming' principle, the students wanted to ban any lecturers or visiting speakers whose views they considered 'offensive'. They demanded the right to be given 'trigger warnings' when a set book contained passages which might be found 'disturbing', such as Scott Fitzgerald's *The Great Gatsby*, because it includes scenes of 'violence by men against women'. They condemned as 'cultural

---

[39]See James Bartholomew, 'The awful rise of virtue-signalling', *Spectator*, 18 April 2015.

[40]In fact, the demand for 'safe space' had originated back in the late Eighties when small groups of radical feminists had come together to exclude anyone who was not 'LGBT' (Lesbian, Gay, Bisexual, Transgender), to reinforce their sense of shared identity against the 'gender prejudice' of the outside world.

appropriation' any 'patronizing' Western borrowing of the customs or clothing of other nations or tribal groups, as when calling for student canteens to stop serving 'Tunisian stew', or the playful wearing of Mexican sombreros. It was this wish to be protected from anything which contradicted their own rigid ideology that caused these ultra-sensitive souls to be ridiculed as 'snowflakes'. In 2016 even the gay celebrity Stephen Fry mocked them for having been 'infantilized'.

But the ultimate irony here was what had happened to that central principle of political correctness. Like an idea come full circle to the extent that that it had finally turned in on itself, the real victims now seen as needing official protection were the 'snowflake' students themselves.[41]

So fierce was the groupthink intolerance (not to mention group hatred) behind all this that it threw up many other contradictions, such as when in 2015 students at Cardiff University wanted to ban a lecture by the onetime feminist icon Germaine Greer. Their charge was that she was guilty of 'transphobia', for saying that she couldn't regard a man who wished to switch gender as really a woman, because he hadn't grown up with the experience of being a woman from birth.

In April 2016, when an LGBT campaigner refused to share a platform at a meeting at a Kent university on 're-radicalising queers' with the veteran gay-rights campaigner Peter Tatchell, he was astonished to be accused of having signed a letter which had

---

[41]With the approach of Christmas in 2017, Professor Kyna Hamill of Boston University revealed that the song 'Jingle Bells' was 'racist', because it had first been performed in 1857 by white men 'blacked up' as 'Nigger minstrels'. She claimed that 'the legacy of "Jingle Bells" is one where its blackface and racist origins have been subtly and systematically removed from its history.'

In Britain, after a slight fall of snow, University College, London, one of the world's leading universities, sent out an official tweet to inform its students that the university would be open as normal, beginning with the words 'Dreaming of a white campus?' This provoked hostile comments from two students claiming that UCL was being racist. The following day the university authorities apologized, saying, 'We chose our words very poorly yesterday when thinking of [Bing Crosby's] "White Christmas". We're sorry and we'll choose our words more carefully in the future.' The offending tweet was removed.

'incited violence against transgender people', and of having used 'racist language'. He cited this as an example of the 'witch-hunting, accusatory atmosphere' closing down 'open debate' on campuses.[42]

Hitting the news and the internet in the summer term of 2017 was a perfect illustration of what Peter Tatchell was talking about when a small US college was engulfed in mass hysteria which echoed what happened to Stanford in the 1980s. After a politically correct sociologist became president of Evergreen College in Washington state, he had set up a 'Committee on Diversity and Equity' to look into how far the college was infected with 'racism'. Packed with black and white radicals, the committee had produced a wildly partisan report, finding that racism at Evergreen was indeed 'rampant', and recommending drastic measures to root out this evil. One faculty member, Bret Weinstein, for 14 years the college's professor of evolutionary biology, held impeccably liberal, non-racist views. But he was so disturbed by the nature of the proposed measures that he began to question in meetings and through emails whether they would not in effect close down free speech, preventing the college from functioning in the proper open-minded and truth-seeking spirit of a university.

By May 2017, with Evergreen now almost wholly in the grip of the radicals' ideology, Weinstein had been branded as the chief hate figure on campus. Fearful of incurring the militants' rage, students and other faculty members who privately sympathized with his views had been cowed into silence. Events came to a head when the militants proposed that all whites should leave the campus for a day, or be attacked for not showing solidarity with their 'anti-racist' agenda. A video posted by the militants themselves shows Weinstein surrounded by a screaming mob of black and white students, trying to engage them in reasoned dialogue while they chant, 'Hey hey, ho ho, Bret Weinstein's got to go.'[43]

---

[42]See 'Peter Tatchell: snubbed by students for free speech stance', *Observer*, 13 February 2016.

[43]All this and more can be seen on YouTube under 'How social justice activists took over a college and drove some professors out': https://youtube/Pf5fAiXYr08.

When the situation got out of hand someone (not Weinstein) called the police. Attempts were made to deny them entry to the building and the campus, until the president asked them to leave the college. For a couple of days Evergreen was reduced by raging mobs to anarchy, with occasional acts of violence against those identified as dissenters. Weinstein himself, faced with death threats, decided to remove his family from the area to a place of safety. A month or two later, he was informed by the president that the college no longer wanted his services.

That same summer, there were not dissimilar scenes at the University of Toronto, centred on Dr Jordan Peterson, a professor of psychology and for 30 years a clinical psychologist. He had won a large following for leading a campaign against an amendment to Canada's Human Rights Act and Criminal Code which sought to criminalize the use of 'gender-specific pronouns' such as 'he' or 'she'.[44] On one occasion, recorded on *YouTube*, he attempted to make an open-air speech on the university campus, in front of both supporters and opponents. He began by insisting that he wasn't going to discuss 'sexual politics', but only wished to defend the 'freedom of speech'. As if to prove his point, the video shows him surrounded by yelling protesters who first drowned him out with deafening blasts of electronic noise from a loudspeaker, then cut off his microphone. As he tried to continue at the top of his voice, the protesters chanted abuse so loudly in unison that he eventually had to walk away.[45]

This was the other side to the 'safe space' movement: its need to stage angry public demonstrations to protest against anything it could find which could conceivably be perceived as 'offensive'. A notable instance had already been the 'Rhodes Must Fall' campaign

---

[44]The new law did not outlaw any use of 'he' or 'she' but made it an offence to use them where it might offend someone who wished to be referred to only by 'gender-neutral pronouns', as in the use of 'zie' for 'he/she', 'zim' for 'him/her', 'zir' for 'his/her' and 'zis' for 'his/hers'.

[45]For this video and others similar see 'Dr Jordan Peterson speaks at UoT rally for free speech', https://www.youtube.com/watch?v=vFcn775CqAg.

in 2015, which began on the campus of the University of Cape Town (UCT), when black students showered a statue of one of the university's historic benefactors, Cecil Rhodes, with human faeces and demanded its removal. This was because, more than a century earlier, Rhodes had played a leading role in the advance of British colonialism in southern Africa, and thus been an oppressor of millions of black Africans. When the demonstrators claimed that the university was 'institutionally racist' and that South Africa's education should be 'decolonised', they used Facebook and Twitter to inspire similar protests at other South African universities. One leader of the movement used Facebook to praise Adolf Hitler and Robert Mugabe, and said in a radio interview that 'Jews are devils.'

Later that year one of the original UCT protagonists, Ntokozo Qwabe, came to Oriel College, Oxford, where he and others launched a similar campaign for the removal of a small statue of Rhodes, scarcely visible on the front of the college, to which again he had been one of its greatest benefactors. Qwabe saw nothing incongruous in the fact that he was only at Oxford thanks to a scholarship endowed with Rhodes's money, on the grounds that this had all been stolen from Africans in the first place.

Initially the politically correct college authorities seemed sympathetic to the campaign's demands, which also included the need to 'raise awareness' in the university of the evils of Britain's colonial past. Only when donors threatened to withhold £100 million in funding from the college was it ruled that the statue could remain.[46]

By 2017 a similar craze for removing or toppling 'offensive' statues of historical figures had caught on in America, particularly those of nineteenth-century notables from the southern states who had

---

[46]This episode inspired similar campaigns elsewhere in Britain, as in Bristol, where one of the city's greatest benefactors had been Edward Colston, who in the seventeenth century had made much of his money from the slave trade. In 2017 the city council finally ruled that his name should be removed from the Colston Hall, Bristol's main concert venue.

played a prominent part in the Confederates' defence of black slavery in the American Civil War.

This provided yet another example of how one extreme form of groupthink tends often to arouse another in opposition to it. On 11 August several hundred 'white supremacists', 'neo-Nazis' and members of other far-right groups gathered on the university campus at Charlottesville, Virginia, to protest against the proposed removal of a nearby statue of Robert E. Lee, the general who commanded the Confederate forces at Gettysburg and in the later stages of the Civil War.

That night, when the right-wing demonstrators held a deliberately Nazi-style torchlit procession and were confronted by an opposing group of students, there were scuffles. But next morning a much larger white supremacist mob assembled, many armed, and were met by a large angry crowd of black and white liberal counter-demonstrators, shouting enraged abuse in the other direction. When the two sides clashed in violent scuffles, this culminated in an incident where one white racist drove a vehicle into the opposing crowd, killing a woman and injuring 19 others. This made headlines round the world.[47] But when these ugly scenes prompted President Trump to deplore the 'hatred, bigotry, and violence' shown by all involved, this inflamed liberal opinion even more, for his failure to direct his condemnation only at the white racists.

Indeed, Trump also questioned where this craze for removing statues might end. No historical figures had been commemorated by more statues in America than those greatest of the country's founding heroes, George Washington and Thomas Jefferson. Since both men had owned slaves themselves, would there now be demands for all these to be removed as well?

One answer was given to Trump ten days later when, on 21 August, protesters posted on the internet a video of themselves

---

[47]For a full account of the 'Battle of Charlottesville', see Joe Helm, 'Recounting a day of rage, hate, violence and death', on the *Washington Post* website, 12 August 2017.

destroying with a sledgehammer one of America's oldest statues, that of Christopher Columbus, which had stood in the centre of Baltimore since 1792. Columbus's crime, as the discoverer of the New World, was apparently to have 'initiated a centuries-old wave of terrorism, murder, genocide, rape, slavery, ecological degradation and capitalist exploitation of labor in the Americas'. It seemed the only crimes for which Columbus had not been responsible were 'homophobia' and 'transphobia'. Compared with that charge sheet, even the offences of Washington and Jefferson paled into insignificance. At least this might not end with demands that the USA should change the name of its capital city.

3. Gender Wars (ii): The Contradictions Multiply

There could be no better illustration of the confusion and contradictions political correctness had finally led to than the contrast between two different episodes which made headlines in the late summer and early autumn of 2017.

The first, summarised at the start of this chapter, was the sacking by Google of one of its senior software engineers, James Damore. His error, in the eyes of Google's CEO Sundai Pichar, was to have suggested, in a long and carefully argued email, citing scientific and psychometric evidence, that there might in some respects be both biological and psychological differences between men and women. In the eyes of the man who fired him, this was so obviously 'offensive' that Damore could not be kept on the payroll, because his views were an affront to the company's 'basic values'.

We have seen how this belief that any perceived differences between men and women are purely a 'social construct' and a 'cultural artefact' went way back to Germaine Greer in the early Seventies, and the kind of set texts which were part of the Gender Studies course run by ultra-feminists at Stanford in the late Eighties. But since then the idea that differences between the sexes are only a product of 'cultural conditioning' had caught on so widely that it had been moving to the centre of politically correct thinking. That little boys like to play with pretend guns and little girls to play with dolls was, it was now argued, only because they have been made victims of socially enforced 'gender stereotyping'.

A few weeks after the Damore episode, however, a huge scandal exploded over revelations that Harvey Weinstein, the most powerful film producer in Hollywood, had for many years been known to be an obsessive sexual predator on women, using the power of his position to force his attentions on dozens of aspiring actresses in an extreme version of the practice long known in the movie industry as use of the 'casting couch'.

This set off a widespread response on Twitter and other 'social media' from vast numbers of women wanting to sign up alongside Weinstein's victims with the words 'Me too', implying that they too had been victims of sexual harassment by men. While the Weinstein affair was still making daily headlines, with further accusations leading to the disgrace of other well-known figures in show business, a weird shadow of this scandal exploded into the news in Britain, where for days on end the media went into overdrive with revelations of how one politician after another had similarly behaved in a 'sexually inappropriate' manner, with scores of women (and even in one case a man).

One senior Cabinet minister was forced to resign after a female journalist claimed that 15 years earlier he had 'touched her knee' in an interview. Another resigned over allegations that he had sent 'inappropriate' text messages to a Conservative activist, and watched pornography on his office computer. Other front-page headlines in the space of a week included, 'Minister sent his PA to buy sex toys'; 'Top Tory's bathrobe pass at a male aide'; 'Minister: "I was victim of Fallon's vile sexism"'; and 'Labour tried to cover up rape'.

This all became so Kafkaesque that one named Tory MP led the news with 'allegations' made against him so unspecified that he hadn't been allowed to know what they were. A senior member of the Welsh Assembly even committed suicide for similar reasons. Despite being publicly named as the subject of other 'allegations' of a sexual nature, he had likewise not been told the nature of these accusations or who they had come from.

One feature of all this hysteria was how seedily degrading all these stories were. At least when in the Sixties John Profumo had featured in the most famous political sex scandal in post-war British history, he had actually gone to bed with the girl in question, who had willingly consented. In all these latter-day allegations of 'sexual harassment', the politicians had come across as no more than emotionally immature 'sex pests', so self-centred and unable to control their physical urges that they had lost any sense of how to relate to another human being.

But rather more relevant was the fact that all those accused of this demeaning behaviour were male. Not one of these stories featured a man being 'sexually harassed' by a woman, because these men had behaved as only men do, having lost all self-awareness and sensitivity as to how a man should behave towards a woman. These men had all grown up in a society which, following the sexual revolution of the Sixties, had seen sex elevated into an obsession and the old social inhibitions against 'improper behaviour' widely cast aside.

There was, however, another side to the unhappy consequences of the 'liberated' view of sexual behaviour which had so widely prevailed since the Sixties, and this reflected not just on the men involved but even more on the women.

A growing feature of life in recent years had been the number of young women who, having engaged with a man in consensual sex and later been rejected or otherwise come to regret it, had then accused their former partner of having raped them. In December 2017 this was highlighted by the two-year-long case of Liam Allen, an engineering student standing trial on six cases of rape and six more of sexual assault on an unnamed woman. So serious were the charges brought against him by the Crown Prosecution Service (CPS) and the police that he faced the likelihood of a 12-year prison sentence, and being given a criminal record for life, wholly destroying his planned future career prospects.

Only three days into the trial did the defence barrister manage to obtain the evidence, previously withheld by the police and the CPS, of 40,000 emails, texts and other messages recorded on the woman's phone, which revealed not only that she and the accused had enjoyed a 'consensual' sexual relationship, but that, when he had broken this off, she had also obsessively pestered him for months with requests that they might continue to enjoy 'casual' sex together. This so destroyed the prosecution's position that the shocked CPS barrister withdrew his case, and the judge ruled that the student could 'leave the courtroom as an innocent man without a stain on his character'.

But this left a huge question mark over the conduct of the police and the CPS themselves, for neglecting to check out this evidence, or even suppressing it, and therefore failing in their legal duty to ensure that the defence was given information so crucial to the case.

It then emerged that, in response to feminist pressure groups and the demands of political correctness, both the police and the CPS had for some time been looking to take incidents of rape much more seriously, and ensure that many more men were charged and found guilty of raping women (who, unlike the men they had accused, were guaranteed complete anonymity).[48] This policy had been particularly driven by Alison Saunders, the woman who, since, 2013, had been the director of the CPS. She had made it clear that one of her top priorities was greatly to increase the number of convictions for rape, requiring the police to be much readier to believe women claiming to have been victims.[49]

Yet at just the time when this case, like all the others mentioned above, was exemplifying the unhappy consequences of those long-ago dreams of sexual freedom, setting the sexes at odds as never before, the prevailing groupthink, as exemplified by the sacking of James

[48]Less than a week after the Liam Allen case became a national scandal, a second rape case collapsed for a similar reason: that the police had withheld evidence which could have cleared the accused. In consequence, the Metropolitan Police announced a review of all recent rape cases. See 'Yard to review all rape cases,' *Daily Telegraph*, 20 December 2017.

[49]The number of prosecutions of men for rape subsequently rose by 30 per cent in a year. This principle that 'victims' should automatically be believed had already been widely accepted in cases of alleged 'child abuse', often with disturbing and controversial consequences, as we shall discuss later in the book.

Damore, was trying to pretend that, biologically and psychologically, the sexes were essentially no different, and any apparent distinctions between them were just a 'cultural artefact' brought about by 'social conditioning'.

In the previous few months there had been further conspicuous evidence of how strongly this make-believe was now being promoted by the cheerleaders for political correctness. In June, for instance, the former tennis star John McEnroe had provoked a storm of protest by saying in an interview that although the American champion Serena Williams was 'the best female player ever', if she had to play on the men's circuit 'she'd be, like, 700th in the world.' Miss Williams tweeted back, 'Dear John, I adore and respect you,' but 'please keep me out of your statements that are not factually based.'

But of course, McEnroe did have the facts on his side. He might not have been necessarily right that Miss Williams would lose to every single one of the world's top 700 men. But even she had admitted that she would be beaten by the then-world number one, Andrew Murray, and she would certainly have been beaten by many more.

The BBC and others were now likewise trying to promote the idea that women playing cricket, football, rugby and other team sports should be taken just as seriously as their male counterparts. But all the evidence showed that, when it comes to most sports, not least for obvious physiological reasons, a few women might be better than a lot of men, but some men are considerably better than all women. Otherwise, in tennis or athletics, men and women would be allowed to compete with each other on equal terms. But the world's fastest female sprinters would have lost to Usain Bolt every time.

Similarly, before the 2017 BBC Proms season began, the BBC announced that female composers would now be 'leading the charge' to show that they were the equal of their male counterparts. But this only prompted a feminist website, Women in Music, to observe that female composers were still contributing a mere 8 per cent of that season's concert programmes.[50] As I playfully observed at the time in my newspaper column:

> although there are many areas of life where women excel over men, the preferred message is that women are really equal in those areas where men do, for reasons of biology and psychology, excel over women. When it comes to our growing confusion over gender differences, we may recall W. S. Gilbert's famous reply when the cry went up 'Votes for Women'. For long he was scorned for retorting 'Babies for Men'. But we now read that 'leading doctors' want the NHS to discuss funding for men to be given 'womb transplants'. We know Gilbert was a highly imaginative comic writer. But even he might be left speechless at the weird muddle we are getting into.[51]

Such is the nature of groupthink, however, that no sooner has one position seemingly been established than it needs to advance still further. For some years pushing its way to the top of the politically correct agenda had been the new obsession with 'transgender', and the importance of allowing people to switch from the sex they had

[50]It was more than once claimed on the BBC that the only reason why female composers had not previously been more prominent in the history of classical music was that women had been the victims of sexual discrimination. Particularly cited was the example of Felix Mendelssohn's sister Fanny, who because of social prejudice had been forced to publish some of her songs under her brother's name (just as the Brontë sisters and George Eliot at much the same time had published their novels under pseudonyms which concealed their gender.

Another recent vogue had been productions of Shakespeare, in which the male title role was played by an actress. Examples included a female Hamlet, a female King (or 'Queen') Lear, and an actress playing Julius (or 'Julia') Caesar, Although this was justified on the grounds that female parts in Shakespeare's day had been played by boys, and was fashionably acclaimed as a breakthrough in recognizing that men and women should be regarded as wholly interchangeable with each other, this politically correct gimmick did tend to make total nonsense of the psychological dynamics of the plot.

[51]Shortly after this I was informed by my newspaper that one of the subjects I was no longer allowed to write about was what they called 'gender wars'.

been born with to the other, or even to choose not to belong to any gender at all.

In its way this was a logical extension of the belief that gender differences are only a 'social construct', and that whether people believe themselves to be male or female is not decided by biology but only a product of 'cultural conditioning'.[52] It had become fashionable to identify people as 'gender-fluid'. By 2017 quite a medical and academic industry had been called into being, to give psychological and medical help to those uncertain of their 'gender identity', and to arrange hormone treatment, surgery and 'conversion therapy' to allow them to 'transition' to a sex other than that they had been born with.

More generally it was becoming politically correct to support people's right to 'self-identify' with whichever gender they wished to be 're-assigned' to, and then be treated by society accordingly. As we saw at the start of the chapter, the Church of England issued instructions to all its 4,700 primary schools that boys should be allowed to wear high heels and girls should not have to wear skirts, for fear of giving offence to other children who were themselves 'transgender'.

As early as 2009, the columnist Richard Littlejohn had noted that Britain's police, post-Macpherson as keen to appear politically correct as any public body in the land, already included not only a Gay Police Association, a Black Police Association, a National Muslim Police Association and even a Pagan Police Association, but also now a 'National Trans Police Association'. This existed, according to its website, 'primarily to provide support to serving and retired police officers, police staff and special constables with any gender identity issue, including, but not exclusively, Trans men, Trans women, people who identify as Transgender, androgyne or intersex, and people who cross dress'.[53]

---

[52]Statistics for those 'self-identifying' as 'transgender' or 'non-binary' are notoriously hard to pin down, but both in the UK and the US this appeared to be much less than 0.1 per cent, or significantly less than one in 1,000 of the population.

[53]Richard Littlejohn, *Daily Mail*, 14 August 2009, op.cit.

But even this new drive for 'diversity' and 'equal rights' was now producing its own bizarre contradictions, as one politically correct agenda collided with another. No one was more resentful of the new transgender obsession than the more radical feminists, who strongly objected to men who had 'changed sex' being allowed to use women's changing rooms or be sent to female prisons. This had gone back to the case of Martin Ponting, a man then calling himself a woman but retaining his male genitalia, who had been found guilty of raping two women, one of them disabled. But when he insisted on being sent to a female prison, he had promptly begun to make sexual advances to other inmates.

In September 2017, when the chairwoman of the Commons Women and Equalities Committee was leading calls for an amendment to the 2010 Equality Act, to change the legal definitions of 'man' and 'woman', a group of feminists arranged a meeting to discuss 'What is gender?' This so outraged the militant transgender activists, who classified them as 'Trans-Exclusionary Radical Feminists' or TERFS (with such slogans as 'TERFS must die'), that they determined to prevent the meeting taking place. When the feminist group congregated at Speakers' Corner in Hyde Park to be told the secret venue arranged for the debate, they were met by a chanting mob of 'transgenders'. While the two groups screamed abuse at each other, one 60-year-old bespectacled feminist photographing the scene was smacked in the face by a burly 'hooded, male-bodied' trans, who smashed her camera to the ground. This was justified by other trans activists, who claimed that they were made to feel 'unsafe' by the 'systemic violence' of those who disagreed with them, and that physical retaliation was only 'self-defence'.

A rather more profound development in this ever more hysterical focus on transgender, however, was the experience of James Caspian, an academic and psychotherapist at Bath Spa University. Himself gay, Caspian had become one of Britain's leading experts on transgender issues, much respected in the field. For some years, however, he had been increasingly troubled by evidence that a rising number of people, particularly women, had, after 'transitioning' to the opposite sex with the aid of surgery and drug treatment, then become desperately unhappy and wanted to change back again. 'Some of these young women', he explained in an interview, 'were saying that they felt they had made a mistake, but had been influenced by a kind of social pressure ramped up by the internet'. When he raised his concerns with colleagues, one said, 'I didn't think we were supposed to talk about that.' He went on:

> Discussion is being suppressed by a small, but vocal minority in the LGBT community who seem to have an agenda to push the boundaries of trans rights, whatever the cost . . . I think we have arrived at a point where people are afraid to say what they think, and that's not a good thing in my field.

The more Caspian pursued his researches, the more they showed that this had become a much more serious and troubling problem than generally recognized. Eventually, therefore, he applied to his university for a grant to produce a full academic study, entitled 'An examination of the experience of people who have undergone Gender Reassignment procedures and/or have reversed a gender transition'. He said he was well aware that his findings would not be regarded as 'politically correct' but, with the transgender issue now being so one-sidedly promoted to society in general, 'all over the internet' and even 'brought into the classroom', he felt it was of great importance that the other side of the picture should be recognized, explored and properly discussed.[54] In other words, he had shown the courage to step outside the groupthink bubble, to look carefully at the evidence and to think (and to feel) for himself.

---

[54]In December 2017 it was reported that the Lancashire Care NHS Foundation Trust had sent out to primary schools a questionnaire to be filled in by all 10-year-old children, asking 'Do you feel the same inside as the gender you were born with? (feeling male or female).' They were also asked to tick a box to confirm their true gender as 'boy', 'girl' or 'other'. See 'Trans survey for 10-year-olds', *Daily Telegraph*, 11 December 2017.

What he was not prepared for, however, was that in November 2016 his application would be unequivocally turned down by Bath Spa, on the grounds that 'the posting of unpleasant material on blogs or social media may be detrimental to the reputation of the university.' As it turned out, when this was revealed, nothing could have been more detrimental to the university's reputation than the reason it had given for rejecting a serious academic study on such an important subject. Once again it reflected nothing more than the power of groupthink not just to close people's minds but to shut them off from any human reality.[55]

So what was the 'reality' all this had led to? For a further look, we need two more briefer chapters.

---

[55]According to the US-based Trans Student Education Resources website in January 2018, it was appropriate to use the all-embracing acronym LGBTQQIAPP+ as denoting 'a collection of identities short for lesbian, gay, bisexual, trans, queer, questioning, intersex, asexual, aromantic, pansexual, polysexual (sometimes abbreviated to LGBT or LGBTQ+). Sometimes this acronym is replaced with "queer".'

2

Hatred and Make-believe Rule, OK?

Cathy Newman: 'Jordan Peterson, you said that men must, quote, "grow the hell up." Tell me why.'

Dr Jordan Peterson: 'Well, because there's nothing more ugly than an overgrown infant. People who don't grow up don't find the meaning in their life that sustains them in difficult times, and they're certain to encounter difficult times. And they're left bitter and resentful, without purpose, and adrift, and hostile, and vengeful, and arrogant, and deceitful, and of no use to themselves, and of no use to anyone else, and no partner for a woman, and there's nothing in it that's good.'

Newman–Peterson interview, Channel 4 News,
16 January 2018

The lure of drill videos and the gang life they glorify is horribly understandable. Apart from the violence, there is little difference between joining a gang and a sports team. Both offer teenage boys what they crave: a challenging activity, competition with their peers that allows them to make friends and prove themselves . . . In the absence of an alternative, these teenage boys have created their own version of *Lord of the Flies*. Our inability to give them what they need to thrive within law-abiding society has consigned a generation to nihilism and bloodshed.

Harriet Sergeant on 'knife gangs', *Spectator*,
14 April 2018

For a final picture of where all these 60 years of growing confusion had led to, we can scarcely do better than take a brief glimpse at what was making headlines in the early days of 2018.

As the new year opened, greeted with the now customary displays of fireworks across the world, none were more spectacular than those in Australia and London. The 'rainbow display' exploding above Sydney Harbour Bridge was apparently designed to celebrate Australia's legalization of 'same-sex marriage'. Those lighting up the sky over the London Eye were intended, we were told, to promote 'gender equality'.

A few days later in Hollywood, hundreds of actresses turned up in black dresses to attend the annual Golden Globes awards ceremony, to chant the message that 'Time's up' for sexual predators such as Harvey Weinstein and countless more. But with no apparent sense of irony, photographers inevitably homed in on those women whose black dresses were skimpiest and who displayed the most daring cleavage. The highlight of the evening was an acceptance speech by the black media star Oprah Winfrey, whose shouts of 'Time's up' prompted an orgy of speculation that she should run for president in 2020.

Over the weeks that followed, not a day went by without further headlines relating to the great 'gender war', indignant Twitterstorms and the ever-growing pressure to conform with political correctness in general. In Britain, the top priority of a chaotic reshuffle of her ministers by a beleaguered Theresa May was said to be the need for more 'diversity', and a government which 'looked more like the country it serves'. This apparently meant promoting more women MPs and those from ethnic minorities. But the reshuffle was so lacklustre that scarcely anyone noticed which nonentity had now been moved to what job.

Few issues had now come to generate more resentful emotion than the idea of the 'gender pay gap' between men and women. This was now given a further boost by the very public resignation of the BBC's female China Editor, when she discovered that she was paid less than two of her male colleagues. But similar anger was soon being directed at many other prominent organizations, including the supermarket giant Tesco, with its 22,500 employees. A leading London law firm announced that it was bringing a mega-law suit on behalf of the women working on Tesco's checkouts. Its case was that they were paid only £8 an hour, in contrast to the £11 an hour earned by men working in its distribution system. Coupled with a claim by the women for years of back pay, it was said that this could cost Tesco a record £4 billion. But it then emerged that the many men working on the shop tills were paid exactly the same basic £8 an hour as their female colleagues, while women working in distribution earned the same £11 an hour as their male counterparts. In other words, when like was compared with like, for the vast majority of Tesco's staff the pay rates for women and men doing the same work were exactly the same (as the law had required since 1970). There was no 'gender pay gap'. And the further the debate raged over what Theresa May herself had described as 'a burning injustice', the more it emerged that the issue was far more complicated than such an emotively crude oversimplification.

May herself had required Britain's large companies to provide figures for their own workforce, and when these were published, at first sight they seemed to confirm the picture she herself imagined. Overall, across all their employees, men were indeed paid 18 per cent more than women. But this was seriously skewed by the fact that there were many more men than women at the very top of those companies, sometimes earning astronomically more than the vast majority of those below them. When this tiny minority was stripped out, the picture became very different. Among younger employees, incomes for men and women were very much the same. Take away part-time workers, and the gap shrank to a barely noticeable 1.8 per cent.

The gap really began to open up when so many women ceased working to have children. Even if they later returned, this interruption to their career often meant that they had stepped off the promotion ladder. Again, one reason why there were so many more men in very senior positions was that the more ambitious of them had never had to break off to look after a family, and were prepared to work exceptionally hard and single-mindedly to get to the top. The much smaller number of women who were similarly motivated no longer found discrimination on the grounds of their gender a bar to that kind of success. Indeed, such was the changed mood of the times that on many occasions the very fact that they were female worked in their favour when it came to promotion and the financial rewards that went with it.

In a different context, that same mood of the times was reflected in a startling new recruiting campaign for the British Army, which for some years had been struggling to win new recruits. In keeping with the Army's chief purpose and its proud record, previous Army campaigns had carried the slogan 'Be the best', showing men in such traditionally masculine roles as fighting in the front line or driving tanks. But now its recruiting had been outsourced to Capita, a public company largely run by former employees of local government.

Their new advertising went to the opposite end of the spectrum. It was no longer targeted as before at the mainly white, would-be tough young men who might previously have been prime candidates for life as a soldier, attracted by the prospect of belonging to an elite, disciplined fighting force, developing useful skills and enjoying masculine adventure. The new recruiting drive was directed exclusively at women, gays, Muslims and other members of ethnic minorities, who it hoped to welcome into what had now been branded as 'the Belonging Army'.

Only later did a leaked official document reveal that this new approach was very much directed from the top of the Army itself. With the full backing of the head of Britain's armed forces, General

Sir Nick Carter, a new 'Compulsory Objectives' scheme ruled that any male soldier who failed actively to work for making the Army 'a modern, diverse and inclusive workplace' could not expect promotion.

By contrast, in these early months of 2018, there was growing public alarm over the dramatic explosion in knife crime, particularly in the poorer parts of London. In 2017 there had been 80 fatal stabbings in London. In the first three months of 2018 there had already been 50 more. Non-fatal stabbings, according to the police, were now running at '300–400 a month'.

This knife culture, which had spread from the US, centred on gangs of hooded teenagers and young men, many from ethnic minority backgrounds, for whom stabbing members of other gangs had become the test of their masculinity. Most were on drugs and they incessantly boasted of their stabbings on the internet, notably through 'drill videos' posted on YouTube, accompanied by violent rap songs describing their latest 'hits', for which 'high achievers' could make a hefty income from the number of 'likes' they registered. The first star 'drill rapper' in the US, Chief Keef from Chicago, had been signed up to a multi-million-dollar deal at the age of 16. Another, Lil Mouse, was only 12 when he was 'discovered'.

The British Army may now have gone out of its way to avoid appealing to masculinity in its latest recruiting campaign. But the urge of young men to demonstrate their masculinity and to compete and show off had not disappeared. It was now resurfacing in its darkest, most nihilistic form, in the gangs who roamed the streets of London, measuring their testosterone-fuelled manliness by the number of other teenagers and young men they could stab and even kill, in order to crow about it in the most lurid fashion on the internet.

Many of these socially alienated young males, betrayed by a society that no longer gave them the education, the opportunities and the values that might have enabled them to grow up into responsible members of society, were black. Although they themselves would have known little of history, there were others who, nominally on their behalf, would have seen them as victims of Britain's dark racist past.

A female *Guardian* columnist noted that Britain's great naval hero Admiral Horatio Nelson, commemorated by London's most famous statue, in the square named after his most famous victory, had served in the West Indies in the days of slavery at the end of the eighteenth century. He had befriended local white planters who derived their wealth from their army of imported black African slaves. It was time, she suggested, to remove the statue of this 'racist' from his column in Trafalgar Square.

Had this just remained a suggestion by a *Guardian* columnist, it would have been seen as no more than might be expected from the country's most politically correct newspaper. But it was seized on by Historic England, the official body charged with looking after Britain's historic heritage, to propose, accompanied by a picture of Nelson's statue being smashed by a wrecking ball, that this should start a national debate over which other statues of historic figures should be removed for similar reasons.

As another legacy of Britain's colonialist past, in March 2018 a Sunday newspaper revealed what appeared to be the most shocking example yet of the mass abuse of young, often under-age white girls by Asian gangs of mainly Pakistani origin. In the Shropshire town of Telford in 2013 seven Muslim men had been sentenced to prison for the serial abuse of some 200 girls. But new evidence had now come to light to suggest that this mass criminality had been on a much greater scale than previously reported, involving since the 1980s anything up to 1,000 victims, and even the killing of at least five people to prevent them revealing to the authorities what was going on. Again, there was evidence that this had been known for years to local police and social workers, who had done nothing. But equally telling was the silence of the 'Me Too' generation of feminists, who clearly regarded the fate of these young girls as not part of their battle for female equality.

If this was just the latest of such scandals allowed to fester out of sight through the official belief in 'multi-culturalism', another contradiction emerged a few weeks later.

Inspectors from Ofsted, the state body charged with regulating standards in Britain's schools, had gone into the Yesoday Hatorah senior school for girls from Orthodox Jewish families in Stamford Hill in North London. The school had an exemplary record for its academic results, discipline and general behaviour. But the only thing which seemed seriously to worry the inspectors was that the girls were not being taught about 'sex', because this was contrary to the school's strict religious principles. Nor was there any mention of homosexuality. The inspectors even grilled the girls about internet dating, although this too was not just against the school rules but would certainly have been prohibited by the girls' parents.

What made this even more remarkable, however, was that Ofsted was also nominally responsible for policing scores of Muslim schools, where almost identically strict religious rules applied. Yet out of respect for their 'cultural traditions', there had never been any instance of Ofsted complaining about the similar ethic in these schools. Somehow, when it came to Jewish children, it seemed, the principles of 'multi-culturalism' no longer applied.

By contrast, no part of the education system, either in Britain or North America, had long been more of a hotbed of politically correct groupthink than their universities. Typical of what was now going in many of them was an announcement by the philosophy faculty of Oxford University in March 2018 that, to attract more women students, its 'diversity and equality officer' was to draw up a new reading list. After 2,500 years when all but a tiny handful of the world's leading philosophers had been men, 40 per cent of the authors on the new reading list were now to be female. This was a variant of the kind of 'positive discrimination' first pioneered at Stanford back in the 1980s. Students would be asked to read texts not because of their intellectual merit or place in the evolving history of Western thought, but simply because of their authors' gender. To make room for them on the list, many eminent philosophers of the past would now have to be ditched from the syllabus.

Equally notable was the way the young stormtroopers of political correctness were now focusing so much of their rage on the very idea of any right to freedom of speech and thought (other, of course, than their own). At King's College, London, a debate on free speech organised by the university's Libertarian Society was broken up in violent disorder by a masked mob of self-declared 'Anti-Fascists'. Bursting into the lecture room, they screamed abuse and threw punches at anyone in range, using precisely the tactics pioneered by Hitler's Brownshirt gangs in 1930s Germany.

Even more symbolically apt was a meeting organised by the Law Faculty at Queen's University in Canada, to discuss 'The rise of compelled speech'. The chief speaker, in an imposing Gothic hall packed with a 900-strong audience, was Dr Jordan Peterson, the Toronto University psychologist who had by now become famous for his campaign against Canada's new law making it a criminal offence not to use prescribed 'gender-neutral personal pronouns' such as 'zie' and 'zis' when addressing people who had 'self-identified' as 'transgender'.

Introducing Peterson, the moderator of the meeting cited this and other examples of how official bodies in Ontario were now requiring lawyers, teachers and organizers of summer camps to promote politically correct ideas. He was loudly interrupted by a protester in the gallery screaming that this was 'a 'f***ing lie. There's no such thing as compelled speech.' A yelling gang of protesters then surged through the hall, two of them invading the platform to stand in front of Peterson with a crude banner reading 'Freedom to smash bigotry'. After a minute or two of shouting, the demonstrators were ushered out of the room. When Peterson observed, 'That's pure narcissism at work, by the way,' this met with a huge cheer.

He then enlarged on how vital were freedom of speech and thought to any civilized society. In light of what they had just witnessed, he noted in particular the damage being done to young university students, encouraged by 'pathological professors' who wanted them not to think for themselves but only to brainwash them into a particular form of 'radical ideology'. 'A university is an absolutely remarkable institution,' he said, 'and to see it brought down by people whose behaviour would be out of place at a four-year-old's birthday party is something abysmal to behold.'

Peterson could not have needed a neater demonstration of his message than the sound from outside the hall of an even larger mob of students chanting abuse and continuing to bang on its large stained-glass windows (eventually breaking one of them), which lasted throughout the rest of the hour-and-a-half-long proceedings.

One reason why Peterson had recently become to so many people a charismatic figure was the part he had played two months earlier in an interview on British television. This was such a revealing landmark in the history of political correctness that it merits a final section to itself.

THE CATHY NEWMAN–JORDAN PETERSON INTERVIEW

One of the more obvious characteristics of those in the grip of any form of groupthink is that they prefer on the whole only to mix with people who share their own beliefs and mind-set. If they ever encounter people who disagree with them, they prefer to do so in a group, in order to shout them down. Only occasionally do they find themselves confronted with someone from outside their bubble articulate and clever enough to expose just shallow and irrational their mind-set is.

Such an occasion was the television interview on 16 January 2018 between Jordan Peterson and Cathy Newman, a famously aggressive interviewer on *Channel 4 News*. When this was posted in full on YouTube, it instantly became such compulsive viewing on both sides of the Atlantic that within a few weeks it had registered more than 10 million views and attracted over 100,000 comments.

Peterson was in Europe to publicize his latest book, *12 Rules for Life*. In the previous year he had built up a huge following, above all through YouTube, for his lectures and interviews, which showed him to be the most penetrating critic yet of what politically correct ideology was doing to Western society. In particular, drawing on the authority of his 30 years as a clinical psychologist working with thousands of patients, and his time as a professor of psychology, Peterson warned of what was happening to men as they were no longer encouraged to become positively masculine, and to women as they became possessed by the idea that they should forget the instinctive attributes of their femininity, to compete with men on supposedly 'equal' male terms.

From the very first question Newman fired at Peterson it was clear that, as a committed feminist herself, she was out to demolish this professor as no more than just another bigoted, narrow-minded, 'alt-right' misogynist. In a scornfully challenging tone, she began, 'Jordan Peterson, you said that men must, quote, "grow the hell up." Tell me why.'

'Well', he replied, 'because there's nothing more ugly than an overgrown infant.' 'People who don't grow up,' he went on, warming to his theme,

> don't find the meaning in their life that sustains them in difficult times, and they're certain to encounter difficult times. And they're left bitter and resentful, without purpose, and adrift, and hostile, and vengeful, and arrogant, and deceitful, and of no use to themselves, and of no use to anyone else, and no partner for a woman, and there's nothing in it that's good.

It was an unexpectedly dramatic opening, and it went on from there for nearly half an hour, as it became increasingly obvious that Newman had a preconceived image of the kind of man she thought she was dealing with, while Peterson continued to demonstrate by his thoughtful, carefully worded, factual replies, often with a smile, that he was nothing of the kind.

One feature of the interview which particularly caught widespread attention was the way Newman again and again tried to accuse Peterson of being things he was not: hostile to women, in favour of a 'gender pay gap', guilty of 'vast generalizations' and 'transphobic'. Each time Peterson gave yet another reply she didn't expect, she would try to squeeze him back into her preconceived picture of him by responding with, 'So what you're saying is . . .', and then giving an absurdly upside-down caricature of what he had said. On each occasion, he politely but firmly had to correct her by pointing out that her version bore no relation to what he had actually said or thought at all.

The high point of this textbook demonstration of how groupthink always tries to distort the views of its opponents into a form that can make them seem ridiculous came when, around 22 minutes in, Newman was asking Peterson what right he had to 'offend' transgender people by refusing to call them by the gender pronoun they preferred. He pointed out that he had never done anything of the sort. He had only opposed the Canadian law mandating the use of 'gender-neutral' pronouns, because this was a wholly unacceptable abuse of the right to free speech. He went on to suggest that, throughout the interview, she had been going out of her way to be as disagreeable and offensive to him as possible, which he had found 'rather uncomfortable', but that she had every right to do so ('Good for you'). But if, he went on, she was undoubtedly doing her job in exercising her own right to be offensive, how could she then complain about other people being offensive? 'You're exercising your right to freedom of speech certainly, to risk offending me. And that's fine, more power to you . . .'

At this point, for the first time in the interview, Newman looked nonplussed, then said, 'I'm just trying to work that out, I mean . . .'

Watching her struggling for words for more than ten seconds, Peterson leaned forwards and said with a smile in his voice, 'Hah, gotcha!'

Although the interview continued for several more minutes, with Newman threshing around ever more wildly in her attempt to lay a glove on him, this was the key moment. And what the majority of those who commented on it took from it was that it was an object lesson in how those who are locked in a particular mind-set cannot think outside it. Many viewers took delight in beginning their comments with the words, 'So what you are saying is . . .' For all her evident desire to crush Peterson, Newman had not really understood a word he was saying. All she could repeatedly do was attack that caricature-image of him that existed only in her own head. And with every word he uttered, he had shown that she was operating as if in a parallel universe.

In other words, she gave a perfect illustration of what happens to anyone who has become possessed by groupthink. There is nothing they want more than to exercise their morally superior scorn for anyone who does not share their mind-set. But when the real world occasionally manages to intrude on their bubble, with facts and evidence and rationally argued points, there will eventually come a moment when like Newman they are nonplussed and lost for words.

We shall see this happen again many times in the course of this book. But first we shall take a rather deeper look at how and why Western society had worked itself up into such an unprecedently confused, unhappy and divisive state.

3

The Real Nature of 'Political Correctness'

Never was any age more devoid of real feeling, more exaggerated in false feeling than our own . . . the radio and the cinema are mere counterfeit feeling all the time, the current press and literature the same. People wallow in emotion, counterfeit emotion. They lap it up, they live in and on it . . . and at times they get on very well with it all. And then, more and more, they break.

D. H. Lawrence, Apropos of *Lady Chatterley's Lover* (1929)

Nothing quite like what we have been looking at in the past two chapters has ever happened to any society before in history. To set it in a wider perspective we might imagine a little group of time travellers transported forward from the time when our story began, in the early 1950s, into the world of the twenty-first century. Obviously, there would be no end to what would surprise them about all the ways in which the world had changed. They would naturally marvel at all the astonishing technological innovations which had transformed life almost out of recognition since their day. They would be amazed by the unimaginable material prosperity enjoyed by so many people in this new twenty-first-century world.

But as they came to learn a little more about how people lived in this seemingly utopian new society, nothing might surprise them more than to discover how much of that old framework of moral values and social conventions by which they had lived in the early Fifties had now disappeared. And of course, much of the unwritten purpose of that framework had been to hold society together by providing a protection against individually selfish and socially disruptive behaviour.

They would be startled to learn, for instance, of the massive increase in every kind of crime: in drug-taking, in gambling; in the casual use of once-taboo swear words. Above all, they might be taken aback to find how conspicuously obsessed with sex Western society in particular had become: sexual imagery of every kind; the availability of pornography; public discussion of sex; even young children taught about sex in schools (with little mention of 'love'); and the extent to which sexually promiscuous behaviour had come to be so widely taken for granted.

They would be amazed by the extent to which the institution of marriage had collapsed, so that 43 per cent of all marriages in Britain (and around the same in the US) now ended in divorce, with an even greater number of breakdowns in the relationships between men and women merely living together. They would be still more astonished to learn that it was now possible for people of the same sex to get married, and even to adopt other people's children.

Indeed, our time travellers might well wonder what all this disintegration of traditional family life had done to children in general. They would not be wholly surprised to find one commentator observing that 'according to various studies', children who had suffered the emotional trauma of their parents divorcing or splitting up 'do worse at school, are more likely to suffer mental or emotional problems, more likely to be unemployed or end up in low-skilled work, more likely to be in trouble with the police, more likely to take drugs, more likely to be promiscuous'.[56]

---

[56]Rod Liddle, 'Divorce destroys society. Don't let's make it easier,' *Spectator*, 25 November 2017, https://www.spectator.co.uk/2017/11/divorce-destroys-society-dont-lets-make-it-easier/

But of all the changes of those intervening 60 years, nothing would have puzzled them more about this new world than its preoccupation with what was now known as 'gender'. On learning that it was now fashionable to believe that, psychologically and biologically, there was no difference between men and women (and that you could even be sacked by one of the world's most powerful companies for denying this), they would stare in disbelief. Wherever they went they would see males and females still looking as distinct from each other as ever: in their appearance, their hair, their clothing, their voices and manners of speech. The vast majority of people they saw pushing baby buggies down the street were still recognizably female. Could it really now be believed that these differences were not rooted in biology but all just a 'social construct', the result of 'gender stereotyping'?

No experience had been generally more important in the lives of our time travellers than that they had lived through those five extraordinary years of the Second World War. In that tough and testing time, men and women alike had risen to the challenge, many aware that at any time they or people they knew might be killed, and united in one all-important cause that called on all their reserves of endurance. For all involved, such stern masculine values as duty, discipline, patriotism, responsibility and respect for authority had been at a premium.

Men at that time, whether serving in the front line of battle or not, had, in the best sense, been 'expected to be men', and there was never any doubt about what this meant. Even today, we can see it mirrored in old films showing those wartime Allied leaders, such as Churchill, Roosevelt or de Gaulle. They were all unmistakably men of fully masculine weight and authority. Indeed, we can see the same ideal of firm and masterful masculinity still represented by the leading male film stars of the years immediately after the war: in Hollywood's Gary Cooper, James Stewart, John Wayne, Gregory Peck and Charlton Heston, or Britain's Jack Hawkins, Kenneth More, James Robertson Justice and many more.

But what made the screen characters played by such actors admired fictional heroes rather than villains was that they were not just outwardly so obviously masculine. They were also presented as selfless, sensitive and compassionate, using their masculine strength to act firmly on behalf of others and the community as a whole. As the Jungians would put it, their outward manly strength of character was balanced and made positive by the more selfless qualities of their inner 'feminine'.

In other words, masculine and feminine qualities are not confined just to one sex. Men and women can have both masculine and feminine traits in their psychological make-up, irrespective of their gender. In essence those attributes which involve any element of strength, whether in a man or a woman, can be seen as 'masculine'. A softer empathetic feeling and sensitivity towards others is seen in psychological terms as 'feminine'. And unless strength is balanced by feeling for others it makes people, regardless of their gender, hard, insensitive to others and self-centred.

Similarly, that part of our brain which tries to think logically and rationally, concerned with order, structure and facts – what is often described as 'left-brain thinking' – is in psychological terms 'masculine'. 'Right-brain thinking', based on intuition and creative imagination, is psychologically 'feminine'. Again, without the life-giving balance of intuitive understanding, the rational calculations of left-brain thinking can become so boxed in on themselves as to lose touch with practical reality.

All these different aspects of our psychological functioning apply to men and women alike. To become fully alive, mature and responsible requires masculine and feminine traits to be in balance. Men may naturally be more obviously governed by the masculine side of their psyche, but this must be balanced by that inner feminine element which Jung called the *anima*: the ability to feel for others and a sense of wider intuitive understanding,

Equally, a woman may well be instinctively more at home with the creative, caring and intuitive, 'feminine' part of her psyche. But this also needs the strengthening balance of the 'masculine' element: what Jung called the *animus*: that strength of mind and character which has typified strong women down the ages, just as it enabled so many women to play their own equally strong and courageous part in those testing years of the Second World War.

What our travellers from those days would discover, however, was that, after the 'sexual revolution' of the Sixties, the sexes were meant to have 'converged'. Men were supposed to have become softer, gentler, more 'feminized'. In the new age of 'equality' and 'women's rights', those sterner masculine values of discipline, authority and order had often come to be seen as no more than oppressive, constricting and life-denying instruments of domination.

Women, on the other hand, were supposed to become more assertive and independent, capable of competing equally with men on male terms. And herein lay the seeds of so many of those contradictions which were eventually to lead the groupthink of political correctness into such bitter and divisive confusion.

THE LOST 'MASCULINE' AND THE LOST 'FEMININE'

What was psychologically so revealing about this supposed convergence between the sexes was not that it achieved a more harmonious balance between men and women, between the 'masculine' and 'feminine' elements in each, but what it showed getting lost on both sides.

Certainly, when men lose touch with their feminine side, their *anima*, they remain stuck in the state of one-sided, 'male chauvinist' insensitivity that typifies all men, according to the caricature presented by feminists such as Germaine Greer. But when men fail properly to develop their masculinity they can in an equally negative way become soft and 'feminized'. Without strength of character, they can become possessed by what Jung called the 'negative *anima*': weak, indecisive, petulant, resentful and just as self-centred as the men who remain one-sidedly masculine.

The converse of all this is what we see when women also lose their own internal gender balance. When Greer and the feminists argued that women should become more assertive and competitive, what they were also rejecting was the potentially softer, more selfless feminine part of themselves. They scorned such attributes as empathetic feeling and an instinctive desire to care for others, which Greer saw as only having made women weak and submissive, laying them open to being dominated by egocentric, unfeeling men.

Women, the feminists argued, should forget their feminine qualities, those which had traditionally placed them at the centre of family life, as strong, caring mothers and grandmothers, as loving wives to loving husbands, as nurses tending the sick, as good and helpful neighbours, and in all those other roles which have made them the quite distinctive but equally important 'other half' to men in almost all human societies down the ages.

Instead, ran the new message, they must learn to live only by the more aggressive values of their *animus*: their inner 'masculine'. But the consequence of losing touch with their own femininity is that they then become possessed by what Jung called the 'negative *animus*': that element in a woman's psyche which can make her just as eager to control and dominate as any one-sided man. Because, unlike a man, a woman cannot usually rely on physical strength to get her way, her negative *animus* seeks to dominate verbally. She becomes hard, argumentative, quick to take offence, imagining that she is speaking in the accents of masculine reason but unaware that the more she is possessed by her negative *animus*, the more dogmatically irrational she can become.

Once we see what is really going on with all these gender imbalances, the more clearly we can begin to understand the confusion into which they have been leading us. When, for instance, Harvey Weinstein and all those other male 'sex pests' are exposed as having no idea of how to treat women in a sensitive, grown-up fashion, this is because they are unable to make any contact with the empathy of their inner feminine. This is why they treat women with contempt, as little more than objects, to be used for the gratification of their own egos. Their stunted, one-sided masculinity has left them emotionally deformed, immature and wholly self-centred.

But equally, we can see what happens to men when they are encouraged to lose touch with their masculinity by becoming 'feminized'. In terms of properly balanced masculinity, we see what a change has come over the values of society in the past 60 years by contrasting two images of the British police. A popular BBC television series in the Fifties, *Dixon of Dock Green*, gave an idealized picture of an ordinary policeman of that time as a solidly masculine but also kindly and understanding father-figure, in no doubt that his duty was to protect the community around him by firmly but fairly enforcing law and order.

Compare this with the picture of the British police we saw at the beginning of the first chapter, where in 2017 they were expected to wander the streets in women's high heels or displaying their blue-varnished fingernails, to 'raise awareness' of 'domestic violence by men against women', or the problem of 'slavery in nails bars'. When a member of the public caustically tweeted that they would do better by 'nailing some criminals', these policemen had become so 'feminized' that they could only petulantly respond by tweeting back that such a comment might constitute a 'hate crime'.

More generally, contrast those heavyweight, unmistakably masculine political leaders of the wartime years with Britain's lightweight and colourless male politicians of later decades. This was one of the reasons why, by the early twenty-first century, when the House of Commons was now almost entirely full of MPs whose values had been shaped in the years after the 1960s, the general reputation of Parliament was on an unprecedentedly downward curve. In the age of Tony Blair and David Cameron, respect for politicians had rarely, if ever, been lower. They tended to be obsessed with image and effect rather than genuine substance or moral principle. The need to appear politically correct had become the order of the day, on every issue from the need for 'diversity' and same-sex marriage to their unthinking belief in 'man-made climate change'. Indeed, in terms of diminished masculine authority, the same had come to be true of many prominent men in almost every area of Britain's national life.

But all this had coincided with the ever more insistent drive to make women 'equal' with men: that relentless pressure to get ever more women into formerly male-dominated occupations, from politics and the boardrooms of major companies to the police, the armed forces and much else.

On occasion this had worked very well, as in the case of the 'Iron Lady', Margaret Thatcher, who – like other strong female leaders elsewhere in the world, before her, such as Golda Meir or Indira Gandhi – had such a powerful 'masculine' component in her psychological make-up that she made her male colleagues seem emasculated by comparison. It was as if, the more inadequate and unmanly Britain's male politicians had become, the more she had emerged to provide all the principled conviction and strength of character they lacked. Often successful, too, had been the marked advance of strong, capable and psychologically balanced women in many other predominantly male occupations, from medicine or running their own businesses to engineering and piloting airliners.

But where this did work, the key to their success lay in those words 'psychologically balanced'. Too often, when political correctness came to dictate that women should be promoted to positions of responsibility not on their individual merits but only because of their gender, the results were much less impressive.

When Mrs Thatcher became prime minister, she was one of only 19 female MPs in Parliament. By 2017 this figure had soared to 208, nearly a third of the House. But by this time, when the public standing of Parliament had already conspicuously declined, scarcely any of these stridently opinionated, virtually interchangeable 'new women' did any more to restore public respect for politicians than their male colleagues. No longer did they stand out as distinctive individuals with minds of their own, as a good many forceful female MPs, both Labour and Tory, had done in the years when there were infinitely fewer of them.

Equally dismal was the performance of virtually all those politically correct women now being promoted on all sides to run civil service departments, government agencies and other public bodies. Some, because of their gender, were moved around from one top position to another so often that they became scornfully spoken of as 'quango queens'. But almost invariably such women were too obviously driven by their *animus*, full of their own importance but behind their backs earning little respect from their subordinates. In their own way they were just as little qualified for their posts as any weak and ineffectual man. Unfortunate too were the often disruptive consequences of insisting for reasons of 'gender equality' that women in the armed forces should be allowed to serve alongside men in ships or combat zones.

If the first rule of groupthink is that it is never properly rooted in reality, the ideological pursuit of this particular view of 'equality' between the sexes was to a significant extent based on no more than collective make-believe. What had gone missing was not just the confidence and authority of positive masculinity in men. For too many of these hard, *animus*-driven women encouraged to compete as 'equal' with men, they had lost any sense of their selfless, empathetic femininity.

Either way, the result was the same. What emerged was not the kind of psychological balance and maturity which naturally commands respect. As with so much else that had happened to society in those decades since the early Fifties, what remained was a picture of people no longer fully developed on either the masculine or the feminine sides of their personality, caught in a state of psychological immaturity, ultimately centred on little more than the promptings of their own ego.

THE HIDDEN KEY: FAKE EMOTION AND THE COLLECTIVIZATION OF THE EGO

It is certainly arguable that that our modern Western society has given greater licence to multifarious expression of the human ego than any before. As early as the Seventies, Tom Wolfe wrote a famous essay on the state of American society aptly called 'The Me Decade'. It was a title which could have been appropriate to any decade since.

But this has not meant that the 'feminine' values of feeling and emotion have vanished. On the contrary, in a particular sense they have come to be projected as one of the most conspicuous features of our age. Consider the wave of collective emotion which in 1997 swept Britain when Diana, Princess of Wales, was killed with her latest lover in a car driven by a drunken driver in Paris. The death of 'the People's Princess', as she was dubbed by Tony Blair, was marked by the mass laying of flowers, the queuing to sign books of condolence, public displays of cards of sympathy in shop windows and obsessive discussion of this earth-shaking event at every turn, in as conspicuous a display of mass emotion as Britain had ever seen. Certainly, there had been solemn expressions of national grief at the deaths of members of the Royal Family before. But as a phenomenon of crowd psychology, reinforced by the relentless coverage given to this shocking event by the media, with much criticism of the Queen for not having 'shown her grief' by lowering the flag atop Buckingham Palace to half-mast, it was of a quite different order.

Not dissimilar in 2015 was the response to the mass murder by Algerian Muslim terrorists of 11 members of the staff of a small-circulation French satirical magazine, *Charlie Hebdo*, after it had routinely published crude, obscene and deliberately offensive cartoons of the Prophet Mohammed.

In no way, of course, did this justify the terrorists' response. But as so often, the groupthink of one group, setting out deliberately to be provocative, had only aroused a far more extreme response from another: the terrorist psychopaths locked in their own opposing form of groupthink.

The following weekend two million people packed the streets around the centre of Paris, chanting for hours '*Je suis Charlie*' and proclaiming their 'solidarity against terror'. Meanwhile 40 world leaders were corralled into a sealed-off side street for a carefully-staged photo opportunity which made headlines across the globe. Almost certainly virtually none of these politicians had previously heard of this little magazine, let alone examined its contents. But they were now eager to proclaim their collective support for the 'right to free speech', in a country whose leading newspapers received lavish state subsidies to ensure that France had the most politically servile press of any Western democracy.

These two episodes, and others not dissimilar, were hailed as deeply moving expressions of popular feeling. Anyone failing to get caught up in it was condemned as wholly lacking in human sensitivity. But how genuinely selfless were these displays of mass emotion? Or were they examples of what D. H. Lawrence foreshadowed (in the words quoted at the head of this chapter), when he wrote that 'never was any age more devoid of real feeling, more exaggerated in false feeling than our own.'

Emotion is such a powerful force in us that it can be detached from its proper object to become an end in itself. Those vast crowds chanting '*Je suis Charlie*' and the politicians who joined in that self-serving photo opportunity were no longer experiencing genuine, individual emotion. They were no longer even experiencing the horror they had doubtless felt when they had first heard news of the atrocity. They had been swept up as one into something quite different: a massive public display of collectivized emotion. They were, as Lawrence put it, 'wallowing', in an orgy of that very 'false feeling' he was describing.

We talk about how our emotions can be 'played on' or 'manipulated'. This is why we can be made to cry by a sentimental film, even though it is only presenting us with a make-believe image having no connection to our own personal situation or indeed reality of any kind. That is what we mean by sentimentality: it plays on our capacity for genuine emotions by allowing us to indulge ourselves in a counterfeit of them.

Few things more obviously make an emotional appeal to us than the image of innocent people made to suffer through no fault of their own. It is why our contemporary media are awash with such stories: interviews and pictures of those caught up in a terrorist atrocity, or a dreadful civil war, or a famine in which thousands are dying, or some other natural disaster. When such a heart-rending event hits the news, multi-million-pound charities are quick to advertise for donations, because they know it will attract a flood of money from moved members of the public. Of course we are moved by such triggers to our emotions: they are appealing to one of our deepest human instincts. Which brings us back to the real, underlying nature of political correctness.

Beneath any form of political correctness is its division of the world into two groups, and its appeal almost invariably starts from the instinct to feel sympathy for one of them: 'victims' – of some kind of oppression, prejudice or discrimination. Once this is taken over by groupthink, even the 'victims' themselves can sentimentalize their plight, as can all those who rally to support them.

The other group, of course, consists of all those who can be seen as responsible for their suffering. And this is what adds that other crucial charge of emotional gratification inseparable from groupthink: the need to express morally superior contempt for all those unfeeling, self-centred 'others' who simply don't understand, and can therefore be dismissively labelled as 'sexists', 'racists', 'bigots', 'homophobes', 'trans-phobes', 'fascists' or whatever scornful term seems appropriate, to the point where this is no longer connected to the reality of whatever genuine injustice may originally have lain behind it, but has become an end in itself.

What matters is the self-righteous satisfaction which comes from denouncing all those wicked others seen as heartless enemies of proper feeling. With the handy little shorthand labels so characteristic of groupthink, they can be reduced, as Janis put it, to no more than 'dehumanized stereotypes'. Their views must be caricatured as so 'offensive' that they should not be permitted to speak at all. They have put themselves wholly beyond the pale. They must be 'no-platformed'.

This, more than anything, gives the game away, because it shows another significant feature of groupthink: welding all those under its spell into the kind of collective egotism we have seen in every example so far. It is after all the essence of what became known as 'identity politics': taking on the shared identity of the in-group you are part of. If you are a militant feminist you are no longer just a woman: you are a feminist woman. If you are a militant black activist, you are not just a human individual but first and foremost a very angry black – just as, if you are a white supremacist, or a Marxist, or a Nazi or a member of a terrorist group, this, more than anything, is what has come to define your identity.

Those carried away by any form of groupthink thus submerge their own personal egos in the collective egos of their group. But that they now share in its common identity helps to inflate their own self-importance. Membership of the group enables them to indulge their own egos, not just in signalling that they share in its state of virtue, but, just as importantly, in displaying ritualized outrage at all those contemptibly unvirtuous outsiders who do not.

Thus groupthink is, by definition, inevitably divisive. It splits the world into in-group and out-group; virtuous 'us' and morally inferior 'them'. This was why political correctness fitted in so neatly with the neo-Marxist view of the world constantly hovering behind it after 1968. It was the fundamental mind-set which ultimately reduced all social questions down to the perennial power struggle reflected in Lenin's famous question: 'Who, Whom?' Who, with all their power and privilege, are doing what to those without them?

Lying behind every form of political correctness was the same stereotyped picture: of society divided between one group with the power, abusing it to make the other its victim. As Germaine Greer wrote in 1970, 'Women are the only true proletariat left' (although other 'victim groups' might not have wished to agree). The Marxist answer to this, of course, is that the victims must rise up to take that power themselves, and thus bring about a better, happier world.

If our time travellers wanted to know whether twenty-first-century society was in general happier and more at ease with itself than the world they had known in those bleak, deprived days of the early Fifties, they would have found the answer to be distinctly equivocal.

For many people life had undoubtedly become very much easier than it had been in that distant, difficult time. With significant exceptions, relations between people of different races had also in many respects become easier. The old divisions between social classes had to a great extent dissolved. Social relations in general had become more informal and relaxed. And one must not exaggerate the extent to which those old values which had held sway until the early Fifties had vanished. It was certainly one measure of how social mores had changed that by the early twenty-first century nearly half of all marriages in Britain and America ended in divorce. But this still meant that more than half survived, and that many of those couples had come to recognize the age-old truth that men and women are indeed psychologically very different from one another, but that they also need each other – instinctively, biologically, socially and psychologically – to make a whole.

In other respects, however, life by the early twenty-first century was not so happy. It had become edgier, more strained and certainly a great deal more confusing. At the beginning of the first chapter, I quoted a journalist asking in 2017, 'Why do we hate and despise each other so much these days?' Insofar as his question had a point, a large part of the answer lay in the all-pervading presence of divisive groupthink. Nowhere did this become more evident than on the internet, that miracle of technology which in many ways was so useful. But in the age of the 'selfie', Facebook and Twitter, it had given new opportunities of expression to the human ego.

It had, for instance, vastly increased the availability of pornography, the most egocentric form of sexual make-believe of all. Not the least incongruity of the belief that any differences between men and women are just a 'social construct' was that millions of men could derive gratification from gazing at images of naked women, not because they had been socialized to do this, but because men are genetically programmed to become sexually aroused by the sight of women's naked bodies (the reverse is not true of women to anything like the same extent). More generally the internet had turned 'social media' into 'anti-social media', giving huge numbers of people the chance to exercise their egos, both individually and collectively, as never before, not least with the licence to broadcast to the world their intolerance of other human beings with an ease previously unthinkable.

Thus had those original Sixties dreams of joyful liberation from old social constraints gradually created a new social and psychological prison. The collective make-believe had collided, as eventually it always must, with a host of quite unforeseen and far from comfortable realities.

In the next part of the book we shall extend our study of the workings of groupthink rather more widely, for which we must consider the particular conditions most likely to encourage groupthink in all its forms to arise and flourish in the first place. In the next chapter we shall take a perhaps unexpected detour into history, and look at some of the most extreme examples the world has ever seen of when groupthink comes to dominate the life of an entire society (apart, that is, from the more intolerant perversions of religion), with consequences for that society that tend to unfold according to a particular and recognizable pattern. We can then return to look at more examples of how and why it has become such a conspicuous feature of the world we live in.

Part II

Groupthink and Times of Change –
A Detour into History

4

Times of Change: How Dreams Become Nightmares

Bliss was it in that dawn to be alive,
But to be young was very heaven.

William Wordsworth, *The Prelude*, recalling the early
days of the French Revolution

There was a mighty ferment in the heads of statesmen and poets, kings and people. According to the prevailing notions . . . nothing that was established was to be tolerated . . . It was a time of promise, a renewal of the world . . .

William Hazlitt, *On the Living Poets*, looking back on
that time in 1818

We may say then that in all our revolutions there is a tendency for power to go from Right to Center to Left, from the conservatives of the old regime to the moderates to the radicals or extremists. As power moves along this line, it gets more and more concentrated, it narrows its base in the country and among the people.

Crane Brinton, *The Anatomy of Revolution*

Like Saturn, the Revolution devours its children.

Jacques Mallet du Pan (1793)

One reason why our time has become so prey to groupthink is unquestionably that in the past 60 years the world has been going through the most intense period of change ever. On the back of astonishing technological advances which in the early post-war years would have seemed unimaginable, long-established certainties, assumptions and values have melted away like snow. So many familiar old reference points were disappearing. In such a bewilderingly new and unfamiliar world people were removed from the old mental and moral framework which could have helped them make sense of it, and recognize what they accepted as reality. People became increasingly inclined to take on board what they were told to think and believe by others: by the media and above all by the intoxicating new spirit of the age.

In his book *The Lonely Crowd*, the American sociologist David Riesman famously described the three ways in which people can be categorized according to the primary source of the values and beliefs by which they live. Through the greater part of human history most people have been predominantly 'tradition-directed': that is to say they have taken on the values and beliefs passed on to them by the traditions and long-established conventions of the society into which they were born. Particularly in times of great change, however, they may become what Riesman called 'other-directed'. They take on the newly fashionable values and beliefs of those around them and the new mood of the times – and thus more easily susceptible to different forms of groupthink.

Then there was Riesman's third, much smallest category: the people he described as 'inner-directed': who live by values and beliefs they have worked out individually, thinking for themselves, and are thus ready to question the groupthink around them.

History has of course presented us with many examples of how, in periods of intense change, highly infectious forms of 'other-directed' groupthink can carry people forward en masse towards consequences they had never remotely foreseen. A particularly vivid illustration is the pattern we see infolding in those great revolutionary upheavals which rocked England in the 1640s, France after 1789 and Russia after 1917.

THREE AGES OF REVOLUTION

In each of these periods of exceptional turbulence, we see how people who were living in an essentially tradition-directed society began to rebel against a long-established ruling order they had come to see as constricting and oppressive. In each case, as the old order came to be challenged in the name of greater freedom – 'rights', 'liberty', 'equality' – it initially seemed to be giving way to the dreams of a better, less constricting world. But once the impulse for radical change took hold, it developed its own momentum, becoming ever more extreme in its demands until eventually, the old order having been overthrown altogether, a new order emerged much more oppressive and intolerant of any dissent than the one it replaced.

In *The Anatomy of Revolution*, the American historian Crane Brinton traced an underlying pattern between those three periods of upheaval. They shared certain basic components, even though they didn't always appear in the same sequence. But in crucial respects their course and eventual outcome were remarkably similar.

(i) Seventeenth-century England

In the first of these revolutions, a long-brewing sense of grievance and resentment at the autocratic powers of the King, Charles I, finally found its focus in 1641, when the English Parliament united to mount a determined challenge to his authority. Initially Charles was forced to give way, by surrendering his two most powerful and unpopular advisers to be imprisoned, one to be beheaded immediately, the other later. But as relations with Parliament became ever more fraught, they led in the summer of 1642 to the second stage of the story, the outbreak of open civil war.

The country split down the middle, between the supporters of the old order and those who wanted a new and very different order. Each side, the Royalists and the Parliamentarians, became possessed by its own form of groupthink, increasing seeing even old friends and neighbours as hated enemies. For two years the Royalists enjoyed military successes. But by 1644, with the Parliamentary forces ever more dominated by fanatical Puritans under the direction of Oliver Cromwell, the tide turned. In 1645, thanks to Cromwell's tightly disciplined New Model Army, Parliament was victorious, and by 1646 the King was in effect its prisoner.

But with the old framework of society gone, what next? Cromwell's army was now much more radical in its views than many members of the Parliament in whose name it was acting. The war's conclusion produced a torrent of demands, from various even more extreme activist groups such as the Levellers, that the revolution go much further, in pursuit of more fundamental popular rights.

For the time being, however, the Parliamentary moderates still carried the day, hoping to establish a new constitutional monarchy, under which the King could remain on the throne under much greater parliamentary control. But when in 1648 England faced the external threat of a Scottish invasion in support of the King, a second civil war began, in which again Cromwell's army was victorious. This outside intervention catalysed a new, more militant, phase of the revolution, in which a more extreme view prevailed.

In January 1649 Cromwell and his allies executed the King and declared England a republic, ruled by Parliament. But when this was followed by yet another invasion from Scotland, this time with Charles's son at its head, its defeat by Cromwell saw him emerge as England's undisputed strong man.

The Puritans had already begun to impose their joyless creed over English life, in everything from permitted forms of worship and the smashing of 'Papist' stained-glass windows and statues in churches to the banning of such traditional popular customs and pleasures as the celebrating of Christmas, maypole dancing, horse racing, drinking, playing music and the theatre. Now, step by step, Cromwell disbanded

Parliament, first expelling all its remaining non-Puritan moderates, then in 1653 closing down its 'Rump' altogether. Appointing himself as Protector (later Lord Protector), in the name of the 'suppression of vice and the encouragement of virtue', he put England under the military rule of Puritan major-generals, answerable only to himself.

But the English were wearying of these years of change, conflict and disorder. Faced with an even more overtly despotic form of government than the revolution had been launched to challenge, many began to hanker for a return to quieter, less confrontational times. After Cromwell's death in 1658, leaving a virtual vacuum of power, they were only too relieved in 1660 to welcome back Charles II as their rightful king. The ever more extreme make-believe of the revolutionary years was finally exhausted, and a modified version of the old order was restored.

(ii) Eighteenth-century France

A century and half later we see in the French Revolution a different version of the same pattern. Again, once the revolutionary groupthink had taken hold, the moderates were gradually replaced by a smaller, more fanatical group of extremists, who then fell out with one another, until this finally led to the crisis which brought the revolutionary fever to an end.

As in England, stage one saw a growing mood of discontent finding its focus in 1789 with an explosion of popular anger, this time directed not just against an autocratic King, Louis XVI, but also, in the name of 'liberty, equality and fraternity', against France's entire ruling social order. A joyful sense of liberation saw the powers and privileges of the monarchy, the aristocracy and the Catholic church drastically curbed. This was the time of which Wordsworth later recalled, 'Bliss was it in that dawn to be alive.'

Stage two of the revolution, lasting nearly two years, was a prolonged debate as to what sort of government France should now be ruled by. This was still dominated by relatively moderate conservatives, happy to see the continuation of a constitutional monarchy with reduced powers. But opposing them was a grouping holding more radical views that would later split into two factions: the Girondins and the even more extreme Jacobins, led by Robespierre. When in 1791 the National Assembly finally agreed a new constitution, which would allow the King to stay on the throne, Louis was ready to sign, even after he and his family had attempted to escape abroad, only to be returned to Paris and kept under guard at the Tuileries Palace.

But as had happened in England, a new factor now entered the equation: the threat of intervention by external powers. Prussia and Austria had declared support for the 'beleaguered monarchy', and the prospect of the revolution now having to defend itself against foreign enemies was to trigger the revolution into a new and more radical third phase.

In the summer of 1792, an Austrian army entered France with a declaration that, should any harm befall Louis and his family, 'an exemplary and eternally memorable revenge' would follow. This was greeted in Paris with rage against the King, while Robespierre's ally Danton set up the Paris Commune to seize control of the city. August saw Danton's Commune sack the Tuileries, massacring the king's Swiss Guards and forcing Louis and his family to flee for refuge to the National Assembly. But the Assembly's response was to suspend the monarchy and take the royal family to a mediaeval prison. When a Prussian army also then entered France, and was defeated, a newly-established National Convention, now dominated by the Girondins, proclaimed France a republic.

Already, however, a split had emerged between the Girondins and Robespierre's more extreme Jacobins, together with their Commune allies. With the mood in Paris ever more feverish, Robespierre called for Louis XVI to be executed. In January 1793 he was taken to the guillotine before a vast cheering crowd.

Over the next four months, with a major Royalist uprising in the west of France (the Vendée), relations between the Girondins and the Jacobins reached breaking point. In May, Robespierre called for an insurrection against the Convention, and a week later armed supporters of the Commune took over the Convention, forcing its members to vote for the arrest of 29 leading Girondins.

This *coup d'état* in Paris provoked protests and revolts right across the country. By now the Jacobins' wish was to eradicate every last vestige of the ancient regime, from the Christian religion to France's entire traditional system of weights and measures (along with a great deal more). Almost the entire traditional mental universe in which the French had lived was to be re-made from scratch.

When in September the Convention passed a 'Law of Suspects', allowing the arrest and trial of anyone suspected of being disloyal to the revolution, this marked the start of the fourth phase of the revolution: the nightmare known as the Reign of Terror. A month later the new government guillotined Marie Antoinette, followed by 21 Girondin deputies, with many more Girondin supporters to follow, including Madame Roland, who cried out from the scaffold, 'O Liberty, what crimes are committed in your name!' As the Royalist Jacques Mallet du Pan famously observed from exile in England, the revolution was now 'devouring its children'.

Even Danton called in vain for 'indulgence towards opponents' and 'national reconciliation'. But the Jacobins' murderous groupthink was now spiralling ever further. As the guillotining of 'enemies of the revolution' continued in Paris, one after another the provincial revolts were ruthlessly crushed. After the defeat of the Vendée, more than 16,000 prisoners were butchered. When Toulon was re-taken from the counter-revolutionaries, it was thanks to the tactics of an obscure young artillery officer, Napoleon Bonaparte, who months later was promoted to become general in charge of the revolutionary army in Paris.

In 1794, with all places of worship in Paris now closed, and Notre Dame Cathedral re-dedicated as a 'Temple of Reason', the Terror raged on. In March Robespierre, who had now formed secret police under the Committee of Public Safety, declared to the Convention that 'the foundations of a popular government in a revolution are virtue and terror, the Government of the Revolution is the despotism of liberty over tyranny.'

Ever more revolutionaries were themselves now being sent to the guillotine by the Revolutionary Tribunal, including Danton. In June and July more people were sentenced to death than in all the previous 14 months. The Convention gave itself the right to arrest its own members.

Finally, on 26 July, Robespierre made a wildly inflammatory speech demanding the punishment of 'traitors' in the Committee of Public Safety itself. The following day the Convention voted for his arrest, and at two in the morning on 28 July he and his closest supporters were arrested and sentenced to death without trial by the Revolutionary Tribunal. That evening, he and 21 of his closest supporters were guillotined.

It left France in a state of stunned shock. This was the moment when the revolution finally collided with the reality of what all those early dreams of liberty, equality and fraternity had led to. One conspicuous response, particularly in Paris – part of what became known as the 'Thermidorean reaction' – was surrender to every kind of worldly pleasure prohibited under the 'Reign of Virtue': riotous drinking, gambling, erotic display in the dress of both women and men, with sexual licence to match.

For the next few years France limped on, rudderless, under a new five-man 'Directory'. The only unifying source of national pride was the succession of military victories won over the Austrians in Italy by a French army under General Bonaparte, which continued in 1798 when he occupied Egypt. But in his absence French armies suffered defeats in Italy. Finally, in November 1799, Napoleon returned from Egypt to stage the coup which made him the new ruler of France.

(iii) The Rise and Fall of Napoleon

Although the rise of Napoleon did not represent the same kind of groupthink that characterized the revolutionary years, it was very much part of the story. Like Cromwell before him, he was the 'strong man' who stepped into the chaotic vacuum left by the climax of the revolution. The astonishing military and political successes won through his skill as a general and the force of his insatiable ego fired up the collective egotism of an admiring France. But the pattern of his career in fact reflected, in a quite different way, how the groupthink of the revolutionary years had begun with idealistic dreams, only to draw France down into a self-destructive nightmare.

For over a decade, France's new ruler seemed to enjoy dream-like success as he conquered much of Europe, proclaiming himself Emperor along the way. But it is in the nature of boundless ambition that it can find no point of rest where it is content to remain: it swells until eventually it over-reaches itself, in what the ancient Greeks would have recognised as *hubris*, bringing about its inevitable *nemesis*.

This was Napoleon's fateful decision in 1812 to respond to reports that Russia might invade part of his European empire by invading Russia itself. Although initially implausibly successful yet again, his *Grande Armée* sweeping all before it, step by step it was led to that hellish retreat through the frozen wastes of a Russian winter. Of the 400,000 men Napoleon had led into Russia in the heat of summer, only 40,000 remained alive.

Reality was now closing in on Napoleon's make-believe from all sides. At last virtually all the major powers of Europe were uniting in opposition to his megalomania, forcing him by 1814 to retreat to Paris, abdication and exile to Elba. Even now he enjoyed one last, brief dream-turned-to-nightmare adventure in those 'Hundred Days' when, having escaped to reclaim power, he finally collided with the reality of Waterloo, and was consigned to perpetual exile. Once again, as in England in 1660, this paved the way for the return of the monarchy, and a modified form of the pre-revolutionary old order.

(iv) Twentieth-century Russia

Just over a century later, we see a variant of the pattern in Russia. But this time, when growing chaos, unrest and long-standing discontents found their focus in February 1917 in a wave of mass protests and uprisings against the ruling order under the autocratic Tsar Nicholas II, there were two very significant differences.

One was that, in Lenin's Bolsheviks, there was a single small, tightly disciplined extremist group, with its own clear Marxist-Leninist agenda, which had long been waiting to seize power. The other was that, when the moment came, the hold it eventually established on power was so ruthless and complete that it would not soon bring about its own self-destruction, but rather would last for decades to come.

So great was the chaos into which Russia had fallen by 1917, with its disorganized armies retreating in the war with Germany, that when the February revolution came it immediately prompted the Tsar to abdicate. Amid wild and inchoate hopes, the new Russian republic embarked on a brief period of moderate parliamentary rule. But any dreams of a new, more democratic society were soon shattered by the October Revolution, and the seizing of power by the Bolsheviks.

Again, the collapse of the old order prompted a bloody civil war between the Reds and the Whites, fighting for a restoration of some version of the old regime. But, thanks not least to the military skill of Trotsky, Lenin's most capable general, the Bolsheviks emerged triumphant, and Lenin was able, in the name of 'the Dictatorship of the Proletariat', to set about destroying every vestige of the old social order. By the time of his death in 1924, he had even managed to re-conquer most of the newly independent countries which had made up Russia's disintegrated empire, now re-born under the 'dream symbol' of the hammer and sickle, as the Union of Soviet Socialist Republics, the USSR.

When Stalin out-manoeuvred Trotsky to the leadership, he steadily tightened the grip of his totalitarian rule in as complete an example of enforced groupthink as the world had ever seen. Private enterprise was banned, private property expropriated, religion all but outlawed in the name of the new atheistic quasi-religion of Communism.

As with so many religions before, it needed to maintain its illusion of an enforced 'consensus' by conjuring up an endless supply of 'heretics' who had to be constantly vilified and ruthlessly eliminated. By 1927 Stalin felt strong enough to expel from the now all-powerful Party his old ally Trotsky and the group of 'Oppositionists' around him, sending the arch heretic into exile (later to be murdered in Mexico by agents of Stalin's secret police).

By the early 1930s, Stalin's collectivization of agriculture, and expropriation of the land and grain stores owned by the peasants, led in the Ukraine to an immense famine, deliberately driving millions to death by starvation. In 1936 the revolution began seriously to 'devour its children' in quite epic fashion, in the three years of Stalin's 'Great Terror', as he vengefully turned on millions more, including many of his former 'Old Bolshevik' colleagues, along with countless other members of the Communist Party and virtually all the senior officers of the Red Army.

This was Russia's equivalent of the Jacobin Terror, except that in its scale and duration it was infinitely worse. By now the greatest crime in the Soviet Union was to be suspected by Stalin's ubiquitous secret police, the NKVD, of failing to conform in every respect to the Party's 'correct thinking'. This encompassed not just any hint of criticism of Stalin's new 'Socialist Utopia', trumpeted ubiquitously by an endless stream of propaganda, but every tiniest detail of life. No one was permitted to say or think anything that was not in line with 'correct thinking'. Totally condemned was the heresy known as 'individualism'. To belong to the collective in mind, body and spirit was all. Officially dictated were the books that could be written or read, the kinds of music it was permitted to compose, the prescribed 'Socialist Realist' style of painting artists had to follow. Even the laws of science had now to be decided on by the Party.

As George Orwell so vividly conveyed in those regular 'hate sessions' described in *Nineteen Eighty-Four*, a crucial feature of Stalin's nightmare new world was the need to whip up collective rage at all those 'enemies of the people' who were perpetually out to 'sabotage' the ideals of the revolution. Such hate figures were invariably reduced to Janis's 'dehumanized stereotypes', to be demonized as 'subversives', 'deviationists', 'bourgeois reactionaries', 'foreign spies', even 'running dogs of capitalist imperialism'. Anyone on whom could be pinned one of those damningly dismissive little labels so familiar from most forms of groupthink could expect to be arrested, imprisoned, shot or sent off to join millions more in that ever-growing network of hellish prisons and camps across the Soviet Union that would one day become known as 'the Gulag Archipelago'.

Not the least aspect of the dead weight of enforced groupthink on which Communism rested was its claim that the revolution had all been brought about in the name of liberating and empowering those oppressed 'victims' at the bottom of the social hierarchy: Russia's millions of 'workers and peasants'. The entire framework of the old pre-revolutionary order might have been swept away, but no one in the new Soviet Union had suffered more than those same workers and peasants, who for the Communists were merely an abstract concept, used to justify the Marxist make-believe that they were fighting to set the downtrodden masses free from all that had made their lives so miserable.

Instead, as in previous revolutions, only more so, the old ruling order had been replaced by an even smaller and infinitely more repressive self-perpetuating elite, which was to continue in power for 70 years. In this respect, the most obvious difference between the Russian Revolution and those earlier examples was that the nightmare it led to did not run its course much sooner before a return to some semblance of 'normality'. Indeed, following the Second World War, the Soviet Communist regime only extended its empire further, imposing its groupthink over the whole of eastern Europe, while in 1949 the same totalitarian ideology, with much the same results, took over the most populous country in the world, China.

Only in the 1980s did it become apparent that the entire edifice of Communism had been built on make-believe, kept in being by force, fear and unending lies. It was incapable of delivering on any of its endless flow of propaganda, or inspiring any genuine emotional commitment from most of those hundreds of millions it ruled over. At last, with remarkable speed, the whole illusory structure just crumbled, leaving its subject peoples to stumble back into some semblance of the real world. Later we shall briefly re-visit those last years of Soviet Communism, because they have something important to tell us about how people who have been relentlessly exposed to groupthink can eventually escape from it.

Crane Brinton did not live quite long enough to see the final fate of the Russian Revolution. But we can conclude this venture into history with a spectacular illustration of the pattern which Brinton didn't include, because it did not match his definition of a 'revolution'. This was the rather different version of groupthink which engulfed Germany in the years after 1933, eventually drawing much of the world into war.

(v) Hitler and Germany

By the end of the 1920s, Germany was a far from happy country: humiliatingly defeated in the First World War, with a weak, unpopular government, an economy sinking into a deep depression, and millions unemployed. Stage one of groupthink – what may be called the anticipation stage – is the conditions which allow it to take hold. The resulting sense of national unrest in Germany finally found its focus in 1933 in the hypnotic demagogue, Adolf Hitler, who was promising to revive the broken economy and restore a sense of national pride.

His seizure of power marked the start of stage two, the dream stage. Hitler's demonic energy and wish to 'make Germany great again' seemed to promise many Germans the national revival they craved. His Nazi version of groupthink was swiftly imposed on the entire country, with the aid of incessant propaganda, torchlight processions, mass rallies and a ruthless secret police, and designed to give the impression that, behind the 'dream-symbol' of the swastika, the German *Herrenvolk* or 'master race' had been welded together into one mighty in-group, united in 'consensus'.

As with all such extreme forms of groupthink, however, this was reinforced by Hitler's ceaseless demonization of all those out-groups in society he could denounce as 'enemies', from his former Brownshirt allies and the Communists, to the Jews and other *Untermenschen* (sub-humans) who did not fit into his make-believe 'Aryan' vision of the German nation.

Thus, through the Thirties, he rode a tide of success, his ambitions reaching ever further. He revived the economy by building up a powerful military machine as an expression of Germany's collective ego. Without opposition he was able to occupy and absorb ever more territories into his new 'Greater Reich', until in 1939 his invasion of Poland finally triggered war.

Like Napoleon before him, Hitler saw his armies sweeping through most of Europe, until the apogee of 1941 when, again like Napoleon, he sent his armies surging into Russia. But when they were abruptly halted in the winter mud and snow at the gates of Moscow, his mad vision met for the first time with a serious check (even though the simultaneous entry into the war of his equally single-minded ally Japan turned the war into truly a global conflict).

Hitler's enforced retreat from Moscow marked the start of a third or 'frustration stage'. Only weeks later, in February 1942, as if to sustain the heady momentum of the dream, came the order for the extermination of 'the entire Jewish race', initiating the Holocaust. That summer, in Russia and North Africa, he made one final push to keep his dream alive, only for it to end in the defeats of Stalingrad and El Alamein. In 1943, as the tide turned on every front, with his armies in Russia and now Italy in retreat, his U-boat fleets being sunk in the Atlantic, Germany's cities being bombed day and night, Hitler was entering the 'nightmare stage', where reality was finally closing in on him.

In 1944 things only became worse by the day, as Allied armies tightened their grip from all sides. In 1945 came the final 'collision with reality'. All that remained of Hitler's edifice of make-believe collapsed literally in ruins around him. As he himself had said in a pre-war speech, 'I go the way that Providence dictates, with the assurance of a sleepwalker.' So had the sleepwalker led Germany into a dream that evolved inexorably into a nightmare from which, for him and tens of millions of others, there was no waking.

CONCLUSIONS: THE 'FANTASY CYCLE'

In the introduction I noted that, second only to the more intolerant perversions of organized religion, history has provided no more extreme examples of systematized groupthink than totalitarian ideologies such as Communism and Nazism.

We have seen how the very act of challenging the familiar framework of what had come to taken as 'reality' divided society into two generalized groups. One tried, increasingly ineffectually, to hold on to and defend the old order. The other became possessed by its vision of how a new form of society could be established in its place.

But once the old framework was gone, the desired goal turned out to be so elusive that the efforts to reach it became ever more extreme and detached from reality.

Here is the central conflict: two diametrically opposed forms of groupthink, each obeying the rule proscribing any dialogue with the other, each creating a hostile caricature of the other. In the case of the three revolutions, as Brinton put it, we see that

> tendency for power to go from Right to Center to Left, from the conservatives of the old regime to the moderates to the radicals or extremists. As power moves along this line, it gets more and more concentrated, it narrows its base in the country and among the people.

The examples of Napoleon and Hitler might seem to be very different. Unlike the 'bottom-up' revolutions, where the groupthink came from below in rebelling against an established ruling order, Bonapartism and Nazism were imposed 'top down' by charismatic, hyper-egotistical leaders who managed to identify their own boundless personal ambition with the interests of their nation so effectively that the people, either by persuasion or force, were carried along by it. But in each case, the make-believe eventually over-reached itself, arousing such a countervailing response from the outside world that the fantasy edifice created by their megalomania was finally brought crashing down.

In this respect we can see Nazism as a right-wing fantasy, perverting patriotism into an extreme form of nationalism. For right-wing forms of groupthink, the 'in-group' is always based on the nation, the race, the tribe, with other nations, races and tribes a despised 'out-group'. Nazism based its appeal on the masculine values of order, discipline and authority, on loyalty to the 'Fatherland', and on a form of racist ideology so narrowly exclusive that it believed in the right of a single 'master race' to exercise ruthless domination over all others.

Communism, on the other hand, is a left-wing fantasy, in that it purports to be based on the compassionate values which champion the dispossessed at the bottom of society. Marxism's appeal lies in its claim to be fighting for these oppressed 'victims', wherever they might be in the world, against the heartless, corrupt ruling classes at the top of society who abuse and exploit them.

This fundamental distinction between right-wing and left-wing ideologies explains the quite different ways in which they are generally perceived in the modern world. In the post-war era, because of the only too obvious crimes committed by the Nazis, there has become no more commonplace term of condemnation than 'fascist', no matter how little similarity with Hitler's original Nazis. The term has been applied not just to any political group which appears overtly racist, but to any standing for such 'masculine' values as authority, order and discipline. One of the most obvious targets has been the police. Indeed, it can often be applied indiscriminately to anyone who represents authority in any guise – even a teacher trying to preserve order in his classroom or a strict parent imposing discipline on his children. Since the Second World War, to describe anyone as a 'fascist' or 'far-right' has become one of the most damning terms of abuse, conjuring up subliminal associations with the perverted human behaviour which led to all the evils of Nazi Germany. Apart from 'paedophile' or 'child abuser', no term is calculated to inspire more automatic revulsion.

But the emotional attraction of the Marxist or left-wing paradigm is that it is the very opposite: selflessly designed to champion the world's underdogs against those seen to be oppressing them. This is why it has always been much easier to overlook or even excuse what has invariably happened whenever Marxist groupthink has managed to seize power over a society. The supposedly idealistic Communists create a new ruling order which, in crucial respects, is little different from the brutally authoritarian regimes imposed by their right-wing opposites.

As Orwell so vividly portrayed in *Animal Farm*, it did not take long for the Soviet Communists, with their proclaimed dedication to be fighting for society's underdogs, to reveal themselves as simply its new, even more tyrannical and corrupt overdogs. Behind their pretence to care for the powerless and oppressed, any new Communist ruling order is based on the same values driving the regimes set up by fascist or other right-wing authoritarians: ruthless discipline, murderous intolerance of dissent, ostentatious displays of military power and the quasi-religious cult of an all-powerful leader. In this respect, the collective deification of Lenin, Stalin and Mao becomes interchangeable with the '*Führer*-worship' of Hitler.

It is an archetypal pattern in collective human behaviour. First there is an 'anticipation stage', where pressure builds up in a society to make a decisive break with the past. When this new energy finds a focus and the break is made, this leads on to a 'dream stage', where for a while it seems the liberating new make-believe is carrying all before it. But precisely because this make-believe knows no limits, it leads to a 'frustration stage' where it is driven to push on even further in pursuit of that elusive goal, in ways even more detached from the real world. By now, uncomfortable contradictions are beginning to intrude, until the ever more extreme groupthink brings about a 'nightmare stage', where the supposedly idealistic vision which originally inspired it has been turned completely on its head. This eventually leads to some sort of 'collision with reality', where the groupthink is brought face to face with the unforeseen consequences of where it has all been leading. We shall be seeing different examples of this sequence – in particular (despite the joking claim that 'anyone who claims to remember the Sixties can't have been there') in how the events of that period unfolded.

5

The 'Fantasy Cycle' and the 'Swinging Sixties'

> For each age is a dream that is dying or one that is
> coming to birth.
>
> A. W. E. O'Shaugnessy (1844–81)

In Irving Janis's identification what I have called the 'three basic rules' of how groupthink operates there was one aspect which he didn't include, even though it applied to every one of his own case studies. This was the five-stage pattern whereby the loss of contact with reality implicit in all forms of groupthink eventually brings about a collision with reality and its own destruction.

I was first drawn to this recurring pattern in history back in the 1960s, when I was working on my first book, *The Neophiliacs* (1969). This was an attempt to analyse that avalanche of change in the late Fifties and Sixties which transformed Britain, socially, morally, culturally and politically, into an almost unrecognizably different country. When I subtitled that book 'The Revolution in English Life in the Fifties and Sixties' I did not of course mean to equate what had happened to Britain during that time with the far greater historical upheavals we have been looking at. But when I came to look at how the events of that period unfolded, two things had struck me.

One was the extent to which so much of what characterized those hectic years had turned out to be bubbles of collective make-believe, from Anthony Eden's doomed Suez adventure in 1956 to the hysteria

Britain plunged into only a few years later, as it became obsessed with all the evanescent excitements of the 'Swinging Sixties'. The other was how often throughout that period Britain's collective mood had gone through striking shifts, even from one year to the next.

Although the joke that anyone who claimed to remember the Sixties couldn't have been there was meant to convey how all memories of that seminal decade had become blurred together in a fog of drugs and deafening pop music, as I further observed in *The Neophiliacs*, there was actually a clear pattern to the different stages through which the period unfolded. We cannot get a proper perspective on so much of the groupthink of the twenty-first century without tracing their origins back to that remarkable spell of history now more than half a century ago. Few people under the age of 60 can have any idea just how dramatically the changes of those years shaped the modern world in which they have grown up, and created the mental universe they have come to take for granted.

As the Western world finally emerged in the mid-Fifties from the shadows of the Second World War, nothing gave people the heady sense that they were entering a future almost unimaginably different more than the sudden arrival of a new kind of material prosperity. Of course, this was underpinned by such a flood of new scientific and technological advances that arguably the human race can never again experience quite such a radical break with the past. None was quite so dramatic as the coming of the space age, when mankind for the first time reached out beyond the confines of our own planet. So rapid was its progress that little more than a decade separated the Soviet Union's launch of *Sputnik*, the first satellite, into space in 1957, and the first Americans landing on the moon in 1969.

But this was just one of the plethora of technical advances marking off those years from anything the world had seen before. Global jet air travel became commonplace; the use of plastics became ubiquitous; medicine was revolutionized by antibiotics; the first commercial computers set off an electronics revolution which within a few decades would lead to the internet and the Worldwide Web, and become crucial to the functioning of almost every form of economic activity. No novelty of those years had more immediate impact on people's everyday lives than the arrival of television, which even by the end of the Sixties was already being hailed as having shrunk the world to an 'electronic village'. In a quite different context, the discovery of the astonishingly complex structures and purposes of DNA, another scientific breakthrough of the Fifties, had far-reaching and unexpected consequences.

All these innovations transformed the way in which we perceived the world.

A further transformation in the Sixties was the profound shift in consciousness that gave rise to what became known as 'environmentalism'. Suddenly human beings became uncomfortably aware not just of what damage they were now doing to the natural world around them, but that they were the first species on Earth capable, through nuclear weapons, of destroying all life on the planet. This fundamental shift in perspective was to prepare the ground psychologically for the ease with which, twenty years later, it was accepted that the future of the planet was also threatened by man-made global warming.

Those years also saw the launch of the single most ambitious political project of our time: to weld together all the peoples of Europe under a supranational form of government such as the world had never seen before.

But what happened in the late Fifties and Sixties, particularly in Britain, once again reflects how any period of social upheaval creates a conflict between those carried away by the liberating new spirit of the time and those defending the crumbling old ways of looking at the world. And the psychological impact of that tidal wave of change was reinforced by two other factors. One was Britain's growing realization that it had lost its place as a world power. The other was the dissolving of much of Britain's old hierarchical class system.

In *The Neophiliacs* I told how those who lived by that traditional framework of values and assumptions became an 'Old Guard', vainly trying to resist the values of the 'New England' emerging to replace it. More than in any other country, this divided the British into two opposing groups, defined by generation and class: youth against age; what may be called the 'lower classes' against the 'upper classes'; the imagined new future against a past which no longer seemed relevant.

When in the late Sixties I analysed what had happened to Britain during those years, I tried to show how often their heady excitement had led people into different kinds of escape from reality. But it was only when many years later I came across Janis's work that I saw how often these various forms of collective make-believe had in fact been shaped by those defining rules of groupthink.

The story began with what I called 'the strange conservative interlude' of the early Fifties. By this time the mood of radical left-wing idealism which led to the Labour election landslide of 1945 had petered out, as by the end of the Forties Britain found itself still struggling through rationing and all the deprivations of the 'age of austerity'. In 1951, under the slogan 'Set the people free,' the Conservatives were returned to power under the ageing world statesman Winston Churchill. Britain still saw itself as a world power, at the centre of an empire which still spanned the globe, still able in 1952 to join America and the Soviet Union as the world's third nuclear power. In 1953 this sense that the country was returning to its past glories was reinforced when millions of viewers were able to gaze for the first time at little black-and-white television screens to watch all the historic rituals of the Coronation, as their new young Queen was crowned in Westminster Abbey, surrounded by hundreds of male hereditary peers in ermine robes and coronets.

Morally and socially, as we have seen, Britain was still an intensely conservative, class-conscious, law-abiding society (crime during these years dropped to a record low). Cinema audiences took patriotic pride in a rash of films extolling the heroic feats of the British during the war, along with cosy Ealing comedies reflecting a society in which everyone was still clearly identified by their place in Britain's traditional class structure. Rationing and post-war austerity were finally coming to an end. As long-unobtainable goods returned to the shops, a commonly heard term of praise was, 'It's just like pre-war.' And when in May 1955 the 81-year-old Churchill retired, the Conservatives, led by his equally upper-class successor Anthony Eden, were returned to power with an increased majority. But the mood was now beginning to change. And the way in which it did so was to unfold twice over through that recognizable five-stage pattern.

ANTICIPATION STAGE: FINDING THE FOCUS

The probability is, I suppose, that the monarchy has become a kind of ersatz religion. Chesterton once remarked that when people cease to believe in God, they believe not in nothing but in anything.

Malcolm Muggeridge, 'Royal Soap Opera',
New Statesman, 22 October 1955

Oh, heavens, how I long for just a little ordinary enthusiasm. Just enthusiasm, that's all. I want to hear a warm, thrilling voice cry out 'Hallelujah! Hallelujah! I'm alive!'

Jimmy Porter in John Osborne's *Look Back in Anger*, 1956

Eden gets tough! Let the crybabies howl! It's GREAT Britain again!

Front-page headline, *Daily Sketch*, November 1956

By the autumn of 1955 there was a new restiveness in the air. The arrival of commercial television, with its brash American-style ads and quiz shows, made the staid, deferential BBC look suddenly dull and old-fashioned. Thousands of young 'Teddy boys', in the dandyish uniform that marked them out, ran amok through the streets of south London after catching on a cinema screen Britain's first glimpse of American rock 'n' roll. One widely quoted magazine article popularized the use of the term 'the Establishment', to describe the way Britain was being suffocated by the excessive influence of a cosy upper-class elite. Another, castigating the way in which obsessive press coverage of the Queen and her family was trivializing them into little more than a 'Royal soap opera', used language about the monarchy more disrespectful than anything heard in Britain since Victorian times. But it was the following year, 1956, that brought the double earthquake which set the rebellious 'new England' on its way and simultaneously rocked the 'Old Guard's traditionalist view of Britain to its foundations.

Culturally the most significant event of 1956 was the full-scale arrival from America of the craze for rock 'n' roll, which swept through the younger generation like a hurricane. The new styles of clothing, dancing, the 'hip' and 'groovy' slang words which went with the hypnotic new music opened up a new fantasy world which split them off from the older generation like nothing before, as everyone outside their new bubble could be dismissed as boring 'squares'.

Quite independently of this new 'teenage culture', another sensation of the year was the emergence of the 'Angry Young Men', a group of young writers from 'lower-class' backgrounds, of whom the most prominent was John Osborne with his play *Look Back In Anger*. Its 'lower-class' young hero Jimmy Porter, living in a tiny rented flat in 'a Midlands city', ranted against the stifling tedium of a country whose life had become dominated by an 'upper class' lost in its dreams of the past. 'Oh, heavens', he exploded, 'I want to hear a warm, thrilling voice cry out "Hallelujah! Hallelujah! I'm alive!"'

Politically, however, by far the most significant event of 1956 was in June when the new Arab nationalist ruler of Egypt, Colonel Nasser, seized the Anglo-French-owned Suez Canal. Already faced with armed uprisings across Britain's colonial empire, in Cyprus, Kenya and Malaya, Prime Minister Eden's response could have provided Irving Janis with another exemplary case study for his list of political fiascos brought about by groupthink.

Through the late summer, as Eden's anti-Nasser rhetoric became ever more hysterical, he and his supporters enjoyed a 'dream stage' as they imagined the revenge they were about to take on this upstart 'wog'. By late October, when it became clear that Britain and France were planning a military invasion to seize back the Canal by force, British opinion was split down the middle. One half was raucously cheering Eden on, with headlines such as 'Eden gets tough! Let the crybabies howl! It's GREAT Britain again!' The other half looked on aghast.

No sooner had British troops landed than Eden's fantasy collided with reality. America warned that it was about to launch a disastrous run on the pound, still a global currency. The Soviet Union, which at the very same time was sending its tanks into Hungary to put down a mass uprising against Communist rule, went even further, threatening to 'shower London with nuclear rockets'.

Britain's instant, humiliating retreat left Nasser in undisputed control of the Canal. Eden resigned, after a fiasco which had not only brought home to Britain more than anything else that it was no longer a world power, but also dealt a blow to the complacent self-image of Britain's traditional ruling class – although this might not have seemed immediately obvious when Eden was succeeded as Prime Minister by another elderly, patrician Old Etonian, Harold Macmillan.

The events of 1956 might have sown the seeds of much that was to come. But as 1957 unfolded, the turbulence of 1956 gradually died away. By the end of the year, when some of the Angry Young Men published a book of essays entitled *Declaration*, in which John Osborne fulminated against royalty, religion and the 'waffling cant' of the 'well-off and mentally underprivileged' who 'rule our lives', such heated language already seemed to belong to another time. Even the original frenzy of the craze for rock 'n' roll seemed to be calming down, although the nature of pop music had now been irrevocably changed.

The national mood was again shifting. The attention of the British was now beginning to focus in a quite different direction.

FIRST 'DREAM' STAGE: BRITAIN DISCOVERS 'AFFLUENCE'

> Indeed, let's be frank about it, some of our people have never had it so good. What is beginning to worry some of us is, 'Is it too good to be true?'
>
> Harold Macmillan, 30 July 1957

Over the next two years, the chief preoccupation of the British was their realization that they were now living in what was being called an 'affluent society'. On a tide of new 'buy now, pay later' hire purchase, the British of all classes were indulging in the greatest spending spree they had ever known.

Only four years after the end of food rationing, they were getting used to being 'consumers'. Ever more British families were now, for the first time, buying cars, refrigerators, washing machines, television sets. The first supermarkets were appearing. Startlingly modernistic steel, glass and concrete mini-skyscrapers in a wholly new style of architecture were rising above London's skyline.

But somehow, seeming to preside over this rush into a new future, was the new Conservative prime minister. When as early as June 1957 Harold Macmillan observed that 'Some of our people have never had it so good', he did not mean it as a boast. He was trying to warn of the dangers of rising inflation. But this was the phrase with which he was to become identified.

In 1958, with the polls showing a huge surge in his popularity, the well-known left-wing cartoonist Vicky caustically took the comic-strip image of Superman to portray Macmillan as 'Supermac'. But this was the admiring nickname that stuck, and in 1959 he led his Conservative Party back to power in a landslide, prompting him to declare that 'The class war is obsolete'. It seemed that Britain's ruling elite had successfully claimed proprietorship over the country's new sense that life for almost everyone had never been better. But with the coming of a new decade, the prevailing mood was again about to change.

FRUSTRATION STAGE: STRAINS APPEAR

> A dogged resistance to change now blankets every segment of our national life. A middle-aged conservatism, parochial and complacent, has settled over the country.
>
> Anthony Crosland, Labour politician, *Encounter,*
> October 1960

It was not just in Britain that the arrival of the Sixties brought a further dramatic shift of mood. In America the 70-year-old President Eisenhower was about to retire, after eight years when the US, even more conspicuously than Britain, had been enjoying a quite unprecedented prosperity. But there was now a widespread sense that, under its oldest-ever president, it had become suffocatingly complacent: a mood crystallized in 1960 by the spectacular emergence of the charismatic young politician who was about to succeed him.

John F. Kennedy's image of youthful energy and idealism, and his charge that America had become 'a tired country', needing to be revitalized by a new, 'dynamic' style of leadership, made him a perfect 'dream hero' for the new decade.

In Britain Harold Macmillan, only four years younger than Eisenhower, had already been trying to respond to the impatient new mood. In his 'wind of change' speech in April, he not only told the South African parliament that the days of white supremacy in Africa were over, but also signalled his intention to set about liberating virtually all Britain's own remaining colonial empire as fast as possible.

But for Britain's standing in the world there were other, more disturbing warnings. It was becoming painfully evident that many of the great, once world-leading industries on which the British economy had long relied were now in decline. There was a sudden vogue for books and articles by a new generation of bright young Oxbridge-educated journalists asking, 'What's wrong with Britain?' and clamouring that Britain must learn to 'modernize'. In particular they liked to contrast Britain's obsolescent economy with the 'dynamism' of the six European countries which in 1957 had set up their 'Common Market'. Macmillan's initial response in 1959 had been to organize a rival to 'the Six', the European Free Trade Association (EFTA). But in the summer of 1960, when he re-shuffled his Cabinet, he also appointed Britain's first Minister for Europe, Edward Heath, a former grammar-school boy who virtually alone in British politics, had long been urging that Britain should join 'the Six'.

Meanwhile that telling phrase 'with it' reflected everyone's sense that Britain was now on an ever-accelerating conveyor belt of change, in everything from pop music and fashion to architecture and car design, and the social pressure to be considered in tune with this heady rush into an ever more exciting future. What came to be known as 'Northern realist' films, for example, glamorized the 'irreverent vitality' of the 'lower-class' young growing up in Britain's industrial cities.

But nothing more symbolized the new Britain than the revolution in attitudes to sex, with 'daring' strip clubs offering unprecedented shows of female nudity. In 1960 the landmark prosecution for obscenity of D. H. Lawrence's novel *Lady Chatterley's Lover*, the test case of a new law intended to end the censorship of 'serious literature', was touted as a showdown between the new 'permissive society' and those stifling old moral rules which now seemed to belong to another age. The book's supporters lavished scornful abuse on the 'bigots' and 'Victorian prudes' vainly trying to defy the advance of the 'New Morality', quoting with particular delight an absurdly self-caricaturing question put to the jury by the Attorney-General for the prosecution: 'Is this a book you would wish your wife or servants to read?' But no less ridiculous were some of the more sententious arguments in defence of the book, such as the claim by the trendy young Bishop of Woolwich that having sex was 'in a real sense an act of Holy Communion'.

The trial thus became a classic instance of two opposing forms of groupthink decisively pitted against each other. The jury's verdict was hailed as a stunning victory for free speech and the New Morality, but in reality its most significant result, quite unforeseen by those who naively drafted the liberalizing new law under which the case had been brought, was not so much to promote 'serious literature' as to open the floodgates to what would become an almost unlimited deluge of pornography without any pretension to literary merit.

Even now, opinion polls were showing that the majority of young people in Britain would still vote Conservative. The Labour Party was in crisis over a bid by the largest trade unions to force Britain into abandoning its nuclear weapons, only narrowly beaten off after a fighting speech by its leader Hugh Gaitskell. But Macmillan was increasingly desperate to be seen to be keeping up with the times.

In June 1961 he startled the world by announcing that Britain would be applying to join those 'dynamic' countries in their Common Market. By throwing its destiny in with Europe, Britain would thus be turning its back on the Commonwealth and its imperial past. Little did he realize how drastically (if not for this reason) public opinion was about to turn against him, and all he and his class and generation stood for.

NIGHTMARE STAGE FOR 'OLD ENGLAND'

This is a letter of hate. It is for my countrymen. I mean those men of my country who have defiled it. The men with manic fingers who are leading the sightless, feeble betrayed body of my country to its death. You are its murderers and there is little left in my own brain but the thoughts of murder for you . . . There is murder in my brain and I carry a knife in my heart for every one of you, you, Macmillan, and you, Gaitskell . . . till then, damn you, England. You are rotting now and soon you will disappear.

John Osborne, *Tribune*, 28 August 1961

The ranks are drawn up and the air resounds with the armourer's hammer. When battle is joined, one can only hope that blood will be drawn.

Jonathan Miller, on the opening of the Establishment, 'London's First Satirical Nightclub', *Observer*, 1 October 1961

The late summer of 1961 brought another dramatic change of mood, not just in Britain but globally. In August, the erection of the Berlin Wall was followed by a boast from Nikita Khrushchev that the Soviet Union was now capable of making a hydrogen bomb 50 times more powerful than the bomb which destroyed Hiroshima. For the first time since 1945 this set off a real fear that the world could be heading for a nuclear war.

In Britain, Bertrand Russell, for the Committee of 100, a new, much more militant core group of CND, the Campaign for Nuclear Disarmament, described Macmillan, Kennedy and Khrushchev as 'the wickedest people in the history of man'. Another member, John Osborne, responded with his 'Damn you, England' letter (quoted above). Two weeks later, when the Committee announced it was planning an unprecedented demonstration in Trafalgar Square, it was prohibited by the authorities. But the demo still went ahead, resulting in the police, to general howls of 'Fascists', forcibly removing 1,314 protesters, the largest mass arrest in British history.

A different expression of Britain's new rebellious mood that autumn was the spectacular craze for 'satire'. The hit of the London theatre season was a new revue, *Beyond the Fringe*, in which four young Oxbridge graduates mocked all the values of 'old England', from films celebrating Britain's heroics in the Second World War to a typically platitudinous Church of England sermon.

When it opened in May, the critics had scarcely noticed a sketch in which Peter Cook caricatured Macmillan as a senile Edwardian patrician, in dismal contrast to the youthful vigour of the new US president. But by the autumn this parody of Macmillan as a hopelessly out-of-touch, upper-class relic of a bygone age was being hailed as the centrepiece of the show. Satire was suddenly all the rage, with the launch by Cook of 'London's first satirical nightclub', the Establishment, and the satirical magazine *Private Eye*. For both, the bumbling Macmillan was a favourite targets.

It was now clearer than ever how conflict in Britain was becoming defined along lines of age and class. One of the most conspicuous features of British life since the mid-Fifties had been the ever-growing prominence of the young, who seemed so much more attuned to the changing times than an increasingly bewildered older generation, and not least the emphasis on the 'lower-class' origins of the new celebrities. In a telling television interview in January 1962 with the pop singer, Adam Faith, even the Archbishop of York insisted, 'I'm one of those who feel that sex is a thoroughly good thing, implanted by God. I'm not one who belongs to the generation who thought it was a sort of smutty thing that you could only talk about hush-hush.'

Just three years after being hailed as 'Supermac', Macmillan was quite out of his depth. Everything that could go wrong for him and his government did. The economy was in trouble, unemployment rising, crime soaring. So intense was his sense of frustration that in the summer of 1962 he sacked a record seven members of his Cabinet. It had no effect on his government's plummeting popularity.

Although negotiations over Macmillan's bid to join Europe had stalled in interminable discussions over technicalities, it became the central issue of the autumn's party conferences. In the longest speech ever made at a party conference, the Labour leader Hugh Gaitskell warned that by throwing in its political destiny with Europe Britain would be turning its back on 'a thousand years of history'. But when Macmillan a week later won a standing ovation from 4,000 Conservatives for his speech in favour of joining, most were wearing badges bearing just the one word: 'Yes'. They were now blindly in support of a policy which only two years earlier they would have scorned as contrary to all their Party stood for.

That autumn, the mood of the time was darkening. In October, the world was suddenly transfixed by the Cuban missile crisis, perhaps the most dangerous in the world's history, when for nearly a fortnight it seemed to be teetering on nuclear catastrophe. In London, several lauded new plays were markedly blacker and more obsessed with sex and violence than anything before. One depicted a serial killer ritually slashing voluptuous nude pin-ups on a 'patriotic altar of Union Jacks' before committing suicide.

When November saw the launch of *That Was The Week That Was* (*TW3*), the Saturday night show on which David Frost and a team of young actors brought 'satire' to a mass-audience, it fast became the most hypnotically watched programme in BBC history. Its mockery of Macmillan and all the values of 'old England' could not have marked a more startling departure from everything the BBC had previously stood for. That same month, having for months aroused frenzied excitement among teenagers at the Cavern Club in Liverpool, the Beatles saw their first record, 'Love Me Do', reach seventeenth place in the pop charts. On Boxing Day, snow began falling across Britain, where it was to remain for most of the next three months, in the coldest winter the country had experienced for over 200 years. It was an appropriate harbinger of the extraordinary year about to unfold.

1963: 'OLD ENGLAND' GIVES WAY TO THE 'NEW UNREALITY'

> On the island where the subject has long been taboo in polite society, sex has exploded into the national consciousness and national headlines. 'Are we going sex crazy?' asks the *Daily Herald*.
>
> *Time magazine*, March 1963

> I do not live among young people fairly widely.
>
> Harold Macmillan to the House of Commons at the height of hysteria over the Profumo affair, 17 June 1963

> 1963 – The Year of the Beatles
>
> Title of special *Evening Standard* supplement at the end of 1963

To this day, Britain has never known a year like 1963. It was the watershed of the 'English revolution'. It is impossible to more than summarize its essence, so relentless were the sensational developments throughout those twelve months. It was the year when 'Old England' finally fell apart and gave way to that youthful, classless, permissive, iconoclastic 'New England' emerging since the mid-Fifties.

As an appropriate prelude, the year began with Britain shrouded in fog, as blizzards buried the country in feet of snow, paralysing much economic activity for weeks on end. From out of the murk in January came the year's first two shocks. One was the unexpected death of Hugh Gaitskell at the age of only 56, to be replaced as Labour leader after weeks of intrigue by the very different figure of Harold Wilson. The second was the vetoing by France's President de Gaulle of Britain's bid to join the Common Market. Macmillan's 'European dream' was over.

His government was embroiled in several minor 'sex and security scandals', but by February rumours were swirling around London of another scandal, this time involving a senior minister and so serious it could bring down the government. In the same weeks, as the Beatles' second record, 'Please, Please Me', raced to the top of the charts, it became clear that this new pop group was a phenomenon the like of which Britain had never seen.

In March the ever more feverishly discussed scandal was first raised in the Commons by Labour MPs. Although John Profumo, the Secretary of State for War, was still not being publicly named, this was enough to prompt him to deny that he had been guilty of any 'impropriety' with Christine Keeler, the model with whom he had been having a relationship. This would eventually prove his downfall.

The same month saw other signs of how rapidly Britain was changing. Just upstream from Parliament the new Millbank Tower became, at nearly 400 feet, the tallest building in London, although it was only one of the new skyscrapers now transforming the city's skyline. Topping the best-seller lists, a new book, *Honest To God*, by John Robinson, the Bishop of Woolwich, claimed that 'in the Space

Age' our 'nursery-book image of God must go,' along with virtually the entire traditional teaching of the church. A report proposed the greatest-ever revolution in Britain's railway system, whose puffing steam engines had for so long been a key image of the national character: more than half of all stations and lines were to go, and steam was to become a thing of the past.

In April the poisonous rumours surrounding the Profumo affair were dominating British politics. It was a hypnotic, phantasmagoric saga, with shadowy new characters like Ivanov, a mysterious defence attaché from the Soviet Embassy, joining the cast by the day. The rumour mill went into overdrive, throwing up other scandals like the naked 'headless man' alleged to be a Cabinet minister involved in a society divorce case, and another known only as 'the man in the mask'.

By May all this had become blurred together into a single intoxicating vision of how Britain's entire ruling class seemed to have been caught up in wholesale sexual depravity, further spiced up by hints of a threat to national security. But its extraordinary power to excite people's minds derived from its continuing basis in shadowy rumour and suggestion that people were only too eager to believe.

This was such a remarkable psychological phenomenon that, when I came to write *The Neophiliacs*, I coined the term *nyktomorph*, derived from two Greek words meaning 'night shape'. I was thinking of when our vision is obscured by darkness or poor light to the extent that we cannot properly make out what we are looking at, and may be tricked into imagining it to be much more significant than it really is – suspecting that dim movement in the shadows to be a burglar, a potential mugger or a wild animal.

In fact, as we shall see, the power of the nyktomorphic effect to distort and magnify our perception of reality plays a significant part in many forms of groupthink. The reactions it inspires may include fear, as in times of war or social disorder, when rumours abound. Quite different is the extraordinary fascination exercised by 'celebrities' of any kind, by which often quite ordinary people can be transformed through ubiquitous publicity into glamorous figures worthy of unending interest and fascination, even though in reality we know very little about them.

Certainly by the end of May 1963 the power of the nyktomorph could scarcely have been more in evidence than in the obsession with the Profumo affair. But when on 4 June he flew back from Venice to admit his guilt in misleading Parliament and resigned from all his offices, this only plunged the country into greater hysteria. Faced with MPs and the press in complete uproar, Macmillan was utterly bewildered. The most telling sentence in his response was, 'I do not move among young people fairly widely.' Subsequently one of his ministers recalled that Macmillan had been 'in a terrible state, going on about a rumour of there having been eight High Court judges involved in an orgy. "One", he said, "perhaps two. But eight – I just can't believe it."' At a fete in his constituency, he was described as moving

> like a sleepwalker round the coconut shies, the raffles and the lucky dips. As he posed for a photograph with the tiny daughter of a constituent, one of a group of young hecklers hissed into his ear, 'Take your hands off that little girl. Don't you wish it was Christine Keeler?'

The Labour Party's lead in the opinion polls was now more than 20 points, the highest since polling began. From the start of the crisis, Harold Wilson had been careful to keep out of the fray, reserving his concerns only for the possible 'security' implications. With the Tory government in such full auto-destruct mode, what more did he need to do?

In July, during a royal visit by the King and Queen of Greece, the Queen was the first monarch to be openly booed in the street since Victorian times. The prestigious magazine *Encounter* published a special issue entitled 'Suicide of a Nation'. On a visit to Europe, when President Kennedy stood in front of the Berlin Wall to be cheered by a crowd of over million for declaring, '*Ich bin ein Berliner*,' this made him more than ever the ultimate Sixties 'dream hero'.

On 22 July came the trial of Stephen Ward, the other protagonist of the Profumo affair, who had introduced Profumo to Christine Keeler and been a friend of the Russian attaché Ivanov, for allegedly living off immoral earnings. The evidence dredged up against him looked more dubious by the day, but after a heavily biased summing-up by the judge, Ward forestalled the jury's likely verdict by taking a fatal overdose of sleeping pills.

At the start of August, the nation was transfixed anew by the sensational news of the Great Train Robbery, at the time easily the greatest theft in British history. It seemed a fitting symptom of a crime rate that had been hurtling upwards since 1956, but had been so daringly staged that the gang responsible assumed a strange glamour. In America, at the end of the month, after months of race riots, bombings and other ominous signs of rising racial tension, a million people converged on Washington to hear Martin Luther King deliver his 'I have a dream' plea for harmony between blacks and whites.

In September, thousands queued in London for the unprecedented release at midnight of Lord Denning's report on the Profumo scandal. Racily written, with headings which might have come from a tabloid newspaper – 'The Man in the Mask' and all – it revealed very little that was new, and the more scandalous titbits of rumour were laid to rest. At last, it seemed, the poisonous boil had been lanced. All those nyktomorphs had been brought out into the mundane light of day.

THE TIMES THEY ARE A-CHANGIN'

> When Mick Jagger comes into the Ad Lib in London, I mean, there's nothing like the Ad Lib in New York. You can go into the Ad Lib and everyone is there. They're all young and they're taking over. It's like a whole revolution. I mean,

it's so exciting. They're all from the lower classes, East End
sort-of-thing. There's no one exciting from the upper classes
any more.

Baby Jane Holzer, New York socialite, quoted by Tom Wolfe
in 'The Girl of the Year', *New York magazine*, 1964

If there was one theme underlying the mood of those hectic years,
it was that heady sense of liberation, from old ways of looking at
the world which had suddenly come to seem stifling and outdated.
Once the genie was out of the bottle, change fed on change. The
itch for new excitement and gratification constantly upped its
demands, and nowhere more than in the headlong rush into what
came be hailed as the new 'permissive society'. The shackles of
'Victorian prudery' were thrown off, and Britain embraced all the
delights of the 'Swinging Sixties' and the new age of sex, drugs
and rock 'n' roll – with unforeseen consequences. The more liberal
attitude to sexual behaviour led to a soaring divorce rate, single-
parent families became commonplace and a widespread collapse
of traditional family values brought immense social damage in its
train.

Part of that revolution was the new obsession with the imagery of
sex, portrayed on stage and screen, in print and in the increasingly
routine use of formerly taboo four-letter words. Plays, films and
books competed to become more daring and shocking and push back
the boundaries of what was permissible, in the familiar pattern of
needing to become ever more extreme.

The 'old guard' who questioned this were derided for being
'reactionary bigots' and 'narrow-minded puritans', but in reality
much of this imagined liberation was leading to new forms of
imprisonment, such as an addiction to pornography. In my account
of those years I analysed what I called the 'fantasy cycle': how, when
people get collectively carried away by groupthink not anchored
in reality, the consequences unfold through a succession of five
identifiable stages.

The cycle begins with an Anticipation Stage, when circumstances combine to offer a new and irresistibly exciting way of looking at the world: an 'idea whose time has come'. Initially this leads those caught up in it into a Dream Stage, when for a while all seems to be going gratifyingly well. But because it is to some extent founded on wishful thinking it requires ever more determined efforts to force it into reality. A Frustration Stage is where unforeseen consequences intrude, which become ever harder to deal with, leading to a Nightmare Stage where unforeseen realities close in on every side, culminating in a final 'collision with reality', when make-believe either falls apart or just fades away into disillusionment.

If this was true of many of the dreams of the Sixties, few were more obviously damaging than the ideology which led during those years to the physical transformation of so many of Britain's cities, as vast areas of human-scale older buildings were bulldozed, to be replaced by tower blocks of council flats and grim concrete housing estates.

In 1979, in a BBC television documentary, *City of Towers*, I traced the story of the utopian vision which had brought this about, originally conceived back in the 1920s by the French-Swiss architect Le Corbusier. His dream of demolishing old cities and traditional forms of architecture, to replace them with versions of his 'city of the future' centred on gargantuan concrete buildings, became hugely influential in the 1930s on a younger generation of architects and planners, to whom he held out the beguiling prospect that they could become the true social revolutionaries of the age. In the 1950s and 1960s it was those same believers in the groupthink of the 'Modern Movement', fiercely intolerant of all traditional forms of architecture, who were now in a position to win over the entire political establishment of the time and put Le Corbusier's dream into practice.

For a decade or so this vision of the future remained an almost universally accepted consensus, cheered on by politicians and the media alike. Traditional, low-rise streets were demolished en masse, so that millions of their inhabitants could be herded into the new concrete towers, which had looked so good in architects' models and artists' impressions. But when they were actually built and lived in, they seemed rather less desirable.

Even by the late 1960s there were those beginning to say, 'We have seen the future and it doesn't work.' By the mid-1970s it was generally recognized that a terrible mistake had been made. The dream had led to a social and architectural catastrophe. Thousands of those bleak 1960s tower blocks would eventually be demolished. The whole episode had been another demonstration of the self-deceiving power of groupthink.

6

Groupthink and the 'European Project'

Britain has lost an empire, and not yet found a role.

Dean Acheson, former US Secretary of State,
November 1962

There has been no more ambitious political dream in our time
than what became known to insiders as the 'European Project': the
desire to bring all of Europe together under a single government.
Considering the immense consequences this had for the world, one
of the strange things about *le Projet* is how little is generally known
of where and how it all began.

In fact, no greater myth can be found than the European
Commission's carefully crafted account of how what has become
the European Union came about, celebrated annually on 9 May as
'Europe Day', coincidentally alongside the Russians, who celebrate
'Victory Day', the anniversary of the end of what it calls 'the Great
Patriotic War'. 'Probably very few people in Europe know,' claims the
Commission, 'that on 9 May 1950 the first move was made towards
the creation of what is now known as the European Union,' thus
perpetuating the myth that this was the first (and successful) attempt
at creating the Union.

According to Commission hagiography, in Paris that day, against
the background of the threat of a Third World War engulfing the
whole of Europe, the French Foreign Minister Robert Schuman read

to the international press a declaration calling on France, Germany and other European countries to pool together their coal and steel production as 'the first concrete foundation of a European federation'. What he proposed', the narrative continues,

> was the creation of a supranational European Institution, charged with the management of the coal and steel industry, the very sector which was, at that time, the basis of all military power. The countries which he called upon had almost destroyed each other in a dreadful conflict which had left after it a sense of material and moral desolation.

Thus, concludes the Commission, 'Everything . . . began that day'.

The reality, though, is very different, and demonstrates perfectly the first principle of groupthink. Far from Schuman heroically standing at the centre of the 'Project', he turns out to have been little more than an unwitting stooge, manipulated by one man who had made its his life's work to set up a 'government for Europe'.

That man was Jean Monnet, hailed rightly as one of the fathers of the European Union, but only alongside Schuman. At the time, Monnet, nearing the end of implementing his four-year plan for the 'modernization' of France, had already seen two post-war attempts at creating his 'government' fail: the OEEC, created on the back of the Marshall Plan, and the Council of Europe. With resigned detachment, he had concluded that neither of them could

> ever give concrete expression to European unity. Amid these vast groupings of countries, the common interest was too indistinct, and common disciplines were too lax. A start would have to be made by doing something more practical and more ambitious. National sovereignty would have to be tackled more boldly and on a narrower front.

However, if Monnet was sure that something much 'more practical and ambitious' was needed to achieve the desired goal, then events in the late spring of 1950 conspired to create precisely the opportunity he was looking for.

During 1949, West Germany had finally emerged to self-government under the Chancellorship of Konrad Adenauer. Under its Basic Law, passed on 8 May 1949, the new Federal Democratic Republic, or FDR, was based on a federation of the eleven highly decentralized *Land* governments which, on British insistence, retained considerable power, guaranteed by a constitutional court. In crucial respects the federal government, centred in Bonn, could not act without the consent of the *Länder*. In particular, all international treaties had to be ratified by the *Länder* through their legislative assembly, the *Bundesrat*.

The new Germany, under the guidance of Ludwig Erhard, was already showing signs of a remarkable economic recovery, which raised the question of how the new nation should be assimilated into the western European community. At the Council of Europe in August 1949 Churchill had shocked many delegates by proposing that she should be given the warmest of welcomes. Two of the western occupying powers, the USA and Britain, wanted to see her continue on the road towards full economic recovery and nationhood as soon as possible. But this had provoked a deep rift with France, which wanted to continue exercising control over the German economy, for fear she might once again become too strong a political and economic rival. The argument centred on that old bone of contention, the coal and steel industries of the Ruhr, heartland of Germany's economy and formerly the arsenal of her war machine. In 1948, France had demanded the setting up of an International Ruhr Authority, which would enable French officials to control Germany's coal and steel production and ensure that a substantial part of that production was diverted to aid French reconstruction. It was a curious echo of France's disastrous policy after the First World War. Naturally, the new West Germany was bitterly opposed to such an authority. So were the other two occupying powers, America and Britain.

For over two years the dispute festered, without resolution. But in the spring of 1950 the US Secretary of State Dean Acheson finally lost patience. He issued France with what amounted to an ultimatum. On 11 May there would be a foreign ministers' meeting in London and, unless the French could offer a satisfactory compromise proposal, the USA would impose a solution on all parties. This gave Monnet the opportunity he had been waiting for. For years he had dreamed of building a 'United States of Europe', starting with the integration of the coal and steel industries, not just of France and Germany but other western European countries, under the direction of a supranational authority.

When Monnet came to commit his plan to paper, he was obviously troubled by how much to reveal of its underlying purpose, and he went through nine separate drafts. In the first, the pooling of coal and steel was regarded as 'the first step of a Franco-German Union'. The second opened it up to the 'first step of a Franco-German Union and a European federation'. By the fifth draft, this had been changed to: 'Europe must be organised on a federal basis. A Franco-German Union is an essential element is this.' The seventh demanded that 'Europe must be organised on a Federal basis.' But by the final draft, almost all this was missing. All he would allow himself was a reference to the pool being 'the first step of a European federation', a term so vague it could mean different things to different people.

Although what Monnet really had in mind was the creation of a European entity with all the attributes of a state, the anodyne phrasing was deliberately chosen to make it difficult to dilute the concept into just another intergovernmental body, and so as not to scare off national governments by emphasizing that its purpose was to over-ride their sovereignty.

Once his memorandum was complete, Monnet's next problem was how to get it adopted. He could not act as the champion of his own plan. As a natural behind-the-scenes operator, his style was always to act indirectly. He needed to win over very senior support in the French government, and the obvious choice was the Foreign Minister, Robert Schuman. It would be he that would have to face US Secretary of State Dean Acheson in a few days' time. Monnet knew

Acheson's officials had few ideas to offer, and he would most likely, therefore, be receptive to some new ones.

As a potential advocate, Schuman had other advantages. Born in Luxembourg to a German mother, he was fluent in both German and French. He had then moved to Alsace-Lorraine when it was under German rule, which meant that in 1914 he had been recruited into the German army. Yet in the Second World War, when Alsace Lorraine was again part of Germany, he had, as a French citizen, been arrested by the Gestapo. He was thus a perfect witness to the need to resolve the Franco-German conflict.

To get to Schuman, Monnet approached his *chef de cabinet* Bernard Clappier, telling him to advise his boss that he had some ideas for the London conference. He had expected Clappier to call him back but, by Friday 28 April, Monnet had heard nothing. Fearing that Schuman was not interested, Monnet sent a copy of his memorandum to Prime Minister Georges Bidault. In it, Monnet wrote of the 'German situation' becoming a cancer that would be dangerous to peace. For future peace, he wrote, the creation of a dynamic Europe is indispensable:

> We must therefore abandon the forms of the past and enter the path of transformation, both by creating common basic economic conditions and by setting up new authorities accepted by the sovereign nations. Europe has never existed. It is not the addition of sovereign nations met together in councils that makes an entity of them. We must genuinely create Europe; it must become manifest to itself . . .

Alas for Bidault, who thereby missed his chance of immortality, the memorandum did not reach him. Meanwhile, Clappier had re-appeared full of apologies. Monnet gave him a copy of the memorandum and immediately decided that Schuman should see it. He caught him at the Gare de l'Est, as he was sitting in a train waiting to go to Metz for the weekend. When Schuman returned to Paris, after studying the document, he had adopted the plan wholeheartedly. It had now become the 'Schuman Plan', although in reality it was not his at all. In the final analysis, he was not even committed to it, except as a device to get him off a hook.

Once Schuman had agreed, the contents of the Plan were passed by his office in great secrecy to the German chancellor, Konrad Adenauer, in the hope of securing his provisional agreement. Other governments, especially the British, were not told. According to Professor Bernard Lavergne, a prominent political commentator of the time, who was to publish a highly critical study of the plan,

> The curious thing was that M. Bidault, the Premier, was – at least, at first – not at all favourable to the Plan which, in early May, was suddenly sprung on him by his Foreign Minister, M. Schuman. And oddly enough – though this was typical of M. Schuman's furtive statesmanship and diplomacy – neither was M. François-Poncet, the French High Commissioner, nor the Quai d'Orsay, or even the French Government, properly informed of what was going on during the days that preceded the 'Schuman bombshell' of 9 May.

However, 'as a result of a curious coincidence', Dean Acheson was already on his way to the summit in London, and had decided to go via Paris to confer informally with Schuman. By another 'coincidence', Monnet was present at their meeting. As Monnet disingenuously put it, 'courtesy and honesty obliged us to take Acheson into our confidence.' The plan was also presented to the French Cabinet, but only in a most perfunctory way:

> Only three or four ministers were informed about [the Plan], and when, finally, on 8 May, the Council of Ministers met, no serious discussion took place at all. Schuman gave them a rough sketch of the Plan, and, without really knowing what it was all about, they gave it their blessing.

Schuman then took an audacious step. He would announce 'his' plan by appealing directly to the peoples of Europe, through the media. In a radio broadcast on 9 May 1950 he revealed Monnet's plan to the world, thus creating the foundation myth which led to that day being officially commemorated as 'Europe Day'. 'World peace', he began:

> cannot be safeguarded without the making of creative efforts proportionate to the dangers which threaten it. The contribution which an organized and living Europe can bring to civilization is indispensable to the maintenance of peaceful relations. In taking upon herself for more than 20 years the role of champion of a united Europe, France has always had as her essential aim the service of peace. A united Europe was not achieved and we had war. Europe will not be made all at once, or according to a single plan. It will be built through concrete achievements which first create a de facto solidarity. The coming together of the nations of Europe requires the elimination of the age-old opposition of France and Germany. . .
>
> With this aim in view the French Government proposes that action be taken immediately on one limited but decisive point . . . it proposes that Franco-German production of coal and steel as a whole be placed under a common High Authority, within the framework of an organization open to the participation of the other countries of Europe. The pooling of coal and steel production should immediately provide for the setting up of common foundations for economic development as a first step in the federation of Europe.

After describing how 'the solidarity in production thus established will make it plain that any war between France and Germany becomes not merely unthinkable, but materially impossible,' he went on to say that this would help simply and speedily to achieve 'that fusion of interest which is indispensable to the establishment of a common economic system'.

This was the Schuman Declaration which now occupies pride of place on the EU's Europa website as the document 'which led to the creation of what is now the European Union'. Yet, according to one historian, although the plan was immediately greeted with great excitement by the press, the curious thing was that literally nobody knew exactly what it was about, not even Schuman.

The whole thing was an elaborate charade, a meticulous coup by the puppet-master extraordinaire, Jean Monnet, to a plan he and his colleague Arthur Salter had devised all those years ago, to deal with a different war and an entirely different geopolitical situation. Like so much to do with the history of the EU, even the photograph of Schuman announcing 'his' plan is a fake. Monnet failed to arrange for photographers to be present, so the 'historic' event was reconstructed some days after 9 May.

The great irony was that the model Monnet adopted in 1950 was, in effect, designed to prevent the Second World War, but before it had even been implemented it had failed. And with the world partitioned into superpower blocs, and an uneasy peace increasingly kept by a balance of terror assured by nuclear weapons, his 1920s paradigm was already obsolete.

However, 1950 was just the start. Monnet himself became the first president of the supranational European Coal and Steel Community, hubristically telling some of his colleagues when they met for the first time that they made up 'the first government of Europe'. But he and his allies soon realised there was no way they could achieve their real goal overnight. Their government would have to be built stealthily, step by step, over many years, first by pretending that it was meant to be only an 'economic community', a 'Common Market'.

In 1957 their project was at last set properly on its way with the Treaty of Rome, creating all the core institutions of their future government (based on those of the old League of Nations). This was much more than was needed just to run a mere trading arrangement. But the only clue as to their real aim was the treaty's opening declaration: that its purpose was to work for an 'ever closer union' of the 'peoples of Europe'. And in pursuit of that aim, only the unelected officials of their new European Commission were given the power to initiate the Community's laws.

For years the Project's real agenda of continuous integration advanced steadily. Ever more powers were transferred from national governments to the new supranational government at the centre. More and more countries, including Britain, were added to the original six, and the peoples of Europe generally came to view all this ever more favourably, as the way to a more prosperous and more idealistic future.

But by its very nature, the vision had to be kept advancing towards that still unstated ultimate goal. By the mid-1980s, plans were being laid for an even more ambitious leap forward towards the goal. In 1992, with the Maastricht Treaty, the European Community was transformed into the European Union. Already it had open internal borders, and as the supreme symbol of their supranational Union transcending petty nationalism, it was now to be given its own single currency.

Even now, any outsider who dared question where all this was leading was likely to be dismissed as just a backward-looking 'xenophobe', a petty nationalist who hated foreigners, a 'Little Englander'. But the EU was by now so complex that only very few of those who claimed to admire it had really any idea of how its labyrinthine structures worked, let alone its real nature and purpose. They simply took on trust what they had been told by others, or read in the press, or learned from the BBC (which was always enthusiastically supportive of the EU, but never really understood more about it than its carefully manufactured outward pretensions).

No sooner had all this been set in train, with the new euro launched on its way, than the Project expanded its reach still further. It was about to absorb ten more countries into its empire, covering much of the continent. The time had come for 'Europe' to take the world stage as a 'country' in its own right, by giving it, like the United States of America, its own constitution.

Only now did signs appear that the dream of 'ever closer union' was at last beginning to over-reach itself. When the new 'Constitution for Europe' was rejected by the voters of France and the Netherlands, among the chief reasons given were that the unelected government in Brussels had become 'too remote', 'too bureaucratic'. Even in Brussels there was worried talk about what was described as 'the democratic deficit'. But at least this rejection of the constitution could be circumvented simply by smuggling it back in under another name, as the Lisbon Treaty.

Much less manageable problems were now appearing, however, the first being the immense ongoing crisis blowing up over the euro. And this came about for precisely the reasons the Commission had been warned of by its own experts back in the 1970s, when the idea of a single currency was first being discussed.

In 1977 a committee of senior economists led by Sir Donald MacDougall was asked by the Commission to advise on what would be necessary for a single currency to work. It could only be viable, they concluded, if Europe's 'government' had control of at least a quarter of all its member states' GDPs, allowing it to redistribute massive amounts of money from richer parts of Europe to poorer members. 'Failure to attend to this matter', the report warned, would result in 'stagnation' at least, and 'at worst in secession and dissolution'. And if poor countries such as Greece and Portugal were allowed to join, this 'would add substantially to the problem'.

As is the way with groupthink wishful thinking, all these expert warnings had been swept aside. The cause of integration had to come first – with just the results McDougall had predicted. Greece and Portugal were among the countries which sank, under an ever-growing mountain of debt, into a sea of economic and social misery not seen in western Europe since 1945. This disaster Europe had brought on itself by its obsessive urge to ignore any idea of national interest. But the next seemingly intractable crisis to hit Europe caused countries to become even more concerned for their own interest.

This was the ever-growing flood of migrants and refugees pouring into Europe from the Middle East and Africa. With camps filled to bursting with unwanted migrants and the Mediterranean awash with corpses, the EU seemed quite impotent to stem the tide. One country after another turned desperately to protecting its own national interest by erecting fences to shut its borders.

The key elements of the dream which had originally inspired the 'European project' were being turned on their heads, colliding with the reality of consequences it had not foreseen. It had thought it could ignore democracy and eliminate the 'evil' of nationalism, yet all over Europe populist movements and new political parties were angrily protesting at being ruled by an alien form of government that seemed wholly unaccountable, and oblivious to the needs and wishes of 'the people', who felt much deeper loyalty to their own countries than to any abstract idea of being 'citizens of Europe'.

In 2014 the importance of this sense of national loyalty was brought home yet again, when the EU made hubristic moves to expand its empire even further, by taking over Ukraine, looked on historically as the cradle of Russian identity. Again, the result should have been predictable. The same intense sense of national identity drove the Russian speakers of eastern Ukraine and Crimea into wishing to be ruled by their fellow Russians in Moscow, rather than by some alien government in faraway Brussels of which they knew nothing. It was yet another case of groupthink make-believe colliding with a reality it had tried to suppress, provoking a crisis between the West and Russia, for reasons the West did not begin to understand.

In 2016, for not dissimilar reasons, came the further shock of the UK referendum, by which the British voted to become the first country ever to leave the European Union. Admittedly there was a great deal of deluded groupthink in both sides of the argument as to whether and how the British should extricate themselves from a system of government they too had never really understood. But that is another story, and one by no means over yet.

I have written in detail about this particular story, of which the true outlines are generally so little known, because it is such a striking example of the extraordinary power of groupthink, in some ways comparable in scale to that of the scare over global warming.

The two stories have much in common. They were both originally conceived by only a very small group of people, but eventually emerged as an 'idea whose time had come'. Both soon won huge support from people who did not necessarily understand all the technical details, but found the message irresistibly appealing: one offering a chance to save Europe from its past, the other to save the planet for the future. Each enjoyed a long 'Dream Stage', when all seemed to be going plausibly well, and to criticize or question them was seen as socially and politically quite unacceptable. Each eventually entered a 'Frustration Stage', when unforeseen consequences began to intrude, although for the 'true believers' this only redoubled their determination to press on, regardless of any difficulties.

But in each case, this had then led to a 'Nightmare Stage', when realities began to close in from which there seemed to be no escape. In the case of Europe these were the seemingly insoluble problems of the euro, the endless flood of migrants, and the rise of nationalistic populism against a system which seemed quite unequipped to satisfy its needs and wishes. In the case of global warming, it was above all the refusal of the rest of the world to follow the West in crippling their economies, for a cause in which they had never really believed anyway. And it is that story, the saga of 'global warming', that we explore as our next example of groupthink.

7

Global Warming

Only an insignificant fraction of scientists deny the global warming crisis. The time for debate is over. The science is settled.

Al Gore, *1992*

Nullius in verba

Motto of the Royal Society

If there is an insignificant increase in the temperature, it is not due to anthropogenic factors but to natural factors related to the planet itself and to solar activity. There is no evidence confirming a positive linkage between the level of carbon dioxide and temperature changes . . . when we see the biggest international adventure based on totalitarian ideology which tries to defend itself using disinformation and falsified facts, it is hard to think of any other word to describe this but 'war'.

Alexander Ilarionov, Moscow, 2004

We take note of the decision of the United States of America to withdraw from the Paris Agreement . . . The Leaders of the other G20 members state that the Paris Agreement is irreversible. We reiterate the importance of fulfilling the UNFCCC commitment by developed countries in providing means of implementation including financial resources to assist developing countries . . . We reaffirm our strong commitment to the Paris Agreement, moving swiftly towards its full implementation.

Communiqué issued after G20 meeting,
Hamburg, 8 July 2017

The belief that the earth faces an unprecedented threat from 'human-induced climate change' – such as currently to constitute a 'climate emergency' – has been one of the most extraordinary episodes in the history of either science or politics. It has led scientists and politicians to contemplate nothing less than a complete revolution in the way mankind sources the energy required to keep modern industrial civilization functioning, by phasing out the fossil fuels on which that civilization has been built.

Future generations may look back on this late-twentieth and early-twenty-first-century panic over man-made warming as one of the strangest episodes in our history.[57] But they will only be able to comprehend how such an extraordinary flight from reality could have taken place by understanding the peculiarities of collective human psychology, and in particular the rules defining the nature of groupthink.

In crucial respects the ideology of climate has much in common with previous examples. Like them, it originated with only a very small group of people who had become gripped by a visionary idea. Like them, it was based on predictions of a hypothetical future – or prophecies – which could not be definitively proved right or wrong.

[57] I deal with this issue at greater length at https://www.thegwpf.org/content/uploads/2018/02/Groupthink.pdf.

Like them it therefore became important to insist that this belief system must be subscribed to by a consensus of all right-thinking people, using every kind of social, political and psychological pressure to enforce conformity. And like them this inevitably shaped the response to anyone who would not be a part of it, who therefore had to be condemned as a 'heretic', a 'subversive' or a 'denier', whose dissent had to be more or less ruthlessly suppressed.

In this sense, acceptance of the 'consensus' mind-set was like a contagious condition. Any attempt to question those who had passed under its spell as to why they believed what they did all too often revealed that they didn't really know anything about it at all. Their heads were filled with a ragbag of mantras and gobbets of misinformation (such as that the vanishing of Arctic ice was threatening the survival of polar bears), which were so often demonstrably the very reverse of the truth.

And this was not just true of many members of the general public. It was equally true of people paid or qualified to know better, such as environmental journalists, politicians, indeed a great many scientists themselves. A neighbour of mine was a reputable professor of chemistry at a leading university and, when he spoke about global warming, liked to claim that he did so with the authority of 'a scientist'. But he would then solemnly tell us that the rise in sea levels caused by climate change would eventually submerge our village, even though it was several hundred feet up on the hills of Somerset.

What makes this example different from the others, however, was that it was based on the unrivalled authority accorded in the modern world to science. Unlike those other belief systems, it could ultimately be tested against empirically verifiable facts. It crucially rested on all-important computer model predictions which, as the years went by, could be compared with the objective evidence of what was actually happening.

Nevertheless, for 30 years the way this has all come about has given expert observers increasing cause for puzzlement. In particular they have questioned three key phenomena: the speed with which the belief that human carbon dioxide emissions were causing the world's climate to warm to a dangerous degree came to be proclaimed as shared by a consensus of the world's climate scientists; the nature and reliability of much of the evidence cited to support that belief; and the failure of global temperatures to rise in accordance with the predictions of the computer models on which the 'consensus' ultimately rested.

But there was also the peculiarly hostile and dismissive nature of the response by supporters of the consensus to those who questioned all this – a group that included many eminent scientists and other experts. And so closely did the pattern of collective psychological behaviour conform to the three distinctive features we characterize as 'groupthink' that there is no hesitation in citing the global warming movement as a classic example of the genre.

For its first ten years or so, as we know, the theory that the world was warming as a direct result of the rise in atmospheric carbon dioxide still seemed plausible. But increasingly after 1998 the predictions and the real-world evidence began to diverge. The response of those within the groupthink was not, as the principles of proper science should have dictated, to ask whether the theory itself might in some way be flawed. Instead, the rules of groupthink continued to be in evidence when, during the period spanning the first report of the UN Intergovernmental Panel on Climate Change (IPCC) in 1990 and the Rio 'Earth Summit' of 1992, global warming became adopted as an international scientific and political 'consensus'.

In terms of how this mighty drama unfolded, by far its most significant feature was the divide between the 'developed' countries and the rest of the world, where the power of Western groupthink has always in reality exercised very much less sway.

One of the central ironies of global warming is the extent to which it ultimately became undermined by the core principle placed at the heart of the world's response to it by Maurice Strong, the man who more than any other politicized the issue. As a very rich but strongly left-wing Canadian businessman, Strong had since his teens become convinced that the future of mankind lay in transforming the UN into a world government. He had also become a very skilful political networker at the highest level. In 1972, thanks to his personal links with the head of the UN, he had been appointed to organize in Stockholm a 'world conference on the environment', which led to him being asked to set up, as its first head, a new UN agency, the UN Environment Program (UNEP).

In fact, Strong knew very little about the environment. But he had come to see it as the key to using the UN's prestige to promote a sweeping left-wing agenda. He argued that the natural resources of the earth were the common inheritance of all mankind, and that the rich Western countries, which had benefited so disproportionately from exploiting them, must now be made to fund the poorer countries in the rest of the world to help their economies to catch up.

In 1985, though Strong had by then stepped down as its director, it was the UNEP which joined the World Meteorological Organisation (WTO) in sponsoring a climate conference in Villach, Austria. The meeting, hailed as the 'First Climate Conference', was chaired by Strong's like-minded successor as head of UNEP, Dr Mustafa Tolba.[58]

In 1987 the two men were able to push their agenda significantly further as members of the Brundtland Commission, the body that was to put the word 'sustainable' into the jargon of politicians and officialdom for decades to come. Thanks to their evidence, and citing the recommendations from Villach, the Brundtland report laid particular emphasis on the dangers of 'human-induced climate change', warning that this could raise global temperatures to such a level that it would have serious effects on agriculture, 'raise sea levels, flood coastal cities and disrupt national economies'. The report therefore called for a major global effort to curb emissions of carbon dioxide and other greenhouse gases.

In the same year, Strong played a key behind-the-scenes role in organizing the conference in his native Canada that produced the Montreal Protocol, the first global treaty to 'protect the environment',

[58]https://public.wmo.int/en/bulletin/history-climate-activities, accessed 11 October 2019.

that succeeded in phasing out the use of CFCs, the chemicals thought to be destroying the ozone layer. This enabled Strong to see that, in global warming, he had found an even more powerful theme on which to push his long-time political agenda. In the landmark year of 1988 everything seemed suddenly to be coming together.

First, on a stiflingly hot July day in Washington that summer, a Senate committee heard a cleverly stage-managed rallying cry by another recent convert to the global warming cause, James Hansen, who, as head of NASA's Goddard Institute for Space Studies (GISS), was in charge of one of the world's key official temperature records. The US media had been briefed to be present in force at this hearing, chaired by Senator Tim Wirth and including among the members of its committee Senator Al Gore. The journalists were promised that they would hear something pretty sensational. Hansen's wildly alarmist predictions that the world was heading for a global Armageddon duly made lurid headlines across USA and beyond, including cover stories in *Time* and *Newsweek*. Wirth and Hansen had certainly pulled off quite a coup in raising the threat of global warming to the top of the media agenda.

Quite separately, however, in November that year in Geneva, the inaugural meeting of a new body, jointly sponsored by WMO and UNEP, took place: the IPCC. Although it was sold to the world as an impartial body of world scientists, the IPCC was never intended by those who set it up to be anything of the kind. The two men more than any responsible were Bolin, appointed as its first chairman, and Houghton, chosen to chair 'Working Group I', which would contribute the all-important section on the science of climate change when the IPCC came to compile its first report. Not only were both men totally committed to the belief in 'human-induced climate change', so were almost all the lesser mortals round the table at that first IPCC meeting, representing 34 nations, as can be seen from the statements each submitted on behalf of their respective governments.[59] Within

[59]Report of the First Session of the WMO/UNEP Intergovernmental Panel on Climate Change, Geneva, 9–11 November 1988. https://www.ipcc.ch/meetings/session01/first-final-report.pdf.

just two years, it was proposed, the IPCC would present its first 'assessment report', in which the key ingredient would be computer models programmed to determine the extent to which rising levels of carbon dioxide would warm the world.[60]

When this First Assessment Report appeared in 1990, the global headlines were led by a claim in its Summary for Policymakers that the IPCC was 'confident that the increase in CO_2 alone' had been responsible for 'more than half the world's recent warming' and would 'require immediate reductions in emissions from human activities of over 60 per cent'.[61]

'Based on current models', the Summary predicted that, unless drastic action was taken, global temperatures would increase through the twenty-first century by up to 0.5°C every decade, an increase far greater than anything 'seen in the past 10,000 years'. Although in the previous 100 years temperatures had increased by 0.6°C, the models were now predicting the possibility of a not dissimilar increase every ten years.

But the Summary for Policymakers was drafted by Houghton himself. And a look at the hundreds of pages which it was purporting to summarize showed a rather different picture. Some of the scientists responsible for them had come to very much more cautious, if not contradictory conclusions. One passage, for instance, admitted that:

> global warming of a larger size has almost certainly occurred at least once since the last glaciation without any appreciable increase in greenhouse gases . . . [and] because we do not understand the

---

[60]It was agreed from the outset that the IPCC's assessment reports would be divided into three parts. Working Group I would be responsible for assessing the science and extent of global warming, Working Group II would focus on its 'impact', and Working Group III would consider ways in which that impact could be 'mitigated'. The contributions of Working Groups II and III would be expected to depend on the findings of Working Group I.

[61]Richard Lindzen, 'Global warming: the origin and nature of the alleged scientific consensus', Proceedings of the OPEC Seminar on the Environment, Vienna, 13–15 April 1992 (available on Cato Institute website); also interview with Lindzen, *Die Weltwoche*, 3 March 2007.

reasons for these past warming events, it is not possible to attribute a specific proportion of the recent, smaller warming to an increase in greenhouse gases.

But it was Houghton's alarmist gloss on the actual findings of the report that, as intended, caught the attention of the world's media and politicians, which was just what was wanted by their ally Strong, who was even now preparing for the unprecedented spectacular he planned to stage in Rio de Janeiro two years later.

The great 'achievement' of so-called 'Earth Summit', which Strong organized and chaired in Rio in 1992, was to divide the world into two distinct groups: the 'Annex I' nations of the West, expected to take the lead in drastically cutting their emissions, and the 'developing' countries across the rest of the world, which could be largely exempted from such restrictions until their economies had caught up with those of the West.

Western groupthink, however, dominated at Kyoto in 1997, when practical steps were first agreed to slow down the rise in world temperatures. These would require the richer, developed nations of the West to reduce their carbon dioxide emissions, while allowing those still 'developing' nations, such as China and India, to continue increasing them until their economies had caught up with the West.

Eventually, this division between the West and the rest of the world turned out to be the crux of the whole story. For some years the consensus theory continued to seem plausible, as carbon dioxide levels and global temperatures continued to rise together, just as the computer models on which the consensus relied had predicted. In 1998 temperatures were the highest on record, coinciding with an unusually strong El Niño event in the Pacific.

Between 2004 and 2007, the 'consensus' still seemed to carry all before it, as its claims for the threat posed to the planet by global warming became ever more exaggerated and extreme, as exemplified in Al Gore's documentary, *An Inconvenient Truth*, and the IPCC's Fourth Assessment Report in 2007.

But it was at this time that more serious cracks began to appear in the 'consensus' case. There had been the continuing failure, since the El Niño year of 1998, of global temperatures to rise as the computer models had predicted. This became known as 'the hiatus' or 'the pause'. There were telling examples of how irrationally supporters of the 'consensus' had reacted when they were, for the first time, confronted by world-ranking scientists outside the groupthink. Some scientists from within the 'consensus' tried to come up with modifications to the theory that might explain why the predictions were no longer being confirmed by the evidence. Around 2007, with a startling drop in global temperatures, they for the first time began to wonder whether 'natural factors', such as shifts in the world's major ocean currents, might not be having more influence on shaping the climate than the IPCC's computer models had allowed.

Eventually even the IPCC and the UK Met Office acknowledged that there had been a temperature 'pause' in the years after 1998. But they too tried to explain this away by suggesting that these natural factors were merely 'masking the underlying warming trend', which in due course would re-emerge. Or they suggested that the heat created by man-made warming was only no longer visible because it was 'hiding in the oceans'. This claim was supported by the IPCC's Fifth Assessment Report in 2013, which accepted that '93 per cent' of the extra heat entering the world during the pause had been absorbed by the oceans, with only 1 per cent raising temperatures at the earth's land surface.[62] Other scientists simply ignored the growing evidence that the models had got it wrong, or worse still started to

[62]The IPCC based its claim on two papers. The first, by Church et al. (Geophysical Research Letters, 16 September 2011), was led by John Church, who had long been the most prominent advocate for the 'consensus' view on sea-levels. This was followed by Levitus et al. (in the same journal, 17 May 2012). The 93 per cent claim came from the latter paper. These papers were greeted with huge relief by the 'consensus' as providing a wholly new explanation for the pause in temperatures. By the time of the El Niño spike in 2016 this was enabling them to claim that the pause had never existed – until temperatures again dropped.

manipulate the evidence, as in the wholesale 'adjustment' of the surface temperature records to show that the world was indeed still warming as the theory had predicted.

During this period, though, there was the emergence through the internet of a new counter-consensus, led by technical experts qualified to challenge every scientific claim on which the 'consensus' relied. It was this which, in accordance with Janis's third rule, prompted supporters of the consensus to vilify anyone daring to disagree with them as just 'climate deniers' who were 'anti-science'.

In reality, of course, it was the sceptics themselves, such as Richard Lindzen and Paul Reiter, who were trying to defend proper science. They also eventually included, for instance, such eminent figures in the world scientific community as the two veteran Princeton physicists, Freeman Dyson and Will Happer.

In 2009/2010, the consensus suffered its three most damaging blows yet. The first blow was the release of the so-called Climategate emails – unpublished communications between the little group of scientists at the heart of the IPCC establishment. These had been leaked in 2009 from CRU, revealing just what angst and anger had been aroused among that same intimately connected group of scientists who were now at the heart of the IPCC. In the exchanges of emails all their names were there: Michael Mann, Ben Santer, Tom Wigley, Stephen Schneider, Jonathan Overpeck, Kevin Trenberth and Gavin Schmidt, who was Hansen's number two at GISS and in charge of one of the two main global surface-temperature records. At East Anglia itself, their close ally, CRU director Phil Jones, was responsible for the other surface record, HadCRUt.

What these emails also brought to light was that, just when Mann had been creating his 'hockey stick' graph of global temperatures, Jones's CRU colleague Keith Briffa had already been trying to produce a remarkably similar graph, also based on tree-ring 'proxies', this time from Siberia. But these had also frustratingly seemed to show a marked falling-off of temperatures in the second half of the twentieth century, which showed that they were not proxies for temperature at all. In other words, they had cut off the tree-ring sequence just where it wasn't giving the picture they wanted, and then incorporated thermometer temperatures for recent decades, making them look much warmer than the medieval era.

The second blow came with the collapse in Copenhagen of the long-planned bid to agree a new global climate treaty, again because of a division between developing nations and the West. The third was a series of scandals that revealed that the most widely quoted and alarming claims in the 2007 IPCC report had not been based on science at all, but on claims made in press releases and false reports put out by climate activists.

On both the Climategate emails and the IPCC scandals the climate 'establishment' did all it could to hold the line, with a series of supposedly independent inquiries staged by its supporters. Leading the defence were the senior scientists responsible for the Climategate emails or prestigious figures such as the government's Chief Scientific Adviser, Sir David King, and presidents of the Royal Society, Lord May and Sir Paul Nurse. How ironic, it was observed (not least by many dissenting members of the Royal Society itself), that the defining motto of the oldest and long most respected scientific society in the world had since the 1660s, been *Nullius in verba*, commonly translated as, 'Take nobody's word for it.'

As countless distinguished members of that august society had known since the days of Robert Hooke, Robert Boyle and Isaac Newton, there is no principle of scientific method more fundamental. No new scientific proposition should be accepted as true solely 'on the word of others', unless they can demonstrate that it is properly supported by evidence. To test any hypothesis, one must look at all the evidence, making sure that any which might invalidate the theory has also been fully taken into account.

All this was what the 'carbon dioxide equals global warming' theory had turned on its head. Almost the entire Western scientific community had been so carried away by the simplicity of the theory that they never subjected it to proper three-dimensional scientific questioning. They programmed their computer models accordingly. And the only response considered necessary to an argument suggesting that the theory might in some way be flawed was to ignore or ridicule it.

Even when more evidence began to suggest that the theory was not being borne out as predicted, the response was either to find ways to modify the theory round the edges, so that it could be held intact, or simply to invent new 'facts' to make the theory still seem plausible. Thus, right from the start, the entire house of cards had been based on 'taking other people's word for it', without ever putting the hypothesis to the test or allowing any genuine scientific debate.

Again and again, however hard they tried to torture the evidence into seeming to support their theory, those hard facts kept on intruding to suggest otherwise. That is why, one day, future generations will eventually look back at this story in disbelieving astonishment, and ask, 'How on earth could such a thing have happened?'

But between 2010 and 2014, despite efforts by supporters of the consensus, such as the BBC and the UK Met Office, to keep the alarm going, it became clear that it was no longer possible to sustain the hysteria that had reached its climax in the years before Copenhagen.

Then came what appeared to be a last throw by the 'consensus', with the approach of yet another major global climate conference in Paris in 2015. Documents supplied by every country before the conference, known as INDCs, or 'Intended Nationally Determined Contributions', set out their intended future energy policies. If ever there was a moment when reality should finally have broken in on the West's wishful thinking, it was the publication of all those INDCs.

These made clear that, however much the countries of the West might be planning to reduce their 'carbon' emissions, the rest of the world, led by China and India, was planning by 2030 to build enough fossil-fuel power stations to increase global emissions by almost 50 per cent. China was intending to double its emissions, India to triple them. Almost all the other 'developing' nations in the list of the world's top 20 emitters, along with Russia and Japan, were forecasting significant increases. The overall picture that emerged was that, while the US (still under Obama) and the EU were proposing by 2030 to reduce their annual carbon dioxide emissions by 1.7 billion tonnes, India was planning to increase its emissions by 4.9 billion tonnes and China by 10.9 billion tonnes. It was certainly some deal.[63]

In other words, the rest of the world had no intention of going along with the declared aim of Paris, to agree on the wholesale 'decarbonization' of the world's economy. Yet astonishingly, so lost were developed countries in the groupthink that the Western media failed to recognize what was happening.

This should certainly have been seen as a historically significant moment, in at least two ways. First, it showed what the rest of the world thought of the West's make-believe, as its declared intentions made a total mockery of everything Paris was meant to be about. But the second point is almost as significant. This was the extent to which the politicians and media in the West wholly failed to recognize or report what had happened. No one who learned about Paris only from the press coverage in the West would have had any idea that this was what the non-Western world was proposing. Few journalists, if any, had ever read the INDCs. What they reported was only the propagandist fluff dished out to them by the international climate establishment, as it tried to pretend that anything of genuine significance had been achieved.

The prelude to this, coinciding with another record El Niño event in 2015/2016, was such a pronounced rise in global temperatures as to prompt claims that 'the pause' had ended. But expert analysts across the world found that wholesale 'adjustments' had been made to the figures in the main surface temperature records, giving an impression that the global temperature trend had been rising much more than justified by the original recorded data.

---

[63]For calculations of the actual figures, see P. Homewood, 'Paris won't stop carbon dioxide emissions rising,' *Notalotofpeopleknowthat*, 17 November 2015. The more precise figures he extracted from the INDCs were, for the US and the EU, a drop of 1,856 Mt of carbon dioxide, for India an increase of 4,895 Mt, and for China 10,871 Mt.

One key person who rejected the Paris conclusions was President Trump. In July 2017, he finally called the bluff of one of the most damaging examples of groupthink the world has ever known, by pulling the US out of the Paris Accord. While the Western countries embarked on ever more costly and economically damaging attempts to reduce their emissions, he was the first Western leader to break silence on the actual contents of those INDCs (to which he explicitly referred in his speech as delivered), showing that the Accord had been no more than a wholly empty sham. At long last the West's most important politician had called into question the entire edifice of political illusions so tortuously cobbled together over the previous 30 years. Whatever we may think of President Trump, or the reasons he gave for his decision, his speech finally began to undermine that ramshackle structure.

But he was only able to do so because all those 'developing' countries had shown just what they thought of what the Western world was up to. Beyond some cynical public relations nods to the need for 'renewables', they did not give a fig what the Western groupthink had wanted them to do or say: they would carry on with their economic growth, based on burning vast quantities of precisely those same fossil fuels which the groupthink wanted eliminated from the earth.

Despite the pretences of the communiqué issued after the first G20 meeting attended by Trump in July 2017, the entire geopolitical balance had changed decisively. The only countries left committed to carbon dioxide reductions were now those belonging to the European Union, along with Canada and Australia, between them responsible for just 11.3 per cent of total world emissions. The only other Annex 1 countries in the G20 were Japan and Russia, responsible for another 8 per cent of global carbon dioxide emissions.

They, like all the other countries that agreed the communiqué after the Hamburg meeting of the G20 in July 2017, had committed themselves to building more coal-fired power stations and thus increasing their emissions. With that wholly dishonest document, the make-believe of political groupthink over global warming was more damningly exposed than ever before.

But the ultimate irony was that what had happened in Paris – whether the climate establishment had got its treaty or not – would have had no influence on the future of the earth's climate. This would continue to change, just as it always had done, thanks to that complex interaction of natural factors, such as the shifting cycles in ocean currents and the activity of the sun, the very factors which the scientists carried away by groupthink had long ignored and never even tried honestly to understand.

The crucial lesson of Paris was that it marked the moment when the groupthink was demonstrated for what it was. It continues to hold the Western world in its grip, but it is increasingly obvious that the rest of the world, led by the dynamic and fast-growing economies of the East, is taking little in the way of the measures to which so many western counties are committed. In fact, this is only one more reflection of the remarkable geopolitical shift which has lately been taking place. By one measure after another, politically, economically and culturally, we have seen the Western world starting to lose that pre-eminent place in the world it has enjoyed for several centuries, and the authority that went with it. Other countries, notably China and India, have been moving up to replace and surpass them. China's economy has in recent decades risen to become the second-largest in the world, India's is catching up fast, and by one measure is already in fourth place. There are forecasts that by the middle of the century these two most populous countries will not only have the two largest economies, but also that India might even overtake China.

There have thus been many signs in recent years that the political power and influence of the West, and most notably Europe, have been in relative decline. In this respect the rejection of the West's attempt to get a binding climate treaty in Paris, followed by Trump's withdrawal even from the little that Paris was claimed to have achieved, may well be looked back on as not just the moment when the great climate scare finally began to lose it its power. It may be seen as one of the more significant landmarks in a much wider historical process, the nature of which we are only now dimly beginning to apprehend, and the full implications of which we cannot yet begin to foresee.

Unquestionably we are now entering an entirely new chapter in the story, and one which leaves Europe and Britain looking very uncomfortably isolated. Sooner or later, these new realities crowding in from outside will make it very difficult to sustain the bubble of scientific and political make-believe in which we have been living for so long.

This is why it has become more relevant than ever to recognize what has really been driving this flight from reality for 30 years. It has been a supreme example of the astonishing power of groupthink to carry people off into states of illusion which, by definition, must always eventually end in disillusionment. But the belief in man-made climate change is only one of the countless other instances of the power of groupthink in our world today, all behaving according to those rules identified by Irving Janis.

8

The Strange Story of Darwinism

Belief in the theory of evolution is thus exactly parallel to the belief in special creation – both are concepts which believers know to be true, but never, up to the present, has been capable of proof.

L. Harrison Matthews, introduction to his 1971 edition of Charles Darwin's *On the Origin of Species by Means of Natural Selection, or the Preservation of Favoured Races in the Struggle for Life* (1971)

There was a time when the three towering intellectual figures of the nineteenth century who had done more than anyone to shape the thinking of the modern world were said to be Karl Marx, Sigmund Freud and Charles Darwin. Two of those three bearded prophets have now been more or less toppled from their former pedestals. Only Darwin remains, his reputation higher than ever.

Darwin's 'idea whose time had come' was his account in *The Origin of Species* (1859) of how the evolution of life on earth had come about. Ever since the middle of the eighteenth century, particularly in France and Britain, 'natural philosophers' and early geologists had increasingly come to accept that life on earth had somehow evolved, over aeons of time. But Darwin's masterstroke was his claim to have discovered the mechanism or organizing principle whereby this process had taken place.

In any form of life, he argued, minute variations occur, some of which may make it better adapted to survive. Given long enough, eventually these tiny variations may accumulate in a particular direction, to the point where this leads to the emergence of a wholly new species. Thus, over infinite stretches of geological time, have the simplest forms of life evolved into ever more complex forms, until the 'tree of life' produced *Homo sapiens*.

Darwin's idea appealed to his age for two reasons. One was that in essence it seemed so simple. The other, at a time when science was replacing religion as the most reliable source of authority in explaining how the world works, was that it did away with any notion of a supernatural Creator. He had replaced it with a narrative which explained how evolution could have taken place by a process that was entirely natural, with no need for any 'guiding mind' or purpose. Today, of course, Darwin is revered as the man whose account of how evolution came about has long been accepted by a 'consensus' of the world's scientific community as a theory which has never been successfully challenged.

As a keen young geologist in my early teens at Shrewsbury School, I would spend my Sunday afternoons looking for fossils in the hills of south Shropshire, for which I was viewed by my contemporaries as something of an eccentric. But I was pleased to discover that I was doing much the same as the school's most celebrated old boy, Darwin, had done 130 years earlier. Although at the time I whizzed through *The Origin of Species*, I was so busy looking for trilobites in the local quarries that it left little impression on me, apart from a vague sense that something about his theory might not be wholly convincing.

It wasn't until the 1970s that I was intrigued to find just how many eminent scientists over the years had expressed serious doubts about his theory. This went right back to two of his most distinguished contemporaries: Louis Agassiz at Harvard, the most revered geologist and biologist of the day, to whom Darwin sent an early copy of his book, and Richard Owen, the creator of London Natural History Museum, who coined the word 'dinosaur'. And when I came to read *The Origin of Species* more carefully, what I found really surprising was how Darwin himself had been perceptive enough to spot four major possible objections to his own theory. If any of these could not be satisfactorily answered, he said, he would have to concede that the entire theory would have to be rejected. But even more remarkable was how Darwin himself had tried to answer each of these objections.

1. THE ABSENCE OF 'INTERMEDIATE FORMS'

One serious problem with his theory, Darwin suggested, was that, wherever we look in the palaeontological record, every fossil we find is of a clearly identifiable species. Where are all the fossils which show the transitional stages as one form of life evolves into another? As he himself put it in Chapter Ten, 'Perhaps the most obvious and serious objection which can be urged against the theory is the absence of intermediate forms between one distinct species and another. Why is every geological formation and every stratum not full of such links?'

Darwin's answer was simple. 'The explanation lies, I believe, in the extreme imperfection of the geological record.' In other words, he was arguing that, when more fossils were found, those intermediate forms would come to light.

2. EVOLUTIONARY LEAPS – THE SUDDEN APPEARANCE OF COMPLEX ORGANS, ALL THE PARTS OF WHICH MUST WORK INTERDEPENDENTLY FOR THEM TO FUNCTION EFFICIENTLY

Another possible flaw in his theory, Darwin said, arose from those many episodes in the story, such as the emergence of flowering plants, where evolution had suddenly taken what seemed to be a particularly dramatic leap forward. In particular he cited the appearance of some complex organ, every part of which needed to operate interdependently with the rest for the organ to serve its purpose. How could this have come about just by the accumulation of infinite small variations? This point Darwin recognised to be so serious that he wrote in Chapter Six, 'If it could be demonstrated that any complex organ existed which could not possibly have been formed by numerous, successive slight modifications, my theory would absolutely break down.' But his only answer was to say: 'I can find no such case. No doubt many organs exist of which we do not have the transitional grades.' In other words, he was falling back on the answer he had given to the first problem. As yet, the fossil record was incomplete. When more fossils were found, this objection would be answered.

3. THE COMPOUND EYE AS A PARTICULAR EXAMPLE

Darwin's next objection was a more specific instance of the same problem. How could his theory explain the sudden appearance in the early Cambrian period of the incredibly intricate compound eye, as exhibited in the earliest trilobites and many of the other first vertebrates?

Here he again admitted the seriousness of the problem by admitting that 'to suppose that the eye with all its inimitable contrivances . . . could have been formed by natural selection seems, I freely confess, absurd in the highest degree'. But his answer this time was even more disingenuous. Going on to describe at length various different forms of optical organs, from the simplest to the most complex, all he could offer in conclusion was his assertion that

> when we bear in mind how small the number of all living forms
> must be compared with those which have become extinct . . . the
> difficulty ceases to be very great in believing that natural selection
> may have converted the simple apparatus of an optic nerve . . .
> into an optical instrument as is possessed by any member of the
> Articulate Class.

In other words, Darwin didn't even attempt to describe the process whereby the compound eye could so suddenly have come to appear in the fossil record, already complete with all its complex interdependent parts. He merely assured us that we should have no 'very great' difficulty in 'believing that natural selection could have brought this about'. He offered not a shred of evidence to explain how this could have happened. As in his other answers he was again asking us to rely on an act of faith, just as he had done with his claim that when, in the hypothetical future, enough new fossils came to light, these would eventually reveal those elusive 'intermediate forms' which would prove his theory was right.

4. THE 'CAMBRIAN EXPLOSION'

Darwin finally added to his list 'another and allied difficulty' with his theory 'which is much more serious': the manner in which 'the main divisions of the animal kingdom suddenly appear in the lowest of the fossiliferous rocks.'

What he was alluding to here has indeed remained one of the greatest riddles in the entire evolutionary story: what has become known as 'the Cambrian Explosion'. Although Darwin didn't describe it so precisely, how is it that we find at the start of the Cambrian period 540 million years ago, a vast mass of fossils suddenly appearing which represented no fewer than 26 new animal phyla (as broadly classified by their body plans)? How, according to his theory, could all these much more complex forms of life have suddenly evolved, seemingly from nowhere, since there is no trace of them anywhere in the preceding fossil record? Before this, all the previous pre-Cambrian strata contain the fossil remains of only three very much simpler phyla. And in all the half a billion years since, the fossil record has only added four more. So where at the start of the Cambrian had all those new phyla come from? How could they have come about through the very gradual process which was the essence of Darwin's theory?

Scientifically, this problem has remained just as serious as Darwin said it was. As he confessed in Chapter Ten, to the question of why we do not find rich fossiliferous deposits belonging to the assumed earliest period prior to the Cambrian system, 'I can give no satisfactory answer.' 'The case', he conceded, 'must at present remain inexplicable'.

But this, he recognized, was clearly not enough. He had to come up with some explanation which could make his theory still seem plausible. So what did he do but fall back yet again on his familiar get-out, the incompleteness of the fossil record? 'Buried beneath the vastness of the oceans', he hypothesized, 'must be the strata which contain all the missing life-forms which had been evolving through the later stages of the pre-Cambrian' – the same old leap of faith that one day in the future the evidence would be found to prove his theory was right. For the last time in the book he reiterates his assurance that, when more fossils were found, possibly below the vast unexplored seabed of the Pacific Ocean, we would find the missing evidence of all those 'forms of life which are entombed in the consecutive formations and which falsely appear to us to have suddenly appeared'. On this view, he concludes, with an almost audible sigh of relief, 'the difficulties discussed above are greatly diminished, or even disappear.'

Today, more than 150 years later, when the known fossil record is infinitely more comprehensive than it was in 1859, no such evidence has emerged, and it becomes ever more certain that it never will. Yet on the basis of Darwin's wishful thinking has rested one of the most influential scientific theories in history, still accepted throughout the world as the most convincing explanation for how life on earth evolved.

CHANCE OR DESIGN?

In 1979, prompted by a hugely popular television series presented for the BBC by David Attenborough called *Life on Earth*, I wrote a series of articles in the *Spectator* discussing the chief contending ways in which the debate over evolution had itself evolved during the previous 200 years.

The story began in the mid-eighteenth century, when those pioneering thinkers, such as Pierre Louis Maupertuis and George-Louis Leclerc in France, followed by Charles Darwin's grandfather Erasmus Darwin and others in Britain, first concluded that life had evolved. This contradicted not only the Biblical account of how the earth and all forms of life had been created by God in six days, but also the long prevailing Aristotelian orthodoxy that every species had been created separately. By the nineteenth century, early geologists such as Charles Darwin's friend Charles Lyell had established enough about the fossil record to pronounce that this process of evolution could only have taken place over millions of years.

But as yet this did not seem to contradict the belief that evolution had been brought about by the design of a supernatural mind and power, Ever since the seventeenth century, when the first modern scientists, like Isaac Newton, had made their astonishing advances in human knowledge of the natural laws which govern how the world works, they had been so awed by how ingeniously and intricately it had all been put together, with everything serving its purpose in perfect balance, that men such as Newton and the naturalist John Ray (1627–1705) concluded it could only have been designed and brought about by a divine intelligence.

This view was famously echoed in 1802 by William Pavey's *Natural Theology or Evidence for the Existence and Attributes of the Deity*, in which he argued that, if we are presented with a watch, with all its parts working perfectly together, we can only rationally assume that it has been assembled by an 'intelligence'. And that nature and the created world so exemplify this same 'intelligible' principle on a cosmic scale can only be taken as evidence for the existence of God. But sooner or later, as the idea of evolution took hold, it was inevitable it would raise the question of how it could be reconciled with what was still the official Judaeo-Christian view, that all forms of life had been created separately in less than a week, and only a few thousand years ago.

The first serious attempt to provide a scientific explanation for how life had evolved was put forward only a few years after Pavey's book, and still long before Darwin. In 1809, the year of Darwin's birth, the French biologist Jean-Baptiste Lamarck (1744–1829), put forward his first full statement of the theory that, through a kind of inner will to survive, some forms of life had begun to develop new abilities in their struggle to adapt better to their environment, and that these 'acquired characteristics' could then be handed on to their descendants until this led to the emergence of a wholly new species.

Lamarck's theory won many adherents, but did not provoke any great confrontation with the Biblical orthodoxy. That had to wait 50 more years for *The Origin of Species*, which finally unleashed that storm of very public controversy, largely centred on the horror of many leading British Christians at the thought that human beings might be descended from monkeys. Although Darwin dismissed Lamarck's theory as 'rubbish', there were now three contending accounts of how new species had been created, which in the popular mind were soon reduced essentially to two. At one pole, still to this day supported by a small minority of widely ridiculed 'Six-Day Creationists', is the old Christian orthodoxy that all species were created simultaneously. At the other, now generally viewed as the undisputed master of the field, is that which over 160 years has established Darwin's natural selection as the new orthodoxy of our age.

But one thing the Creationists and the Darwinians have in common is that they both rest their beliefs on an unshakeable certainty that they are right. At one extreme the Creationists rest their faith on the account given in Genesis. At the other, the Darwinians ultimately rest theirs on the belief that new species have been created through an endless succession of chance variations. This was summarised by the Nobel Prize-winning French biologist Jacques Monod (1910–76) in his pronouncement that 'chance alone is the source of every innovation': what he famously described as 'the Monte Carlo game', whereby random combinations of chemicals had brought about a self-replicating molecule which was the crucial precondition to the miracle of life, and which, by purely random mutations, led eventually through natural selection to *Homo sapiens*.

The belief that the whole story of life on earth has come about through Monod's roulette wheel of chance has been echoed before and since by many of his fellow neo-Darwinians, from the insistence of the eminent Harvard palaeontologist George Simpson (1902–84) that 'man is the product of a purposeless materialistic process' to Julian Huxley's 'not only is Natural Selection inevitable, not only is it an effective agency of evolution, but it is the only effective agency.'

What is less widely appreciated is that, ever since Darwin's time, there has been a third position, held by a great many thoughtful observers who have looked at the mysterious process of evolution with a much less certain eye. Beginning with Louis Agassiz and Richard Owen, these have included not just a galaxy of eminent scientists, but also intelligent lay commentators as various as Bernard Shaw and Arthur Koestler. As I wrote in 1979, these 'Creative Evolutionists' (to borrow a term from Shaw) have certainly accepted the fact that complex life has evolved over the past 600 million years. But they cannot accept what they see as the over-simple Darwinian explanation for how this came about. They believe that the process whereby new forms of life emerged has been driven by something other than just chance and random variations. They conclude that many of the great mysteries and riddles of the evolutionary story must have been guided by some other natural 'organizing principle' or 'X-factor', which does not necessarily rely on what religions down the ages have described as 'God', any more than it necessarily entails embracing, like Shaw, a version of Lamarckism.

Over the years these critics have included many more caustically sceptical scientists than generally realized. For instance, C. H. Waddington (1905–75), a Professor of Genetics at Edinburgh, argued that 'To suppose that evolution of the wonderfully adapted biological mechanism has been produced by blind chance is like suggesting that, if we went on throwing bricks together in heaps, we should eventually be able to choose ourselves a most desirable house.' Pierre-Paul Grasse (1895–1985), for 30 years Professor of Evolution at the Sorbonne, similarly asked,

> Where is the gambler, however possessed by his passion, who would be crazy enough to bet on the roulette wheel of random variation? The creation by grains of dust carried by the wind of Dürer's *Melancholia* has a probability less infinitesimal than the construction of an eye through the mishaps which might befall a

DNA molecule: mishaps which have no connection whatever with the future function of the eye. Daydreaming is permissible, but science should not succumb to it.

The real problem for the Darwinians has remained precisely the same as that implicitly recognized by Darwin himself in *The Origin of Species*. For all their certainty that their theory is right, and provides the most plausible explanation for all the evidence we have, they still have not managed to establish the irrefutable evidence which could prove it beyond doubt. For all his outward show of certainty in the first edition of *The Origin of Species*, Darwin remained puzzled to the end of his life, as became clear from subsequent editions and his other later writings, by some of the riddles he himself had identified, such as the failure of the fossil record to contain any examples of those 'intermediate forms'. He had attached much importance to the ability of selective breeding to create an astonishing variety of outward forms within a species (e.g. the difference between a Pekinese and a Great Dane). But they remain the same species, just as when any of the myriad varieties of garden roses is left long enough it will eventually revert to being just a wild rose. Indeed, as early as 1867, Darwin was so stumped by one challenge to his theory that he was almost tempted to abandon it.

A professor of engineering at Edinburgh, Fleming Jenkin, presented him with what appeared to be a crucial logical flaw in his case for natural selection. This was that, although one individual member of a species might emerge with a useful chance variation which fitted it better to survive, it could only breed with another 'normal' member of the same species. So within six generations, the hereditary power of this variation would have been diluted to a mere sixty-fourth: a somewhat flimsy basis on which to build the line of succession between the amoeba and Charles Darwin. Darwin ended up retreating back into a kind of embarrassed Lamarckism, something he had already flirted with in attaching such importance to the process whereby his famous Galapagos finches had developed different forms of beak to crack open different types of seed.

A few decades later, to the delight of Darwin's followers, his theory was (they believed) pulled off the hook on which Jenkin had impaled it by Mendel's discovery of 'recessive' and 'dominant' genes, which significantly lowered the mathematical odds in favour of a beneficial mutation being passed on.

But for twentieth-century Darwinians much greater puzzles remained, for which their theory could as yet offer no adequate explanation. Above all, there were all those quantum leaps in the evolutionary process which required a whole range of complex interdependent factors to have emerged simultaneously. They still could not account for the sudden emergence of the compound eye, complete with every one of the 600 components essential for it to fulfil its purpose; any more than they could explain how the first birds emerged in the Mesozoic, simultaneously equipped with feathers, air sacs, hollow bones, warm blood and all the other features which so distinguished them from their immediate reptilian ancestors.

The Darwinians could not have been more eager to find confirmatory proof of their theory. Even before the end of the nineteenth century they thought they had discovered a perfect example in the transformation of the peppered moth, *Biston betularia*. Although its natural appearance was variegated and brightly coloured, the Industrial Revolution had seen it widely take on an almost all-black coloration. This was hailed as 'the clearest case in which a conspicuous evolutionary process has actually been observed', and for 70 years was held up as a canonical example of Darwin's theory in action. But eventually it had to be recognized that, despite the dramatic change in their appearance, these new melanistic moths were not in any sense a new species, but only a variety of the same old *Biston betularia*.

The twentieth century produced an ever greater mountain of knowledge which seemed to the Darwinians to make their theory ever more convincing, not least thanks to the astonishing discoveries being made in the field of genetics, and particularly Crick and Watson's revolutionary discovery in the 1950s of the structure and functioning of DNA. These revealed how an incredibly complex set of relationships between all the different component parts of DNA functioned as a fundamental building block of life, and opened up a wholly new picture of how evolutionary changes might come about. Here at last, it was claimed, was an explanation for how the genetic coding of an organism might at the same time permit the simultaneous variation of different parts of that organism.

As we shall see, however, it eventually threw up a whole new set of fundamental questions which the natural selection theory was so unable to answer that the Darwinians did not even try. They simply ignored them, or retreated into crudely misrepresenting them in a way which made them look ridiculous.

As so often before, this seeming breakthrough was to turn out to be a false dawn, which only raised new questions even harder to answer. Already Arthur Koestler (in *Janus* and *The Ghost in the Machine*) had been able to portray the efforts of the Darwinians to defend their theory against each new challenge as one of the most extraordinary episodes in the history of science.

Having for so long dismissed the idea of any driver of evolution other than the endless succession of chance variations, they now began to smuggle in by the back door the idea that there might after all be some other 'guiding principle' at work. Jacques Monod, in his essay *Chance and Necessity* (1970), argued that, alongside mere chance, there was an element of hidden purpose implicit in the pattern of evolution, to which he gave the name 'teleonomy', derived from the old Greek word *telos*, meaning 'an end or purpose'. When Aristotle used the word 'teleology', he meant that, when anything is created, its design is dictated by the final purpose it is intended to serve. 'Objectivity', Monod now wrote, 'obliges us to recognise the teleonomic character of living organisms and to admit that in their structure and performance they act projectively, to realise and pursue a purpose'. In other words, the emergence of a new form of life already contains within it some implicit element of the purpose which will enable it to become a better adapted new species.

A few years earlier another unequivocal Darwinian had gone much further. In his best-seller *On Aggression* (1966), the Austrian expert on animal behaviour Konrad Lorenz addressed the highly significant riddle of how one form of life, *Homo sapiens*, had developed a unique propensity to feel and display aggression towards members of its own species, individually and collectively, to the point of killing each other, sometimes on a colossal scale, as in fighting wars or committing acts of genocide, to the extent of becoming the only species to develop the means and power to destroy itself – while also having a unique capacity to act co-operatively to fulfil a common purpose and to feel and show selfless love for others. How could such a contradiction have come about just by the process of natural selection, based as it was at every step up the evolutionary ladder on the 'survival of the fittest'?

Lorenz sought to solve this riddle by recourse to what he mysteriously called the 'great constructors'. He simply could not accept that mankind could possibly be 'unfit' enough to bring about its own destruction, let alone that of all other life on earth. Instead he suggested that the day must come when, as he put it, human beings would become capable of loving not just individuals: 'We shall learn to love our human brothers indiscriminately.' And what did he imagine would instil this new 'commandment' in our hearts? 'The great constructors can, and I believe they will. I believe in the power of human reason, and I believe in the power of natural selection.' From '*Credo in Unum Deum*' Lorenz had come full circle. By yet another act of faith, he had come to believe in the miraculous power of his mysterious 'great constructors' to guide the evolutionary story to a rational and beneficial outcome.

In fact, the Darwinians were at last beginning to contemplate one of the greatest mysteries of all thrown up by their theory: how can we account for all those characteristics which so fundamentally distinguish us from every other form of life on earth? The Darwinians' attempts to resolve this puzzle have been so revealing that I shall reserve discussion of them to the final section of this chapter.

But first we must consider another hugely important and quite unexpected new challenge which advances in scientific knowledge were about to pose to their theory. And particularly significant in terms of the rules of groupthink was how they chose to respond.

'Irreducible Complexity' and the Challenge of 'Intelligent Design'
In 1982, I was asked by *The Times* to write an article to mark the centenary of Darwin's death. I focused on the riddle of all those many 'evolutionary leaps' which required 'a whole complex of biological factors working together in just the right way'. In particular I cited that recent BBC television series, *Life on Earth*, in which David Attenborough had chosen to demonstrate the miraculous power of Darwin's natural selection by holding up in one hand an earthbound shrew, and in the other a bat, using them to illustrate how, by growing a membrane between its front and back legs to become a wing, one had evolved into the other.

But how could this plausibly have happened when, from the moment that membrane began to develop, the shrew was much less well adapted to survive and more vulnerable to predators? So it would have remained throughout the time needed to elapse, according to Darwin's theory, for that useless membrane to gradually turn into a wing that would allow the creature to reach its final properly adapted state as a bat.

Such an obvious question had clearly never occurred to Attenborough, or to the BBC producers who made the film, or to all those critics who gave it unquestioningly rave reviews, or to most of the millions of viewers who hailed his series as one of the most impressive documentaries they had ever watched.

It was not until 20 years later that I came across a remarkable international group of scientists, all brought up to accept the Darwinian orthodoxy, who had first come together in California in 1993 to discuss how their researches had led them independently to conclude that the theory was in fact wholly incapable of explaining the mystery of how life on earth had evolved. They included respected experts in molecular biology and biochemistry, and in essence they had all found they were looking at a far more sophisticated version of those same riddles Darwin himself had found so perplexing. But their new critique of Darwinian theory rested on a fundamentally important new branch of science which only a few decades earlier had barely existed.

The astonishing advances recently made in molecular biology had opened up our understanding of the most basic physical components of life. The more the scientists had learned about the structures and functioning of cells, proteins, amino-acids and DNA, the more they had been struck by the breathtaking complexity of the part these all played in making life possible. How could natural selection 'alone possibly account for all the fathomless complexities of the evolutionary story?

There was, for instance, the awe-inspiring intricacy of the bacterial 'flagellar motor' in cells. Electron microscopy has shown that, self-assembled from some 30 different proteins, these are constructed exactly like a highly sophisticated artificial machine, complete with a rotor, a driveshaft and a propeller, capable of revolving at up to 100,000 revolutions a minute. Altogether the motor is made up of thousands of parts, each of which is essential to enabling the whole assemblage to work. Similar complex interactions are involved in the structure of the proteins themselves, and of the amino-acids which make them up. All of these have to be assembled in precisely the right way and precisely the right order, or they simply could not function.

And what ultimately controls all this are the unbelievably complex coding instructions contained in DNA, containing so much information that, in human terms, it would run to hundreds of pages for every part of the operation. So where had that DNA come from in the first place, to make it possible for a single chemical molecule to replicate itself, without which evolution could not have begun at all?

In 1969 one biochemist in the group, Dean Kenyon from Berkeley University, had co-authored a book called *Chemical Predestination*, which came to be prescribed reading for generations of university students. In it he had argued that amino-acids might naturally have assembled themselves into just the right combination by some form of chemical attraction. But when he was questioned on this hypothesis one day by an intelligent student (who just happened to be called Einstein), Kenyon realized he couldn't offer a satisfactory answer. He spent years completely re-thinking his position, until he concluded that the combining of the amino-acids could only come about through just the right information being passed to them from their DNA.

What Kenyon and all these scientists had, in their different ways, been led to conclude was that there was no conceivable way in which the theory of natural selection could begin to explain such riddles. Everywhere they looked at the most basic building blocks of life they found 'irreducible complexities' which could not possibly have been brought about by those incremental slight variations that were the mainstay of Darwinian theory. It was as if at every point these processes and structures could only work in the way they did had they been somehow specifically 'designed' for the purpose they served. And all this relied on that mass of information needed to direct and control every tiniest detail of how they were assembled and functioned.

Wherever, in any context on this earth, we come across evidence of 'information' which shows a logical structure, we must assume that it originates from some form of 'intelligence'. Hence the name which was given to what all these scientists had agreed was the only conclusion that could be drawn from all the factual evidence they were looking at. It inescapably bore all the marks of some form of 'intelligent design'.

In terms of trying to explain this to the world, they were inevitably faced with a huge problem. They were just reporting the facts of what they had discovered, along with the inferences they had been led inexorably to draw. In no way were they putting forward a new rival theory to explain, like Darwin, how evolution had come about. They were not offering any suggestions as to what the origins of that 'intelligence' might be. They were simply pointing to undeniable scientific evidence which showed there could be no proper scientific understanding of how life had evolved unless it took this crucial and hugely significant new factor into account. But what these scientists were saying would turn all existing evolutionary theory on its head. It was inevitably a direct challenge to the orthodoxy that had been accepted for well over a century by a 'consensus' of all the world's scientific opinion.

How the Darwinian establishment responded to this challenge was extraordinarily revealing. It made no attempt to argue with or even discuss the case for 'intelligent design'. In 1996 the biochemist Michael Behe, who coined the term 'irreducible complexity', published *Darwin's Black Box*, in which he laid out the scientific arguments for intelligent design. Some of the reviews in leading US newspapers were quite favourable, and agreed that the case was well-argued and interesting, but others could not have been more dismissive, claiming that 'intelligent design' was merely trying to smuggle in a 'religious' explanation for evolution, even though Behe's book had suggested no such thing.

It gave the Darwinians their cue to sweep aside 'intelligent design' as not even worth discussing – as just another version of 'Creationism', that belief still shared by Southern Baptists and other Biblical fundamentalists which holds that, as described in Genesis, 'God created the world in six days.' In 2004, therefore, when a school district in Pennsylvania ordered that a brief explanation of intelligent design should be read to classes being taught the Darwinian theory of evolution, a high-profile court action was brought by parents at the school, supported by the US Civil Liberties Union, that this was illegal. After a lengthy trial, the judge ruled in their favour, on the grounds that intelligent design was not science. It was just 'religion in disguise' and should not be taught in schools.

The 'consensus' had triumphantly closed ranks, with no need for the issue to be discussed further. From now on, anyone mentioning 'intelligent design' in public or in print could immediately be dismissed by people who knew nothing about the intelligent design thesis with the most damning word they knew: 'Creationist'. On Wikipedia anyone who had suggested that intelligent design was a serious contribution to science would be dubbed an anti-science 'Creationist' just as routinely as anyone questioning the 'consensus' on global warming was dismissed as just a 'denier'.

In 2009 the celebrations for the 200th anniversary of Darwin's birth could not have provided a greater contrast to the rather muted fashion in which the centenary of his birth had been marked 27 years earlier. There was no way *The Times* in 2009 would have run an article as critical as the one I had written for it in 1982. The BBC in particular put out adulatory programmes on the great man for days on end, as though he had been elevated to a secular saint. The crowning moment, reverentially described by David Attenborough, was a ceremony in the Gothic great hall of the Natural History Museum, where a statue of Darwin was hoisted into place, looking down as if from the east end of a cathedral. It replaced one that had long stood there of Richard Owen, the museum's founder, who had been one of Darwin's earliest and most sceptical critics.

The real irony was that, in honouring their prophet like this, the Darwinians were themselves unwittingly basing their beliefs on no more than a 'revealed truth', requiring a leap of faith on a par with that of the Six-Day Creationists they held in such contempt. Yet in reality it was the despised sceptics who upheld the proper principles of science. It was they who believed in looking objectively at all the evidence, and following only where that evidence led. It was this alone which had liberated them from a bubble of make-believe they had come to conclude could no longer be reconciled with the observed facts.

The Ultimate Riddle: Ego versus Instinct

> The greatest wonder on earth is man . . . master of ageless earth . . . lord of all things living . . . he has learned the use of language, the wind-swift motions of brain; he has found the ways of living together in cities . . . there is nothing beyond his power. His subtleties meet all chance, conquer all dangers, to every ill he found its remedy . . .

[Yet] of all the subtleties of his nature, none is more wondrous than how it can draw him to both good and evil ways . . . nothing vast enters the life of mortals without it being accompanied by a curse.

Chorus of Theban Elders in Sophocles' Antigone

We end with the most revealing of all the puzzles the evolutionary story has presented (apart, of course, from that still completely unexplained mystery of how life itself first came to appear on the earth billions of years ago).

How is it that, of all the countless millions of species to have existed, the evolutionary process eventually produced just one which displays those two absolutely crucial but seemingly contradictory attributes that mark it out from every other form of life? On one hand Sophocles was able to marvel at the mental ability so immeasurably superior to that of any other animal that it enabled human beings to become 'masters of the ageless earth'. On the other this had brought with it that 'curse' which enabled them to be drawn into uniquely 'evil ways', leading them to behave to one another and the world around them worse than any other animal.

To put this into more modern terms, on one hand they had developed a brain much larger than that of any other animal, giving them a wholly new form of higher consciousness and a much greater understanding of the world around them, enabling them to communicate through language and to create all the wonders of human civilization. On the other, this had unleashed all those uniquely damaging impulses which would eventually give them the power to destroy all life on earth. Furthermore, in terms of geological time this all happened so quickly that it could not possibly have been brought about just by the cumulative effect of an infinite succession of natural variations and mutations.

This presented the Darwinian theory with a wholly new challenge. What other factor might account for the riddle first so strikingly identified by Sophocles 2,500 years ago? The key lies in that one feature which more than other distinguishes *Homo sapiens* from any other form of life.

Every other species, in its struggle to survive, lives its life in unthinking obedience to natural instinct. It is that which dictates everything it does, from how it acquires its food to how it relates to other members of its own species. It also dictates how it plays its part in the miraculously complex interdependence of the rest of nature, so that every species depends for its survival on countless others. Above all, instinct dictates how each species complies with that supreme underlying biological one imperative in all forms of life: the need to reproduce itself, and thus to ensure the continuance of its own species.

As individuals human beings are to a great extent just as subject to the dictates of instinct as any other animal. Instinct tells them that they need to eat, to sleep, to form social groups and much else, just as instinct gives them a sex drive. But the difference arises in the unique extent to which human beings have broken free from that all-embracing instinctive framework. In crucial respects, when it comes to the ways in which they act out those instincts, they can vary how they choose to.

Every other animal knows only one way to acquire its food. But the further human beings have moved from a state of nature, the more they have learned a whole range of different means, from planting seeds in the ground to buying ready meals at a supermarket. When they form social groups, these may be as wildly different as a society ruled by a Communist dictatorship and a local golf club. When it comes to making a home for shelter and to protect their young, 'foxes have holes,' as the saying goes, 'and the birds of the air have nests.' But every blackbird's nest looks much like another, because its design is dictated by instinct. The structures human beings call home, however, can take on any form, from a mud hut to Versailles, from an igloo to a 27-storey tower block.

The reason for this is that humankind has developed a unique new level of consciousness. Every animal has a degree of consciousness – even a humble amoeba needs consciousness to identify its food – and as we near the top of the evolutionary ladder many species, such as dolphins, chimpanzees and birds, have considerable intelligence and the ability to learn. But they are still constrained entirely within the framework of instinct. Only the higher form of consciousness developed in *Homo sapiens* has freed it from the need to comply with instinct in every respect.

And a crucial consequence is that humans have the capacity, individually and collectively, to feel and to act egocentrically. It would be absurd to speak of an egocentric fish or a selfish bee. But human beings can act entirely selfishly, cutting themselves off from everything and everyone outside themselves. And this gives rise to all those anti-social forms of behaviour which mark them out from all other species. They can engage in ruthless competition with one another for entirely selfish ends. They can experience jealousy and envy. They can become obsessed by irrational hatreds and resentments. They can get drawn into meaningless arguments with other people who are just as convinced that they are right. They can lie, cheat and deceive one another, and indeed themselves. They can commit every kind of crime, engage in senseless cruelty and irrational acts of violence. They can wage wars with one another. And they can seek sexual gratification in ways wholly unconnected with the purpose for which nature has given them a sex drive. And all this has introduced into human life a unique element of instability.

But of course there is that other, much deeper level of human nature which stands completely opposed to it. On this deeper (or higher) level, human beings wish to live in peace and harmony with each other and the world outside them, and to co-operate in working for the common good. They find fulfilment in feeling and acting selflessly and lovingly in a higher cause than just their own. In essence, they wish to reconnect themselves with that sense of purpose and meaning all other animals enjoy without having to think about it.

Throughout history no human achievements have been more significant than those inspired by the wish to resolve that crucial split in human nature. This is why every society has consciously devised different ways to control and transcend all those egotistical impulses which are so disruptive: most obviously, codes of moral behaviour, and political systems and frameworks of law to promote and maintain social order.

In a deeper way, it is this desire of human beings to experience a sense of connection between their own inner life and others' and with the world outside themselves, which has led them to every kind of artistic expression. They have found meaning in creating the patterns of music, as they join together in singing and dancing; they have created beautiful forms and images in paintings and sculptures, in jewels and clothes and every kind of decoration, in the designs of their buildings, in the rhythms and magic of poetry.

A CONCLUSION

Richard North

Booker (as I called him) sadly died before he could complete this book. Nonetheless, he left copious notes and other material, together with instructions for its completion. They have been augmented by notes taken by his eldest son Nick from long conversations with his father about the book.

Of the sources used in completing the main part of this work, I have used only material written by Booker, with the lightest of editing, making it almost entirely his original work. Two chapters in the main part had to be assembled from scratch – the chapters on Europe and global warming. For both of these I was able to rely on a paper for the Global Warming Policy Foundation, specifically addressed to what Booker called 'one of the strangest episodes in human history' – the advocacy of global warming as an existential threat for humankind (although Booker would have written 'mankind') – supplementing the chapter on the European Union with material from our book, *The Great Deception*, during the writing of which Booker 'held the pen'.

Before he died, Booker suggested one other chapter might be written on Brexit, but as he left no notes on this issue (other than his frequent columns in the *Sunday Telegraph*), this would have required a departure from our self-imposed ordinance against using material which Booker himself had not written. However, since Brexit occupied much of his thinking in the last years of his life, not least because he had spent so much of his energies in the preceding years opposing our membership of the European Union, this book would not be complete without a commentary on post-referendum events and his part in them.

This is especially so as in the 'debate' that developed following the referendum of 23 June 2016 on how to manage our departure from the EU, Booker himself became a prominent target of groupthinkers. The reason was that, very much in collaboration with myself, he departed from the former Eurosceptic 'pack' – redefined as 'leavers' or 'Brexiteers' – to seek a rational, measured departure from the EU. His ideas were based on what was popularly known as the 'Norway Option', which involved re-joining the European Free Trade Association (EFTA) as a basis for remaining in the European Economic Area (EEA). However, many of those with whom we had shared objectives in the pre-referendum 'Eurosceptic' days had veered to what we called an 'ultra' position, rejecting any idea of a managed exit. Instead, they favoured a 'no-deal' exit, relying on WTO rules to enable the UK to continue trading with the EU and the rest of the world.

It is not appropriate here to rehearse the pros and cons of the two positions. Suffice to say that many former, self-declared supporters of Booker took to the online comments section of his column in the *Sunday Telegraph* to denounce him in the most aggressive and sometimes extremely unpleasant terms. Many were still prepared to endorse his work on global warming, with which they agreed, but rejected his 'Norway Option' stance, with which they disagreed.

That this was a classic example of groupthink is graphically illustrated by an article by a one-time friend and colleague, James Delingpole, published on the Breitbart website in January 2019.[64] 'Dellers', as he was affectionately known, was one of Booker's most ardent supporters, especially in respect of his work on global warming, and shared his commitment to Euroscepticism. Yet, when it came to the mechanisms for leaving the EU, their paths suddenly diverged. Delingpole supported a pathway which Booker had

---

[64]https://www.breitbart.com/europe/2019/01/27/why-brexit-on-wto-terms-is-the-best-option-for-britain/

cautioned against, specifically the 'no-deal' scenario, often referred to as leaving 'on WTO terms'.

The context of the article is relevant, as Delingpole had recently appeared on Andrew Neil's politics show, where he had manifestly failed to argue his case, with one journal gleefully reporting, 'Brexiteer rinsed after failing miserably to defend no-deal Brexit.'[65] In his own defence, therefore, Delingpole adopted a defiant tone with a headline reading, 'I'm right – Brexit on WTO terms is going to be just great for Britain.'

Justifying his stance, he then wrote that the 'vast majority of people' in the Brexit debate had 'picked their side based on a mix of gut feeling, personal ideology and circumstances', and not on what he called 'how-many-angels-can-dance-on-the-head-of-a-pin minutiae'. 'We can't all be experts on everything,' he declared: 'On a matter like this which involves wading through small print, we not unreasonably think this a job best left to trusted representatives with a background in international law or finance or politics.' For their 'trusted representatives', most Brexiteers, he asserted, 'will have tended to take on trust the considered opinion of experts like Lord Lilley, Martin Howe QC, Ruth Lea, Patrick Minford and Jacob Rees-Mogg that No Deal is the best option – without feeling the need to acquaint themselves in any detail with the nuances of WTO'.

What characterized these people, though, was that they comprised a group loosely known as the 'ultras', who had taken an extreme (and almost certainly minority view) of how we should leave the European Union. As a necessary part of his justification, however, Delingpole describes this group as 'experts', even though none had previously professed any expertise or great knowledge in the arcane issues relating to the WTO. This especially applied to the Lord Lilley, a former MP, and Jacob Rees-Mogg, the MP who then chaired the extremist European Research Group. To Lord Lilley, however, Delingpole was especially reverential, saying he had 'read and

[65]*New European*, 25 January 2019. https://www.theneweuropean.co.uk/top-stories/james-delingpole-rinsed-after-stuttering-through-bbc-interview-talking-brexit-1-5866045

absorbed documents like Lord Lilley's *30 Truths About Leaving on WTO Terms* and that I find the arguments more compelling than anything I've heard from Remainers'.[66] Had he explored further, he would have detected multiple errors which completely misstated the position, not least this gem: 'Customs declarations and declarations of origin are required for goods traded across the Swiss border but do not result in long delays or lengthy queues for the 23,000 lorries and 2.2 million people that cross every day.'

It is a matter of fact that long queues of commercial vehicles are regularly observed at the main Swiss customs posts, such as that at Berne, and especially after weekends and public holidays when commercial traffic is not processed.[67] But one of Lilley's more interesting deviations from the truth was in another document, published about the same time under the title of *Fact – not Friction*, which set about 'exploding the myths of leaving the Customs Union'. In this document, claimed Lilley:

> The claim that WTO rules require checks to be made at the border is incorrect. Checks of customs declarations are carried out electronically and physical checks often made at importer's or exporter's premises. Even the Union customs code, which requires agri-food checks at border inspection posts 'in the vicinity of the border', allows them to be as far as 40 km inland. This is particularly important for avoiding infrastructure and checks at the Irish border.

As noted by Lilley, the issue of Border Inspection Posts (BIPs) was (and is) particularly important, and it was vital to the Brexiteers' case that they could be positioned away from the border, otherwise they would become tangible evidence of the 'hard border' that both the UK and the EU was pledged to avoid. Yet, for all of his confident

---

[66]https://globalbritain.co.uk/wp-content/uploads/2019/01/GBLL-paper-30-Truths-Final-05.01.19.pdf
[67]See, for instance, this: http://www.eureferendum.com/blogview.aspx?blogno=86888

assertions, there is no reference to BIPs in the Union Custom Code. The relevant law is Council Directive 97/78/EC which, contrary to Lilley's claims, actually states that BIPs must be 'located in the immediate vicinity of the point of entry' into the Member State.[68] That requirement is egregiously misquoted by Lilley, with the omission of the all-important caveat 'immediate', which completely changes the meaning of the official text.

Immediately, though, one sees where Lilley is going with this, as he asserts that the apparent (but non-existent) flexibility allows BIPs 'to be as far as 40 km inland', citing the port of Rotterdam as an example. There, he claims, 'inspection posts are located in the wider region around the harbour up to 20 km from the docks themselves.' This is not true. Rotterdam is not so much a single port as a port complex, stretching from the Maas estuary at the North Sea end, with the Kloosterboer Delta Terminal, into the heart of the city, with an outpost, Dordrecht, on the Oude Maas. In all, it extends over 40 km from end to end, which means that a BIP in the centre of the port complex could be 20 km from the 'border' – i.e., the seaward edge of the complex – yet still within the port complex. In fact, four separate BIPs are registered with the EU in the Rotterdam port area, including one at the Kloosterboer Delta Terminal at the entrance to the estuary, effectively right on the border.[69]

These examples demonstrate with utmost clarity Janis's first example of groupthink: a group of people coming to share 'a common view, opinion or belief that in some way is not based on objective reality'. Lilley, in particular, has constructed a narrative based on misquoting official documents to make a case which in real life cannot be sustained. By his own admission, Delingpole and the many 'Brexiteers' that shared his stance had not settled their views on the basis of any objective reality – they had simply adopted the 'received wisdom' of the group.

[68]https://eur-lex.europa.eu/legal-content/EN/TXT/PDF/?uri=CELEX:31997L0078&from=EN
[69]https://eur-lex.europa.eu/legal-content/EN/TXT/PDF/?uri=CELEX:32009D0821&qid=1563184991622&from=EN

So limited is his knowledge that, on Andrew Neil's show, Delingpole repeatedly professed not to know the answers to problems thrown up, but nonetheless exudes confidence that a solution will be found. At one point, when confronted with the potential effects of a no-deal Brexit on the sheep-farming industry, he said, 'I'm sure we'll find a way round that,' illustrating another feature of Janis's first rule: that there is undoubtedly an element of wishful thinking or make-believe in the make-up of groupthink.

The second rule states that, because their shared view is essentially subjective, those afflicted by groupthink need to go out of their way to insist it is so self-evidently right that a 'consensus' of all right-minded people must agree with it. Their belief has made them an 'in-group', which accepts any evidence which contradicts it, while the views of anyone who does not agree can be disregarded.

And there in his article, as evidenced by its very title, is the living embodiment of the second rule: 'I'm right', proclaimed Delingpole, calling in aid error-strewn sources that served to prove only one thing – that he knew so little about the subject he was not even in a position to tell what was right or wrong. Yet from this position of profound ignorance he was able to assert that 'most Remainers' knew 'just as little about WTO terms as most Brexiteers'. The difference was that their experts – from a vast, Remain-dominated Establishment ranging from the BBC and the Treasury to sundry EU apparatchiks, Big Business and innumerable globalist institutions such as the International Monetary Fund – told a completely different story. In an unconscious display of 'mote and beam' he then concluded: 'Remainers believe it with fervent passion not because they know better but simply because it confirms all their worst prejudices.'

This conveniently takes us to rule three of groupthink, which requires of the 'in-group' to treat the views of anyone who questions their beliefs as wholly unacceptable. The 'groupthinkers' are incapable of engaging in any serious dialogue or debate with those who disagree with them. Those outside the bubble must be marginalized and ignored, although if necessary their views must be mercilessly caricatured to make them seem ridiculous.

An indication of this mechanism at work came when Delingpole wrote Booker's obituary on the Breitbart website, heading it, 'RIP Christopher Booker, the World's Greatest Climate Change Sceptic'.[70] 'Dellers' was prepared to laud (and highlight) his work on climate change, with which he agreed, but the EU scarcely merited a mention. Nothing at all was said about the sharp divergence of opinion on Brexit. Ironically, Delingpole mentioned Booker's work on groupthink, entirely unconscious of his own vulnerability on the issue. This rather confirmed Booker's observation that the power of groupthink to lure people into its grip must never be underestimated. By definition, he has told us, the last people who will ever realize this are the victims of groupthink themselves.

The weapon of choice of 'groupthinkers' seems largely to be marginalization. In the frenzied media environment of the 24/7 news cycle, broadcasters and newspapers are often desperate for copy, and will indulge in any amount of trivia to feed the ravening machine. But if a thesis does not fit the 'narrative' – i.e., conform with prevailing groupthink – it will struggle for a hearing. Thus, not one of Booker's prescient warnings on the effects of a no-deal Brexit, published in his column in the *Sunday Telegraph*, ever saw wider circulation, even in his own newspaper.

Rather, as the *Sunday Telegraph* adopted a stridently 'pro-WTO' editorial stance, Booker's column was cut down in size and relegated to a supplement, where he was invited to confine his writing to commentary on the 'countryside and nature'. When he insisted on continuing his advocacy of the EEA option, the paper – unwilling to risk the opprobrium of firing him – resorted to publishing, almost weekly, critical letters from readers. In breach of a long tradition of advance notification, Booker would usually only learn

[70]https://www.breitbart.com/europe/2019/07/03/rip-christopher-booker-worlds-greatest-climate-sceptic/

189

of these letters when they were published. They were to become what between us we decided was a new genre, the 'Booker is wrong' letter, a semi-permanent feature of the newspaper.

While there was a certain decorum and restraint to these letters, the same could not be said of the online readers' comment facility. There, a torrent of *ad hominem* abuse was allowed to proliferate, with not the slightest attempt to moderate the writing or remove the more offensive posts. This was the final stage of groupthink, as Booker points out. In the third rule, if marginalization of dissenters is not enough, they must be attacked in the most violently contemptuous terms, usually with the aid of some scornfully dismissive label, and somehow morally discredited. The thing which most characterizes any form of groupthink, the rule states, is that dissent cannot be tolerated. In the *Telegraph* comments, this rule was played out to its fullest extent.

What is doubly interesting about the Brexit saga, though, is that it illustrates something Booker said to me about testing theories. If you had developed a theory to explain any how particular phenomenon worked, he said, and a completely new issue emerged with similar driving characteristics, then if your theory was sound, it would also serve to explain the new occurrence. And here we have the theory of groupthink, developed long before Brexit as a word had even been invented, which more than adequately explains the behaviour of the warring parties we see engaged in the Brexit 'debate'. In fact, there isn't a debate at all. The opposing parties simply talk (and sometimes shout) past each other, in the manner of groupthink, never engaging in any serious dialogue or debate with those who disagree with them.

That said, there is a characteristic of groupthink to which Booker alludes, but doesn't develop to any great extent. Had he lived, I'm sure he would have built on it to the extent that it could even become a part of the Janis rule set, or even a separate and fourth – albeit minor – rule.

The clue to this lies in his commentary on Darwin where, as the controversy developed, three contending accounts emerged to explain how new species had been created. But in the popular mind, Booker observes, these were soon reduced essentially to two. At one pole, still to this day supported by a small minority of widely ridiculed 'Six-Day Creationists', is the old Christian orthodoxy that all species were created simultaneously. At the other, now generally viewed as the undisputed master of the field, is what over 160 years has established Darwin's natural selection as the new orthodoxy of our age.

Effectively, we see this in virtually every 'debate' where groupthink dominates. The advocates of 'global warming', for instance, will not allow any nuances. In their world, there are either 'believers' – those who accept that the planet is confronting an unprecedented 'climate emergency' – or 'deniers'.

There is no room for the suggestion that we are still emerging from the centuries-long Little Ice Age which followed the Medieval Warm Period, during which temperatures would be expected to rise naturally; that temperatures have historically been higher (which is why Greenland is called Greenland), as have carbon dioxide levels. In between extremes, therefore, there is a view that a largely natural rise in temperature (such that it is) might have some adverse effects, for which it would be wise to prepare, without accepting that the temperature increase is a potential extinction event. But such a view is rarely heard.

Brexit, an issue with many nuances, is another example where the debate has been reduced to its binary elements: you are either a 'remainer' or a 'leaver', the latter being identified with the more extreme 'no-deal' scenario. Neither in the media nor in the political debate has there been any serious discussion of the centre ground, represented by the 'Norway option'. In fact, when David Cameron visited Iceland (an EFTA/EEA member) in October 2015 – after he had announced his intention to hold a referendum – he chose specifically to warn against the option. He trotted out a number of weary, well-worn untruths, such as the claim that Norway was 'the tenth largest contributor to the EU budget' and was 'bound by the rules of the single market without any say in the decision-making process'.[71] In fact, no EFTA/EEA state contributes to the EU budget and, as regards the decision-making process, there are extensive and well-known formal consultation processes.

When in August 2013 I interviewed Anne Tvinnereim, then state secretary for the Ministry of Local Government and Regional Development – more than two years before Cameron made his claims – she acknowledged that Norway was not there when the EU voted on new laws. But, she said, 'we do get to influence the position.' Explaining the simple facts of international relations, she told me, 'Most of the politics is done long before it [a new law] gets to the voting stage.' The Norwegian government, she added, tries to influence legislation at an early stage.[72]

But what was remarkable about Cameron's intervention was that Dominic Cummings, then the campaign director of *Vote Leave* (which was to become the designated lead campaigner for the 'Leave' proposition), actually agreed with the (then) prime minister: 'Vote Leave does not support the "Norway option" for Britain.' 'After we vote leave', he went on, 'we will negotiate a new UK-EU deal based on free trade and friendly co-operation. We will end the supremacy of EU law.'[73] The 'Norway option' latterly became dubbed by the more extreme leavers as 'BRINO' (BRexit In Name Only), with advocates branded as closet remainers. The centre ground had been condemned by both extremes.

As Brexit divided the country, and remained unresolved by the end of 2019, more than three years after the referendum, we had started to see something much more profound than a dispute about whether we should leave the European Union. Commentators were earnestly writing about 'a crisis like no other in recent British history', citing the

[71]*Guardian*, 28 October 2015. Cameron tells anti-EU campaigners: 'Norway option' won't work for Britain. https://www.theguardian.com/politics/2015/oct/28/cameron-to-confront-norway-option-anti-eu-campaigners

[72]*EU Referendum* blog, 1 August 2013, 'We do not need Brussels to tell us what to do.' http://eureferendum.com/blogview.aspx?blogno=84212

[73]*Guardian*, op. cit.

words of the former head of MI6, Sir John Sawyer, that Britain was having 'a nervous breakdown'. Brexit was compared to an earthquake in which pent-up forces were suddenly released, 'tearing open new fault lines and energizing old ones such as inequality, de-industrialization, globalization, imperial retreat, immigration and austerity'.[74]

This had multiple commentators discussing the theme of a 'culture war', where party politics, to an extent based on class and traditional left/right divisions, had been replaced by arguments of cultural mores transcending normal divisions. But while even the *New Statesman* was prepared to accept the conceptualization of Brexit as 'essentially a culture war, and not a class war', the writer Simon Wren-Lewis asserted that the theme was 'powerful and contains a lot of truth', but argued that this was not the whole story.[75]

Despite well-founded doubts, it is perhaps more appropriate to characterize not Brexit but the UK as a whole as undergoing a series of culture wars, in the plural. Largely (although not entirely) due to influence of social media and the internet, the information society has splintered into many fragments, creating an endless number of what Booker called 'groupescules'.

Why this should be is relatively easy to explain. In Chapter One, relying on material he first assembled to write his book *The Neophiliacs*, Booker recalls life in the Fifties and Sixties. Born in 1948, I was too young to recall much of the early Fifties (although even today I can recall seeing a long queue of cars at a local garage, their owners seeking petrol as a result of shortages induced by the 1956 Suez Crisis), but the late Fifties and early Sixties were very much part of my growing up.

As a family we were very much in the middle-class tradition. My father took the *Daily Telegraph* during the week and the *Sunday*

---

[74]*Independent*, 22 July 2019: Brexit Britain is on the brink of a 'national breakdown'. https://www.independent.co.uk/news/long_reads/brexit-uk-regions-westminster-boris-johnson-remainers-a9009446.html

[75]*New Statesman*, 2 July 2019: 'Is Brexit a culture war or a class war?' https://www.newstatesman.com/politics/staggers/2019/07/brexit-culture-war-or-class-war

Times at the weekend. In pre-transistor days, our valve radio brought us the BBC Home Service and we listened with rapt attention to the news bulletins. Listening at that time had to be planned: the latency of valve radios meant we had to switch the set on several minutes before we could hear anything, while the tuning would invariably drift, requiring delicate manipulation of the dial to bring back the chosen programme. There was no spontaneity in the process. As for television, I was in my mid-teens before the family acquired a single black and white set, and viewing was limited to two channels, BBC and ITV.

The point is that our information about what was termed 'current affairs' was extremely limited. Very few families could afford two newspapers, although almost all – in my area of north London – bought one. As a teenager, I supplemented my pocket money by delivering papers, and even in the avowedly 'working-class' blocks of flats to which I delivered, the uptake was high.

As one might expect, there was considerable polarization of views, but it was very limited in extent. Politically, you were either Conservative or Labour. The Liberals, as they were then, were sort of there, but only at the fringes of my early teenage perception. Politically, we could be well-informed, but only after a fashion. We were constrained by our limited access to information and our restricted choices. But the upside was that there was far greater commonality of view. To an extent we were conditioned by our choice of media, but insomuch as the media were limited, our views within our selected groups rarely diverged to any great extent.

As the years passed, we saw the proliferation of TV channels, with the launch of BBC2 in 1964, the arrival of Channel 4 in 1982 and Channel 5 in 1997. But while the television network took 33 years to expand from two to five channels, within a further six years digital TV was making accessible hundreds of channels, available by satellite and cable, outstripping BBC1 and ITV.[76] And by 2018, 90 per cent of

[76]*Guardian*, 24 April 2003, 'Multichannel TV overtakes terrestrial', https://www.theguardian.com/media/2003/apr/24/bbc.broadcasting

all adults in the UK were classified as 'recent internet users', up from 51 per cent in 2006, the facility having first come online in 1977 and become commercially available in the early Nineties.[77]

With that came email, and then email groups and forums, followed by Facebook in 2005 (originally only available to universities), with YouTube and Twitter making an appearance in the same year. Google, which had been launched in 1998, brought out Google News in 2002 and its blogging platform (Blogger) in 2003 – a publishing tool first developed in 1999. For the UK, the Netflix streaming service came on line in 2012, followed by Amazon Prime Video in 2014 and then Instagram in the same year.

Alongside this explosion of information providers came the technology to access them on the move. The world's first hand-portable mobile phone had been launched in America in 1983, reaching the UK consumer in 1992, the year the first text message was sent. But the real revolution came to the UK in 2003 with the launch of the 3G 'smartphone'. Four years later, Steve Jobs announced the Apple iPhone to the world and personal communication was never to be the same again.[78]

Putting all this together, it is fair to say that in less than two decades, a revolutionary 'information society' has emerged. The speed has been quite remarkable. To illustrate the enormous benefits, I can call on my own experience. When writing the thesis for my PhD back in 1995, I needed to find a dimly remembered reference from a technical journal, the name of which I was not entirely sure of (in a field dominated by many similarly-named journals). Ploughing through back copies of relevant journals in daily visits to Leeds University medical library took me over a month, before – much to my relief – I found the paper I was looking for. When I replicated the exercise recently, using Google search, it took two minutes.

---

[77]ONS, 23 May 2019, https://www.ons.gov.uk/businessindustryandtrade/itandinternetindustry/bulletins/internetusers/2018

[78]https://www.mobilephonehistory.co.uk/history/time_line.php

But while some of the practical benefits are obvious, the social effects are less so. So rapid and extensive have been the changes that some have hardly been recognized, much less fully assessed. Even now, the impact of what is termed 'social media' – and its personalized advertising – on election campaigning is hotly disputed. Even if no one sensible would deny that the technology has been extremely influential, it is difficult to pin down its precise effects.

What does seem evident, though, in the political field if not elsewhere, is that the gift of unlimited information, accessible at minimal cost at the click of a button, has not led to a better-informed debate. Rather, the same phenomenon that I observed in my own youth has been replicated and, if anything, intensified. Confronted with such a wide range of sources, the average users – if there are such people – will select those which they are comfortable, essentially those which tell them what they want to know and confirm their pre-existing prejudices. The only real difference is that, with so many sources, there are no longer the monolithic groups sharing similar viewpoints. The body politic has fragmented into a staggering array of sub-groups, each with their own unique and identifiable characteristics and beliefs. Booker's 'groupescules' have multiplied beyond all recognition. Here, groupthink comes into its own, and makes Booker's research and observations more relevant than he could have imagined when he first started writing this book.

Let us step back for a moment, and note that the habit of specialist groups and professions to adopt their own languages and vocabularies, as marks of distinction, is well known. For many centuries, priests adopted Latin as their *lingua franca*, simply to mark themselves out from lay persons. Similarly, until relatively recently, doctors would write prescriptions and notes in Latin for the same reason. But every profession and most trades have their own specialized vocabularies, the learning of which marks the transition of the individual into the 'secret society' they are about to join. Even in the ancient profession of soldiering, this distinction applies. In my teenage days I was one of a group of newly recruited cadets presented with our Lee Enfield No. 4 rifles, and we were given the task of learning the names of the components of the weapon, a ritual known to generations of soldiers as 'the naming of parts'. There was even a poem by the same title on this ritual, written by Henry Reed in 1942 under the general heading of 'Lessons of War', and referring to this self-same rifle. In this context, it is one of the first steps in marking the transition from callow civilian to soldier. But without being so clearly identified as such, it is a ritual that applies to every trade and profession: one of learning its special vocabulary, knowledge of which distinguishes those who 'belong' from the outsider. In the political and many other spheres, that is the role of groupthink.

With so many different groupings that lack uniform, badges or trades to distinguish them, groupthink becomes the 'glue' that binds individuals to deliver the cohesive whole, giving them their identity. At the same time, acceptance of the groupthink mores peculiar to the group serves as a rite of passage, while its free, uncritical use is a very tangible expression of loyalty. Groupthink, therefore, is not about knowledge or information, but a property, and the very foundation of the modern, otherwise amorphous groupings facilitated by the emergence of the electronic 'information society'.

Booker observed in his earlier notes that politics in general has always been coloured by groupthink. Each political party or faction or grouping naturally has its own sense of seeing the world more clearly than its rivals. And their groupthink and hostility towards those of a different view become more extreme the further they move to the 'hard-left' or 'hard-right' ends of the political spectrum.

But the role groupthink now plays in the political discourse has expanded beyond all recognition. In noting that it was only when he belatedly read Janis's book in 2014 that he realized he had unwittingly been writing about different examples of groupthink through much of his professional life, Booker had stumbled upon a phenomenon increasingly important in modern society – far more than Janis ever experienced. Groupthink has broken its earthly bonds, transforming from a relatively narrow foundation to one that drives our modern politics, and much else besides, dominating political thinking and reactions.

In this, Booker has been prescient in identifying 'political correctness' as the root of the modern iteration of groupthink, and what tends to define the vocabularies different groups adopt. Recently we saw this in action in a Twitter exchange in which Jameela Jamil, self-described as a 'feminist in progress' boasting nearly a million 'followers', remonstrated with a writer for using the term 'blind spot'. 'We don't say blind spot any more just FYI', she tweeted, 'it's ableist. I only recently learned this.'[79] Few statements could better illustrate the nature (and fatuity) of political correctness. Technically, the 'blind spot' describes the small portion of the visual field of each eye that corresponds to the position of the optic disc (also known as the optic nerve head) within the retina. As there are no photoreceptors (i.e., rods or cones) in the optic disc, there is no image detection in this area.[80] Necessarily, blind people (the subject of 'ableist' concern) cannot, by definition, have blind spots. Only sighted people can experience these phenomena. Jameela Jamil, therefore, is not using knowledge or understanding in the pursuit of the avoidance of offence to some unspecific group of blind people. Her insistence that the phrase to which she objects is 'ableist' is not based on objective reality. That she had 'only recently learned this' suggested she had absorbed this as part of the groupthink matrix which had become part of her identity. As groupthink, it must now be enforced on all those who might form part of her circle. The approved term is now 'dead angle', betraying the lack of understanding of the origin of the term. Once adopted, the consistency and rigour with which groupthink is enforced make it a form of 'virtue-signalling'. But particular terms are also used as 'passwords' to the inner sanctum of her group, in the process of 'weaponizing' language, making it the currency of dispute and a screen by which interlopers can be detected and excluded.

Thus, we have gravitated from the particular examples Janis analysed for the basis of his theory. As Booker wrote, they were all political decisions which had ended badly, because a little group of

---

[79]Twitter, Jameel Jamil, 9 October 2019, https://twitter.com/jameelajamil/status/1181968839338102784
[80]https://www.britannica.com/science/blind-spot

powerful men had collectively become so fixated on a single narrow view of what they hoped to achieve that they shut their minds to anything that might contradict it. They were thus caught out by consequences they had failed to foresee. They had seen the world only through the make-believe prism of how they wanted it to be, and the end result had been a very rude awakening, as they bumped into an uncomfortable reality of which they had failed or refused to take account.

We have certainly seen, Booker adds, many more recent examples Janis could well have added to his case studies. One of the more obvious was the recklessly obsessive way in which George W. Bush and Tony Blair launched their invasion of Iraq in 2003. So fixated were they just on toppling Saddam Hussein that they had never given proper forethought to what might follow once that goal had been achieved. Iraq was thus plunged into those years of bloody sectarian chaos for which Bush and Blair were wholly unprepared. But as we have seen with global warming, Janis's picture of the rules by which groupthink works applies to very much more than the particular form of it which was the focus of his study.

This is the real point. Through the communications revolution, groupthink has become a mass phenomenon pervading almost every part of our lives, exercising a pernicious form of control over our language and thinking. We have only to look at the newspapers these days to see items arising from some form of groupthink, large or small, on almost any page, which in turn is more likely to be a webpage on a mobile screen. But then, the institutions themselves have been captured by their own brand of groupthink, and none more so than the BBC. Although not always quite so blatantly as in its coverage of global warming, the BBC has long had a recognizable slant on almost every controversial issue it covers. Rarely, as in the days when it pulled out all the stops to propagandize for Britain to join the euro, are we left in any doubt as to which side of the argument it is on.

But what is staggering is the consistency of the groupthink memes, which seem impervious to change. Back in 2013, shortly after I had interviewed Anne Tvinnereim on the errors surrounding the perception of the Norway option, we had the BBC's then Europe correspondent, Matthew Price, produce a short film entitled '*Would Norway's special EU arrangement work for Britain?*'[81] Critiqued on my own blog, he repeated exactly the same canards we had sought to demolish, including his gross misrepresentation that 'Norway has to obey the trading rules of the European Union. And yet, unlike the 28 member countries that make up the EU, it has no say in what those rules actually are. They are, literally, imposed by Brussels.'[82]

Interestingly, Booker and I had heavily researched this aspect of Norway's relationship with the EU and, in January 2013, he had written in his *Sunday Telegraph* column a piece headed, 'Forget Brussels: now we are ruled by the giants of Geneva', the thesis being that much of the regulation issuing from the EU was being passed down from even bigger, global bodies.[83] Where Norway itself was represented on these global bodies in its own right, we could find a situation where it could have a direct role in formulating global standards which would become EU law, then to be adopted by the Norwegian government via the EEA – law which Norway had agreed in principle long before it had got anywhere near Brussels.

Again in 2013 – a busy year – I interviewed the Norwegian vet Bjorn Knudtsen, who was then chairman of the Fish and Fisheries Product Committee of a United Nations body called Codex Alimentarius, an organization which defines marketing and safety rules for foodstuffs throughout the world, which then form the basis of the EU rules. For Norway, trade in fish and fisheries products is a vital national interest, with 95 per cent of products, worth €3 billion annually,

---

[81]BBC, 3 September 2013, https://www.bbc.co.uk/news/av/world-latin-america-23941315/would-norway-s-special-eu-arrangement-work-for-britain. Later, in a Twitter exchange with another blogger, Price was to admit that he had overstated his case, admitting for instance that Norway could 'lobby to affect EC proposals'. Boiling Frog blog, *EU, Norway and BBC Bias*, 4 September 2013. https://thefrogsalittlehot.blogspot.com/2013/09/eu-norway-and-bbc-bias.html

[82]*EU Referendum* blog, 3 September 2013, 'Norway: more BBC lies', http://eureferendum.com/blogview.aspx?blogno=84298

[83]https://www.telegraph.co.uk/comment/9828433/Forget-Brussels-now-we-are-ruled-by-the-giants-of-Geneva.html

being exported. For an exporting country, Mr Knudtsen emphasized that strict regulatory standards are a necessary and acceptable price to pay for what he termed 'certainty' in the international trading system. But it was equally important that Norway was able to shape the regulation, and be aware of new regulation in good time, to enable its businesses to adapt to them. It thus paid approximately £250,000 a year to host the Codex fisheries committee in Oslo, giving the Norwegian government an early and complete insight into what was going through the system.[84]

With its huge resources and full-time staff able to travel all over the world, and with unparalleled access to a range of sources about which we could only dream, one might have thought the BBC could have done this sort of research and come up with a more measured view of the Norway option. But not only has the Corporation produced its shallow, error-ridden narrative, its journalists, ensconced in their comfortable, protected 'bubble', are also impervious to any alternatives. Bound by their groupthink, they trot out the same trite factoids every time they rehearse the subject.[85] Thus does the 'narrative' evolve into the body of groupthink which defines the BBC's view on the subjects on which they report, passed down unchanged and unchanging through the years to channel their researchers and journalists into the 'correct' form of thinking. The media, therefore, may perpetuate a less extreme version of groupthink but, due to its pervasive nature, it becomes far more pernicious. As long as the media are the guardians of their own brands of groupthink, debate on a wide variety of issues is effectively sterilized, unable to progress.

This might have mattered less had we not undergone our communications revolution, served by the 24/7 news cycle, where reports are delivered to the nation's mobile telephones as often as

---

[84]*EU Referendum* blog, 25 June 2013, 'Codex is the top table,' http://www.eureferendum.com/blogview.aspx?blogno=84061

[85]For instance, see the BBC website for 30 October 2018, 'Brexit: What is the Norway model?' by Chris Morris, Reality Check correspondent. https://www.bbc.co.uk/news/uk-46024649

not while events are still in progress, turning the news into a never-ending soap opera without context or considered analysis. No wonder groupthink has become such a pervasive part of our lives. The pre-formed opinions that constitute the genre are the short-cuts which fuel the cycle. They also form the recognition signals which allow the audiences to absorb the material of which they approve, and shape their own responses.

What Booker has done, though, is to marry the new with the old. He lived his adult life through a period of the most intense change this nation – and much of mankind – has ever experienced. His own profound understanding of collective human psychology has been enhanced by Janis's analysis of groupthink, which can now help us to see in a new light the real nature of a little-understood phenomenon which has very much greater relevance to our lives than has been generally recognized.

In concluding his book, therefore, we need to remind ourselves – as Booker did in his earlier pamphlet – that the widely different examples of how people can get caught up in groupthink have three things in common. One is that their beliefs always eventually turn out to have been based on a false picture of the world, in some way shaped by the make-believe that it is different from what it really is. The second is the irrational degree of intolerance they display towards those who do not share their beliefs. The third is how ultimately their groupthink must always end up in some way colliding uncomfortably with the reality their blinkered vision has overlooked.

Booker ended his pamphlet on an optimistic note, with the comforting observation that every South Sea Bubble ends in a crash. Thus, he asserts, every form of groupthink eventually has its day. This, he says, is invariably what happens when human beings get carried along by the crowd, simply because they have lost the urge or ability to think for themselves. But what we also have to contend with is the effects of the communications revolution. Groupthink now has the never-ending ability to reinvent itself, transforming and multiplying in the 'legacy' media and the constantly mutating social media, where there are few means of checking its proliferation.

The combination of volume and accessibility creates a new challenge for humanity we have scarcely begun to appreciate. But as social media advertising during elections (and referendums) is said to damage the very foundations of our democracy, so the malign effects of groupthink, appearing in multiple forms which can even become the basis of 'fake news', present an even greater danger. More than anything, it is groupthink which is driving the fragmentation of our politics in society as a whole. Effectively, we are moving from the age of enlightenment into a new era where leaden conformity with the prevailing groupthink is the most dominant force in our lives.

I am less of an optimist than Booker was. He always had ultimate faith in the goodness of humanity, and was always willing to look on the bright side. Nor was he wrong in that. There is much good in modern society, and there can be no dispute that technology has brought us untold benefits. But just as it took the nineteenth-century public health laws to deal with much of the physical damage caused by the Industrial Revolution, and the twentieth century to address some of the social aspects, so dealing with groupthink and its proliferation through our communications network is one of our next major challenges.

Booker, with his sunny disposition, was certain we could meet the challenge. I hope he is right. Either way, he has done us a great service in updating and expanding Janis's original work. The great sadness is that he never lived to see his work completed.

AFTERWORD

Nicholas Booker

This is my father's final book but not his last written work. That honour goes to a guide to the lovely Litton village church, the tower of which he now rests near to. It was the final corrections to that modest booklet to which he turned his attention in the week before his death. The last thing he actually wrote by hand was no more than the salutation of what was to have been a thank-you letter to our neighbour's young children. They had sent him a 'Get Well Soon' card which, come to think of it, included a sketch of that same church – the bells of which my father heard strike midnight one last time on 2 July 2019.

When he was told by an oncologist the preceding November that he had no more than a few months to live, possibly just weeks, my father faced down his ultimate deadline with extraordinary grace and practicality. In the run-up to Christmas he set out to write his memoirs. They were to be called *From One World To Another*. He also continued to contribute jokes to *Private Eye* and, right up until February, insisted on filing his weekly *Sunday Telegraph* column.

He had spoken about how much he was looking forward to writing his memoirs for as long as I can remember. There was so much he wanted to cover (and correct!) that he thought they'd possibly run to two volumes. However, by early 2019 he realised he would not be able to finish them and sadly completed just five chapters – mostly wonderful vignettes of our family history and his childhood during World War Two and its aftermath. His final lines recalled pedalling through the Shropshire countryside to go fossil hunting – for Cambrian trilobites and Silurian sea lilies at Wenlock Edge – as Darwin had done little more than a century before him.

It says much about my father that when it came to telling his own story, written in his own words, it would remain untold. Not least because he spent much of the last decade, as those familiar with his newspaper columns will know, writing about the lives of others considerably less fortunate than himself. The importance of family, and shining light where it was absent, were central not just to his philosophy but to the way he lived. And his sense of family extended beyond much loved relatives and colleagues, believing as he did in an interconnected cosmos spanning space and stretching through time.

My father would have been amused by his obituaries, and not in the least surprised. He joked about announcing his death prematurely so he could send in corrections. Whilst the *Guardian* definitely deserved points for trying, my personal favourite was *The Times* which managed to get two of the most objective facts about his life wrong – his place of birth and date of death – not to mention much of what happened during the intervening period.

Archilochus of Paros famously divided thinkers into two types. Those who knew many things were foxes and those who knew one big thing were hedgehogs. One might easily think that my father was a fox – after all he knew, and cared passionately about, many, many things. In a flash he could remember your phone number by breaking it down into a combination of historical dates, Köchel numbers and cricket scores.

Such was his love of nature, he could walk across the chalk downs and through the woodlands of Hardy's Dorset pointing out the wild flowers, birds and butterflies, recall the ebb and flow of their populations over his lifetime and know the week of the year when they might be expected to be first seen. He had penetrated the psychology of storytelling and his greatest work, *The Seven Basic Plots*, will no doubt be his most enduring legacy. Books he had been quite capable of writing, extending his thesis onto art, architecture and music, alas were never to be written.

But my father wasn't really a fox – he was a hedgehog in disguise – seized from a young age by the conviction that somewhere there was a single cosmic idea that would explain how everything in the world, and indeed how the universe itself, fitted together. He believed that the more one is in touch with one's own centre, the more deeply one is aware of a web of meaning, of coincidence and symbolism. That everything is really all part of the *same* great story.

Still just able to see his screen and keyboard (many of the hammered letters had long since fled) he decided to try and continue writing as much as he could of his 'Groupthink book', which you are now holding. Towards the end, on the days when he thought he would be able to make it back up the stairs, he sat at his study desk – by now relying on laborious one-fingered typing. It took tremendous determination. He believed this book might help us see more clearly.

His own eyesight had been worsening for some time. Torches that were once used to find his way up the church path to lock its door each night were now required to help him read, even in broad daylight. Nothing would stop him working or thinking, talking *and* listening.

My father thought this book was worth trying to finish, and warranted such an effort, because as he says in the preface, once he recognised Janis's groupthink thesis could be applied beyond its original purview it 'helped to explain and illuminate so much that [he] had been writing about through most of [his] professional life'. Chapter eight, 'The Strange Story of Darwinism', was the last that he worked on and in his final few weeks he was wrestling with a concluding section. Day after day he would hold up the last pages of that chapter, asking me to print fresh copies again and again. He said he was working out how to add a few paragraphs on altruism.

Sadly, he never wrote them. I can only speculate, but I think what he wanted to articulate was a rejoinder to the dominant modern belief that altruistic acts can be explained by ultimately selfish motives. He was frustrated with what he perceived to be the superficiality of those like Darwin, Hamilton, Price, Dawkins and E. O. Wilson who reasoned that some form of self-interest lay at the heart of all seemingly selfless acts – with explanations ranging from reciprocity, group interest or signalling; to the propagation of genes, whether of the individual concerned or their kin.

He saw this as another example of groupthink – initiated and promoted primarily by evolutionary biologists, who were expounding beyond their expertise into an aspect of human nature, the mysteries of which they could not begin to comprehend from a nihilistic materialist reductionist perspective. Contrary to those who think altruism must really be masked self-interest, my father was with Dante, believing that at the heart of humanity and indeed the universe itself is 'the love that moves the sun and all the other stars'.

This book really completes a line of thought which my father started writing about at the age of just 31. In *The Neophiliacs*, he took us on a hair-raising rollercoaster ride through the late Fifties and early Sixties. The journey culminated in an astounding last chapter entitled 'The Riddle of the Sphinx', the epigraph of which was to become a guiding principle for him, featuring in *The Seven Basic Plots* and his funeral. It comes from the Katha Upanishad and states, 'Who sees the variety and not the unity, wanders on from death to death'.

Decades ago, he had come to see our compulsion to imagine stories as really being about the struggle we all have with our ego – our capacity to think and feel and behave egocentrically. How, unlike animals, we can step partly outside of instinct and the overriding need every lifeform has to survive and reproduce. That it is this unique capacity which divides our personalities in two (and mistakes unity for variety). The ego limiting our vision and separating us from others and the world; and that deeper centre which can reconnect us with our selfless instincts, and if we look hard enough, our inmost identity.

However, it was only in the last few years that he realised one of the patterns he kept on coming up against could be made easier to understand with the introduction of the concept of groupthink. That is the need of egotism, when it becomes collective and defined by a fantasy, to divide people into in and out groups; and in doing so generate groupthink to which those who subscribe to it fall victim, propelling further and further away from objective reality. This process, which leads otherwise sensible people to adopt a fantastical view of reality, is justified by the assertion of it being consensus opinion (typically rested on prestige), and in turn requires them to ridicule or ignore anyone who disagrees.

50 years later, my father had come to believe that groupthink was a particular kind of phenomenon which his younger self had already recognised:

> Not only does one form of fantasy invariably stimulate another, such as the obvious mutual exacerbation of left-wing and right-wing fantasies; not only is the increase in one form of fantasy in society almost invariably accompanied by increase in others, indicating that they not only lead to each other, but actually spring from a common root; but also each form of fantasy, from the standpoint of reality, is functionally interchangeable with any other. The outward forms they take are only of importance on the level of appearances; on the level of reality, the analogy of one form may be applied to all. All fantasy is a form of gamble. And ultimately all fantasy is a form of sickness or madness.[86]

It was whilst writing *The Neophiliacs* that he coined the word *nyktomorph*, meaning night shape, to describe the way we can be 'continually excited by half-formed images and cloudy possibilities' which are so often the object of groupthink. Where Occam had his razor, Booker had his torch – and he persistently shone its light at any number of shadows, that we might better see whether a bear was in fact a bush. Or a rope really a snake.

Whether or not you agree with his examples, we can all recognise groupthink around us. It is worth then considering that Booker believed 'on the level of reality, the analogy of one form [of fantasy] may be applied to all' *and* that 'Who sees the variety and not the unity, wanders from death to death'.

---

[86] *The Neophiliacs: The Revolution in English Life in the Fifties and Sixties.* London: Collins, 1969, pp. 344–5.

My father often repeated the following lines uttered by an old Vietnamese to a *Guardian* journalist during the unimaginable hell of war in the late 1960s:

> Humanity is one. Each of us is responsible for his personal actions and his actions towards the rest of humanity. All we can do is hold back our own brand from the fire. Pull it back, do not add to the flame.[87]

This book and the rest of his extraordinary body of work compels us to look more closely and enables us to see more clearly. My father once had a dream about his own death which ended with him being carried up into a great cloud of light. Love and light. He felt it was a moment of joy, as he glided from one world to another. His tombstone is yet to be raised but on it shall be inscribed the words, 'Let There Be Light'.

I want to close with another passage from *The Neophiliacs* by Christopher Booker – the man my brother and I are so fortunate and proud to be able to call our father.

> In fact, ultimately, all life on the level of reality is one. Each individual man, or animal, or plant, is merely the temporary vessel of a tiny part of that one substance, and their deepest instincts are to preserve it in not just their own species, but in the grand chain of all creation. An offense against one part is an offense against all, and nothing has been more illustrative of man's mounting self-assertion against his natural setting over the last few hundred years, than his steady destruction of all forms of wild life, from the growing pollution of the earth, air, and water, and the destruction of forests, flowers, birds, beasts and butterflies, to the actual extinction of whole species.
>
> At his deepest level, man feels his unity with this whole sum of life, the precious intangible thing that is in him, and of which he

---

[87]Quoted in *The Seven Basic Plots: Why We Tell Stories*. London: Continuum, 2004, p. 695.

forms such a minute fraction. The desire for eternal life, so often seen on the fantasy level as simply a self-centred desire for personal immortality or reincarnation, is in fact a desire having handed on the gift of life to the next generation, for the peace of merging back once again into that whole – a whole which, beyond the material world where it is alone divided into life spans and measures of time, has no beginning, and is therefore truly eternity.[88]

Nicholas Booker
New Delhi, India
January 2020

[88] *The Neophiliacs*, p. 362.

INDEX

INDEX

A NOTE ON THE AUTHOR

Christopher Booker was a founding editor of *Private Eye*, to which he regularly contributed, and also wrote a longstanding column for the *Sunday Telegraph*. His bestselling books include *The Seven Basic Plots: Why We Tell Stories*, *The Real Global Warming Disaster*, *The Neophiliacs* and with Richard North, *Scared to Death*, *The Mad Officials* and *The Great Deception*. Christopher Booker died in July 2019.

A NOTE ON THE TYPE

The text of this book is set in Minion, a digital typeface designed by Robert Slimbach in 1990 for Adobe Systems. The name comes from the traditional naming system for type sizes, in which minion is between nonpareil and brevier. It is inspired by late Renaissance-era type.

The Unfinished
Twentieth Century

◆

JONATHAN SCHELL

VERSO

London • New York

First published by Verso 2001
© Jonathan Schell 2001
All rights reserved

The moral rights of the author have been asserted

Verso
UK: 6 Meard Street, London W1F 0EG
US: 180 Varick Street, New York, NY 10014–4606

Verso is the imprint of New Left Books
www.versobooks.com

ISBN 1–85984–780–3

British Library Cataloguing in Publication Data
A catalogue record is available from the British Library

Library of Congress Cataloging-in-Publication Data
A catalog record for this book is available from the Library of Congress

Typeset in Erhardt by Helen Skelton, Brighton, UK
Printed and bound by Biddles Ltd, Guildford and King's Lynn
www.biddles.co.uk

I dedicate this book to the memory of Bernard Fall
and François Soulis, whose high-spirited generosity and
kindness to me during my first days as a would-be reporter
of the Vietnam war, which claimed both of their lives, set me
on the journalistic path I have followed ever since.

Introduction

WHEN THE SOVIET UNION broke up and the Cold War ended, nuclear weapons all but disappeared from public consciousness. Nuclear weapons themselves, however, did not disappear. At this writing, there are some 32,000 in the world. Lacking the justification given for them during the Cold War, they have yet to acquire any new justification, and seem to float in a moral and political limbo. In the two essays in this book, I seek to take stock of this anomalous state of affairs. In the first, I place the nuclear predicament as a whole in the larger context of the history of the twentieth century. That century divides quite neatly into two parts. The first was a period of global mayhem, including the two world wars, and ended in 1945. The second was a period of comparative calm, in which the mayhem was stilled—at least at the global level—

but was overhung by universal nuclear terror. In the United States, the resort to nuclear terror was justified as a response to the threat posed by a totalitarian Soviet Union. When the Soviet Union collapsed, and the terror was retained, the question arose whether perhaps nuclear weapons had in fact been built for some deeper, as yet incompletely articulated reasons. In *The Origins of Totalitarianism*, published in 1951, Hannah Arendt traced those origins to tendencies in the predominantly liberal European civilization that had given birth to them. "If it is true," she observed then—forty years before the Soviet collapse—"that the elements of totalitarianism can be found by retracing the history and analyzing the political implications of what we usually call the crisis of our century, then the conclusion is unavoidable that this crisis is no mere threat from the outside, no mere result of some aggressive foreign policy of either Germany or Russia, and that it will no more disappear with the death of Stalin than it disappeared with the fall of Nazi Germany. It may even be that the true predicaments of our time will assume their authentic form—though not necessarily the cruelest—only when totalitarianism has become a thing of the past." If Arendt's suspicion is correct, then it may be that the nuclear danger, by outlasting the Soviet threat, has shown itself to be one of the "authentic forms" of danger produced by our civilization. To ask this question, of course, is not to answer it. The answer will come in the decisions that the nuclear powers make about whether to keep or eliminate their nuclear arsenals.

The second essay looks more closely at the post-Cold War policies of the United States, and at the alternatives that are available. Cold War nuclear policy was a concatenation of scientific and political factors. In science, the new factor was the bomb itself. In politics it was the Cold War. The wedding of the two produced a bi-polar, nuclear-armed global confrontation. Its strategic expression was the doctrine of nuclear deterrence. The disappearance of the Soviet Union kicked away the political foundations of this policy. Apparently, out of sheer momentum, the United States continued the policy of nuclear deterrence into an age to which it was no longer politically fitted. In the last several years, a new policy, which is incompatible with deterrence, has won support in the United States: national missile defense. Defenses are justified as a response to a newly salient danger, nuclear proliferation. If nations could truly be defended from nuclear attack by such defenses, they would constitute a full replacement for deterrence. If, on the other hand, defenses are merely added to offensive arsenals, the consequences would seem to be the disruption of deterrence, and the instigation of a new arms race, or several new arms races. To make matters even more confusing, the technical feasibility of nuclear defenses is still undemonstrated. However that may be, the debate on defenses seems destined to be the venue in which the nuclear question in our new period is going to be debated. In short, the entire framework of nuclear policy that served for fifty years has broken down, and no new alternative has been found to replace it. In this policy debate, too, I suggest, the inescapable, underlying question is whether the nations that possess nuclear arms will insist on keeping them indefinitely or are prepared to accept their abolition.

The Unfinished
Twentieth Century

A Tale of Three Augusts

AN AGE ENDED, WE KNOW, when the Berlin Wall fell, auguring, soon after, the dissolution of the Soviet Union. But which age was it? The Cold War was over—that much was clear. Yet many felt and understood that some longer historical period, or perhaps several, had also come to a close. One clear candidate is the age of totalitarianism—a period coextensive with the life of the Soviet Union, which bracketed the rise and fall of Nazi Germany. (China's current government, which has evolved into a strange hybrid that some are calling "market communism," is the only one of the great totalitarian states of the twentieth century that has not actually been overthrown.) Another candidate is the age of world wars, which, as suggested by the war that remained cold, have been rendered unwinnable and therefore unlikely by the invention of nuclear weapons. And when the histories of the two world wars and the two great totalitarian regimes are considered together, they form a third candidate—an age that many historians are now calling the "short twentieth century." The calendar's divisions of the years, they've observed, match up inexactly with history's turning points. According to this way of reckoning, the nineteenth century began not in 1800 but in 1789, with the French Revolution, and came to its close not in 1900 but in 1914, when the First World War broke out, putting an end to the so-called long nineteenth century. The twentieth century, having begun in August of 1914, lasted only until the failed hard-line Communist coup in Moscow in 1991, which, in another pivotal August of the twentieth century, set in motion the Soviet collapse. Some years before, the Russian poet Akhmatova had expressed a similar idea:

> Snowdrifts covered the Nevskii Prospéct ...
> And along the legendary quay,
> There advanced, not the calendar, But the real
> > Twentieth Century.

It is this real twentieth century—the twentieth century of the Somme, of the Gulag, of the Holocaust—that in 1991 startled the world, the historians are now saying, by turning out to be short. On either side of it were the calmer seas of a predominantly liberal civilization. A bolder assertion of this notion was Francis Fukuyama's renowned claim that the liberal restoration of 1991 marked the "end of history"—by which he meant not that the end of days had arrived but, only a little more modestly, that humanity's long search for the best form of government had reached its destination in a nearly global embrace of liberal democracy.

The distinction between the real twentieth century and the calendrical one is based on the convincing idea that the century's bouts of unprecedented violence, both within nations and between them, possess a definite historical coherence— that they constitute, to put it simply, a single story. The proposed periodization is clearly optimistic, suggesting that the tide of bloodshed has reached its high-water mark and is now receding. The failure of the Cold War to become hot and the liquidation in 1991 of the world's last thoroughly totalitarian regime lend substance to the hope. I wish to suggest, however, that this appraisal remains starkly incomplete if it fails to take into account one more age that reached a turning point in 1991. I mean the nuclear age, which opened in another epochal August of the twentieth century, August of 1945. (Somehow in this century August was the month in which history chose to produce a disproportionately large number of its most important events.) No narrative of the extraordinary violence of the twentieth century can possibly be told without taking into account the greatest means of violence ever created.

The Greeks used to say that no man should be called happy before he died. They meant not only that even the most contented life could be undone by misfortune at the last minute but also that the meaning of an entire life might depend on its ending. For a life's last chapter was not merely an event, with its freight of suffering or joy; it was a disclosure, in whose light the story's beginning and middle might need to be drastically rewritten. Or, to vary the metaphor, stories, including the stories of historical epochs, are like pictures of heavenly constellations drawn by connecting dots—in this case, historical facts. The addition of new dots may merely add detail to the picture that has already taken shape, but it may also alter the entire image. The swan will turn out to be a crab; what looked like a whale turns into a dragon. Such was the case, certainly, with the end of the Soviet Union and the Cold War. The Soviet Union's infirmities, we now must suppose, were eating away at its power long before, one fine day in 1991, the empire evaporated. It is understandable that contemporaries are usually startled by events, but historians have no right to present surprise endings to the tales they tell. Their new job will be to retell the story of the Soviet Union in such a way that the sudden collapse at the end makes sense.

So it must eventually be with the nuclear age. The story of a Cold War that was the scene of history's only nuclear arms race will be very different from the story of a Cold War that turned out to be only the first of many interlocking nuclear arms races in many parts of the world. The nuclear dilemma, in sum, hangs like a giant question mark over the twentieth century. To 1914 and 1991 two dates therefore need to be added. The first is 1945 and the second is the as yet unknown future date on which the end of the nuclear age will be disclosed. Whether this conclusion will be the elimination of nuclear weapons (either before or after their further use) or, conceivably, the elimination of the species that built them is the deepest of the questions that need answering when we consider the still-open book of the real twentieth century.

In the United States, the historians' oversight is only one symptom of a wider inattention to the nuclear question. In the first years of the post-Cold War period, the nuclear peril seemed to all but disappear from public awareness. Some of the reasons were understandable. As long as the Cold War lasted, it had seemed almost indistinguishable from nuclear danger—the more so since both looked as if they were going to last indefinitely. One half of this assumption was of course removed by the Soviet collapse. For a while, the public seemed to imagine that nuclear danger, too, had unexpectedly proven ephemeral. The political antagonism that had produced the only nuclear terror Americans had ever known had, after all, really ended with the Cold War. The prospect of a second Cuban Missile Crisis became remote. It was reasonable for a while to imagine that the end of the struggle in whose name nuclear weapons had been built would lead to their end. Perhaps it would happen quietly and smoothly. The Comprehensive Test Ban Treaty would be accepted and succeeded by arms reductions. START II would be ratified and followed by START III, START III by START IV (at some point the lesser nuclear powers would be drawn into the negotiations), and so on, until the last warhead was gone. American presidents encouraged the public complacency. "I saw the chance to rid our children's dreams of the nuclear nightmare, and I did," President George Bush said at the Republican convention in 1992; and in 1997, President Bill Clinton boasted that "our children are growing up free from the shadows of the Cold War and the threat of nuclear holocaust."

The news media took their cue from this official neglect. Nuclear weapons all but dropped out of the news and opinion pages. In the decade since the Berlin Wall was torn down, newspaper readers and television viewers were given little indication that some 35,000 nuclear weapons remained in the world, or that 7,000 of them were targeted at the United States. A whole generation came of age lacking even rudimentary information regarding nuclear arms and nuclear peril. On the tenth anniversary of the end of the wall, few commentators taking stock of the decade bothered to mention the persistence of nuclear danger.

A frightening new landscape was coming into view. To begin with, the presidents who said that they had ended nuclear danger had not acted that way. Clinton's repeated though little-reported "bottom up" reviews of defense policy left the strategy of nuclear deterrence—and the arsenals it justified—untouched. His spokesmen let it be known that nuclear weapons were to remain the foundation of American security for the indefinite future. Russia followed suit—

abandoning a willingness expressed by Gorbachev to eliminate nuclear weapons and stalling on the ratification of the START II Treaty. And so the nuclear arsenals of the Cold War, instead of withering away with the disappearance of that conflict, were delivered intact, like a package from a deceased sender, into the new age, though now lacking the benefit of new justification—or, for that matter, of new opposition.

Meanwhile, newcomers to the nuclear game moved to acquire the weapons. If nuclear powers such as Russia and the United States, which no longer had a quarrel, were entitled to maintain nuclear arsenals, why not countries that, like India and Pakistan, were chronically at war? To insist otherwise would, in the words of India's foreign minister Jaswant Singh, be to shut the Third World out of the "nuclear paradigm" established by the First and Second Worlds, and so to accept "nuclear apartheid." In May of 1998, India and Pakistan, accordingly, fired off their rival salvos of nuclear tests. The antagonism between the Soviet Union and the United States had been "cold," but this conflict was hot. The three wars that the two countries had fought since the late 1940s were in short order followed by a fourth in the summer of 1999. The world's multiplying nuclear arsenals were meanwhile supplemented by a new prominence of their repellent siblings in the family of weapons of mass destruction—chemical and biological weapons, which may become the instrument of choice of nations or terrorist groups worried about the expense and difficulty of making nuclear weapons.

From the very first moments of the nuclear age, scientists have warned the world that it is in the nature of nuclear technology—as of all technology—to become universally available and therefore that, in the absence of political will, the world would tend to become nuclear-armed. In a world boiling with local (and not so local) hatreds, the retrogression of arms control raises the question of whether the Cold War, instead of being the high point of danger in a waning nuclear age, will prove to have been a mere bipolar rehearsal for a multipolar second nuclear age.

A number of voices challenged this status quo by calling for the abolition of nuclear weapons, but their views went largely unreported by the news media that had ignored the dangers of which they warned. Among these voices were leaders of the traditional antinuclear peace movement; the seven governments of the New Agenda coalition, composed of Brazil, Egypt, Ireland, Mexico, New Zealand, Sweden, and South Africa; and an impressive array of retired military officers and civilian leaders, including ex-President Jimmy Carter, Senator Alan Cranston, former commander of the Strategic Air Command General George Lee Butler, and the commander of the allied air forces in the Gulf War, General Charles Horner. In a series of reports and statements, these people have argued that the end of the Cold War has provided a historically unique but perishable opportunity to remove nuclear danger by eliminating nuclear arsenals everywhere. (Since only eight nations possess nuclear weapons, and of these only India, Pakistan, and Israel have not signed the

Nonproliferation Treaty, abolition means persuading just eight nations to live as would the 182 non-nuclear signatories.) Notable among the new abolitionists were some of the most hawkish figures of the Cold War, including Paul Nitze, drafter in 1950 of National Security Council Memorandum–68, regarded by many as the charter of American Cold War policy. He recently argued that the United States' huge lead in the development of high-precision weaponry created a new military context in which the United States simply did not need nuclear weapons. Considering this advantage, Nitze could "think of no circumstances under which it would be wise for the United States to use nuclear weapons," and therefore recommended that the nation "unilaterally get rid" of them. The emergence of this hawkish strain of abolitionism, in which precision, high-explosive conventional bombing would give the United States a usable military superiority that nuclear weapons could never confer, assured that, should the idea of abolition ever take hold, a debate within the ranks of the abolitionists themselves would be robust. But Nitze's dramatic proposal fell into the media silence that had swallowed up all other proposals for abolition.

Preface to a Century

IT SEEMS TIMELY, THEN, to take a fresh look at the nuclear question in the context of the century that has just ended. The exercise, we can hope, will shed light on both the nuclear dilemma and the story of the century, short or otherwise, in which nuclear weapons have played, and unfortunately go on playing, so important a part. One place to begin is with a work that, as it happens, was first published in *Blackwood's Edinburgh Magazine*, in London and Edinburgh, at the turn of the last century, in 1899: Joseph Conrad's *Heart of Darkness*. Conrad wrote in the heyday of a liberal civilization that had seemed to spread steadily and grow stronger for most of the nineteenth century. Its articles of faith were that science and technology were the sources of a prosperity without limits; that the free market would spread the new abundance across the boundaries of both classes and nations; that liberty and democracy, already established in several of the most powerful and advanced nations, were gaining ground almost everywhere; and that all of these forces were swelling an unstoppable tide of overall human progress. It is, of course, a revival of these ideas—minus, notably, the idea of progress—that has inspired the belief that the twentieth century, or even history itself, ended in 1991. Conrad was not an acolyte of this faith. He was perhaps the most acute among a number of observers who, having witnessed firsthand what the "civilized" countries were doing in the "backward" parts of the world, where colonialism was at its zenith, discerned the shape of a radically different future. *Heart of Darkness* is many things. It is a tale of travel to an exotic place. It is a glimpse, through the eyes of the seaman Marlow, of the atrocities committed by King Leopold's International Association of the Congo. It is an investigation by literary means of the extremes of depravity. And it is, as we today are in a position to appreciate, a topographic map, clairvoyant in its specificity, of the moral landscape of the twentieth century.

"It was like a weary pilgrimage amongst hints for nightmares," Marlow says of his sea journey to the Congo along the African coast. The hinted nightmares turned out to be the waking experience of the century ahead. That century, Conrad apparently understood, was about to open up new possibilities for evil. In *Heart of Darkness*, he seems to thumb through them prospectively, as if through a deck of horrific tarot cards. The concentration camps are there. The black men "dying slowly," "in all the attitudes of pain, abandonment, and despair," whom Marlow witnesses in a grove of trees immediately upon arriving at an outer station, are unmistakable precursors of the millions of men and women who were to die in the concentration camps soon to be built in Europe. The monster Kurtz, the charismatic station chief who murders in the name of progress, and who, although "hollow at the core," was gifted with magnificent eloquence and "electrified large meetings," is a sort of prefiguration of Hitler. Conrad even has a Belgian journalist comment that Kurtz would have made a "splendid leader of an extreme party." Which one? "Any party," is the answer. For, the journalist stammers, "he was an—an—extremist." But Kurtz is not to be understood as a fringe character. "All Europe contributed to the making of Kurtz," Marlow says, in a rare moment of editorializing.

Consider, by way of inexplicably refined forecasting, the likeness of some of Marlow's comments about Kurtz to some comments Hitler makes about himself in 1936. The power of Hitler's voice, carried to the German public over the radio, was a basic element of his power. Conrad notes something similar in Kurtz. Marlow:

> Kurtz discoursed. A voice! a voice! It rang deep to the very last.
> Yet beneath the rich and resonant voice lay an emptiness:
> [...] The voice was gone. What else had been there?

And, for comparison, Hitler speaking at a rally in 1936 about his appeal to the German people:

> At this hour do we not again feel the miracle that has brought us together! Long ago you heard the voice of a man, and it struck to your hearts, it awakened you, and you followed this voice. You followed it for years, without so much as having seen him whose voice it was; you heard only a voice, and you followed.

To give just one more example, anyone who witnessed the monotonous, ceaseless American artillery fire into "free-fire zones" in Vietnam will experience a shock of recognition in the following description of a French naval vessel firing into the African jungle:

In the empty immensity of earth, sky, and water, there she was, incomprehensible, firing into a continent. Pop, would go one of the six-inch guns; a small flame would dart and vanish, a little white smoke would disappear, a tiny projectile would give a feeble screech—and nothing happened. Nothing could happen. There was a touch of insanity in the proceeding, a sense of lugubrious drollery in the sight.

Nor did Conrad fail to take note of those indispensable props of the gigantic, insane, state-sponsored crimes of our time: the obedient functionaries. The "banality" of their evil, famously described after the fact by Hannah Arendt in *Eichmann in Jerusalem*, is foreshadowed in Conrad's description of a minor bureaucrat in the ivory-gathering operation at the Central Station. This man, mistaking Marlow for an influential figure, curries favor with him, prompting Marlow to observe, "I let him run on, this papier-maché Mephistopheles." He adds, "It seemed to me that if I tried I could poke my forefinger through him, and would find nothing inside but a little loose dirt, maybe." Conrad described well the humiliation that so many decent people were to experience in having to take ridiculous personages seriously solely because of the immense suffering they were causing. Face to face with Kurtz in the jungle at night, Marlow comments, "I resented bitterly the absurd danger of our situation, as if to be at the mercy of that atrocious phantom had been a dishonoring necessity." The inspired anti-Nazi diarist Friedrich Reck-Malleczewen, who was executed by the Nazis in 1944, experienced a similar feeling of humiliation when he thought back to an accidental encounter he had once had with another atrocious phantom—Hitler. "If I had had an inkling of the role this piece of filth was to play, and of the years of suffering he was to make us endure," he wrote, "I would have done it [shot him] without a second thought. But I took him for a character out of a comic strip, and did not shoot."

The most remarkable and telling augury of *Heart of Darkness*, however, was the glimpse that Conrad, vaulting ahead in prophecy to 1945, provided of the destination toward which all these preposterous and terrifying tendencies somehow were heading; namely, the threat that, with the help of the Kurtzes of this world, the human species might one day get ready to wipe itself off the face of the earth. After his climactic meeting with Kurtz in the jungle, Marlow further comments, "There was nothing either above or below him, and I knew it. He had kicked himself loose of the earth. Confound the man! he had kicked the very earth to pieces." This foreboding of annihilation was no incidental feature of the work; it returns several times, always at critical moments in the story. The most renowned passage in which it occurs is the legendary addendum "Exterminate all the brutes" that Kurtz pinned to the bottom of the dithyramb to nineteenth-century progress that he left as his legacy. The foreboding recurs even more explicitly when, after Kurtz has died and Marlow is on his way to inform Kurtz's betrothed of the fact, he reports, "I had a vision of him on the stretcher, opening his mouth voraciously, as if to devour all the earth with all its mankind." The technical means for destroying the species lay far in the future, but the psychological and moral preparations, it appears, were well under way in 1899.

The First August: The Beginning of the Real Twentieth Century

AS THE SCHOLAR JESSICA REIFER has pointed out, Conrad's intimations in a single text of virtually all the unprecedented evils, including the threat of self-extinction, that Western humanity was about to visit upon itself and the world in the twentieth century are evidence before the fact of their common roots and essential unity. These "hints for nightmares," however, did not materialize into real historical events in Europe until, during the first of the century's fateful Augusts, the First World War broke out. Then the nightmares followed, one after another, in a chain whose unusually clear linkage points to the underlying continuity.

The judgment that the outbreak of the First World War was the starting point in the twentieth century's plunge into horror did not originate with the inventors of the idea of the short twentieth century; it has been the belief of a remarkably wide consensus of historians. George Kennan spoke for this consensus in his diplomatic history *The Decline of Bismarck's European Order*:

> With the phenomenon of the Second World War before
> me, it was borne in upon me to what overwhelming extent
> the determining phenomena of the interwar period,
> Russian Communism and German Nazism and indeed
> then the Second World War itself, were the products of
> that first great holocaust of 1914–18 .... And thus I came
> to see the First World War ... as the great seminal
> catastrophe of the century ....

As Kennan suggests, the stories of the two world wars
on the one hand and of the two great totalitarian regimes on
the other were as tightly intertwined at every crucial juncture
as the proteins on the strands of a double helix. Total war
and totalitarianism were kin in more than name. From
1914 onward, each fed the other in a vicious spiral of violence.
To begin with, the shock of the First World War is widely
understood to have created the social conditions essential
to the success of the Bolshevik revolution in Russia. In the
words of the historian Martin Malia, "This war disorganized
Russia's still immature political structures to the point
where the Bolshevik Party, a throwback to the violent and
conspiratorial politics of the 1870s, was able to seize power
...." Many understood even at the time that the brutality of
the war had been carried over to the system of rule that
followed. As the contemporary socialist Victor Chernov put
it, "The moral nature of the Bolshevik Revolution was
inherited from the war in which it was born."

That the Nazis' rise to power in Germany was made

possible in good measure by the war is also accepted widely. It will be enough here—without trying to recount the story of the destabilization of German politics and society by her defeat and the harsh terms of the peace settlement—to recall two comments made by Hitler. The first is his remark that "if at the beginning of the war twelve or fifteen thousand of these Hebrew corrupters of the people had been held under poison gas, as happened to hundreds of thousands of our very best German workers in the field, the sacrifice of millions at the front would not have been in vain." The idea of killing Jews by gas was not one that Hitler, who had been a victim of an English gas attack, was to forget. The second comment is his description of his reaction to the declaration of the First World War. "Even today," he wrote in *Mein Kampf*, "I am not ashamed to say that, overpowered by stormy enthusiasm, I fell down on my knees and thanked Heaven from an over-flowing heart."

If in the century's Teens and Twenties total war prepared the way for totalitarianism, in the Thirties, when Hitler carried out the series of aggressions that brought on the Second World War, the process worked the other way around. Hitler's biographers tell us that while at the front in the First World War he felt so much at home in the trenches and so ill at ease in civilian society that he canceled all his leaves. For him, it seems, not war but peace was hell, and there is a sense in which the interwar period was just one more leave that was canceled by a peace-weary Hitler.

The plainest of these links, finally, is that between the war against Hitler and the decision by the United States and England to build atomic weapons. In October of 1939 (more than two years before the United States went to war with Germany and Japan), when the businessman Alexander Sachs visited President Franklin Roosevelt to recommend an atomic-weapons program, Roosevelt commented, "Alex, what you are after is to see that the Nazis don't blow us up." Sachs replied, "Precisely." Throughout the war, the scientists at Los Alamos—many of them refugees from Europe—held before their eyes the prospect that Hitler would succeed in building the bomb first. Evil, even when opposed, has a way of preparing the ground for more evil, and Hitler by this route became a progenitor of the bomb. His extraordinary malevolence induced his adversaries to embrace an evil that otherwise they conceivably might have forgone. Through this indirect paternity were reborn key aspects of the policies that he, more than anyone else, had pioneered. As in a magic trick—appropriately accompanied by a gigantic world-blinding flash and (mushroom-shaped) puff of smoke—the politics of mass annihilation, even as they were going down to defeat in Hitler's bunker, were in 1945 transferred to the care of Washington.

Extermination

WHAT WAS THE NATURE of the new possibilities for evil that Conrad had discerned in the Congo and that the series of calamities inaugurated by the war in 1914 brought, as if through the action of a pendulum swinging in an ever-widening arc, to fuller and fuller realization, until the human species created weapons whereby it could destroy itself? Violence on a previously unimaginable scale was the obvious common denominator. This violence was the basis for the increasing use of that lingua franca of twentieth-century politics, terror—terror as an instrument of rule, which is to say totalitarian rule; terror as a strategy of war, and especially of "strategic" bombing, aimed at breaking the morale of civilian populations; and, finally, nuclear terror, rather optimistically referred to as a "balance of terror." (Terror in nuclear strategy, let us note, is terror in not only its most extensive but also its purest form, inasmuch as its practitioners sometimes imagine that it can be projected forever without actual use of the instruments that produce it.) But something more than a colossal increase in violence and terror was involved. In Kurtz's phrase "Exterminate all the brutes," Conrad gives us the concept we need: extermination. The capacity and will to destroy not just large numbers of people but entire classes of people was the new invention. Policies of extermination, of course, require slaughter on a mass scale, but they aim at more than slaughter. By seeking to eradicate defined human collectivities, extermination aims not only at those groups but at their progeny, who are shut out of existence when the policy succeeds. The distinction is basic. Mass slaughter is a crime against the living; extermination is, in addition, a crime against the future. When Hitler launched the Final Solution, his target was not just the living Jews but all future Jews together with the culture they had created and, if they were permitted to live, would go on creating. Murder is a crime that, by destroying individual lives, violates the legal and moral order of a community; extermination is a crime that, by destroying an entire community, is a crime against the family of communities that make up humankind—a crime, as international law has come to recognize, "against humanity." Genocide—the destruction of a people, whether defined as a race or a tribe or a nation—is the quintessential act of extermination, but it is not the only one. Another is the extermination of social classes, practiced by Stalin and Mao Zedong and Pol Pot, among others. In the Bolsheviks' very first year in power, they discovered a category of crime that they called "objective." A crime was "subjective" when you had done something wrong; it was "objective" when, through no deed of your own, you belonged to a social class that the government wanted to liquidate. As early as 1918, Latvian Latsis, one of the chiefs of the Cheka, the precursor of the KGB, announced the goal in plain language: "We are engaged in annihilating the bourgeoisie as a class." Thus there was no need, Latsis explained, to "prove that this or that man acted against the interests of Soviet power." It was enough to ask, "To what class does he belong, where does he come from, what kind of education did he have, what is his occupation?" The answers to these questions "decide the fate of the accused." "That," he said, "is the quintessence of the Red Terror"—terror that was to cost the Soviet people an estimated fifty or sixty million lives in the coming half-century.

A third target of policies of extermination was cities and their populations. Let us consider two examples. The first is the bombing of Hamburg by the British air force in 1943. As early as July 1940, Churchill, while commanding the Battle of Britain, had called for "exterminating" air attacks on Germany. From then until 1942, the Bomber Command, afflicted by high loss rates and fearful of losing out in interservice rivalry with the Navy and the Army, drifted away from "precision" bombing, which had to be carried out in daylight, into "area bombing," which could be carried out at night. The aim was to destroy the morale of the German people by killing German civilians and destroying their homes. By the end of 1942, giant raids on Lübeck and Cologne had made it clear that the annihilation of entire cities in one or a few raids was feasible. Accordingly, Most Secret Operation Order No. 173, of 27 May 1943, stated, under the heading "Intention," that the aim of the raid was "to destroy HAMBURG." The order estimated that 10,000 tons of bombs would have to be dropped to "complete the process of elimination." And thus it was done, producing a firestorm in the city and killing some 45,000 people in a single night. The second example is Hitler's plan, formed even before his attack on Russia, in June of 1941, for the annihilation of Moscow and Leningrad. Moscow was to be razed because it was "the center of [Bolshevik] doctrine"—for Hitler's larger goal was an "ethnic catastrophe." He intended to dig a reservoir where

Moscow had once been. At first, he planned to spare Leningrad, because it was "incomparably more beautiful" than Moscow; but soon he put Leningrad, too, on the list of cities to be destroyed. His explanation sheds light on the mentality of those who are preparing to exterminate entire human communities:

> I suppose that some people are clutching their heads with both hands to find an answer to the question, "How can the Führer destroy a city like St. Petersburg?" ... I would prefer not to see anyone suffer, not to do harm to anyone. But when I realize the species is in danger, then in my case sentiment gives way to the coldest reason.

The Nazi general Franz Halder concurred with this supposedly cold reasoning: annihilating the two cities, he wrote, would be a "national catastrophe which [would] deprive not only Bolshevism but also Muscovite nationalism of their centers."

A plan was drawn up. Leningrad would be sealed off, to weaken it "by terror and growing starvation"; then the Germans would "remove the survivors in captivity in the interior of Russia, level Leningrad to the ground with high explosives, and leave the area to the north of the Neva to the Finns."

Of course, we know that the two cities survived, owing not to any thaw in Hitler's cold reasoning but to the almost superhuman resistance mounted by the Russian people.

Extermination as a Systemic Evil

JUST AS THE TWENTIETH CENTURY'S policies of extermination—whether of peoples, classes, or cities—enveloped entire human communities, so also they were carried out by entire communities—or, at any rate, by the state authorities that putatively represented those communities. Extermination, a species of crime requiring extensive social resources, is—can only be—a systemic evil. To the extent that popular support was present, the policies amounted to attempted murder of one society by another. Although there can be debate over just how extensive popular support was for Stalin's and Hitler's policies of extermination, there can be no doubt that, through the states that ruled over these peoples, the resources of entire societies were placed at the disposal of those carrying out the policies.

The resources were not just the obvious ones—the secret police, the transportation systems, the concentration-camp administrations, the armies, the bomber forces. They had to include mass cooperation of the kind that control of the state alone provides. When the state becomes an exterminator, and the law, instead of enjoining evil, supports and enforces it—as does the whole tremendous weight of custom, habit, bureaucratic inertia, and social pressure—the individual who might seek to oppose the policies is left in an extremity of moral solitude. Even the voice of conscience, in these circumstances, can become an enlistee in the ranks of the evildoers. People find themselves in the dilemma defined by

Mark Twain when he presented Huck Finn's inner deliberations whether to turn in his friend, the runaway black slave, Jim. Huck's "conscience," he believes, is telling him that it is wrong not to turn Jim in. Nevertheless, Huck decides to do what is "wrong" and hides Jim. Adolf Eichmann, too, heard the voice of an inverted conscience, but he, unlike Huck, obeyed it. At the end of the war, with the defeat of Germany in sight, he had an opportunity to slow down or even halt the transports of the Jews to the killing centers, but instead he redoubled his efforts. "The sad and very uncomfortable truth," Arendt writes, "probably was that it was not his fanaticism but his very conscience that prompted Eichmann to adopt his uncompromising attitude during the last year of the war ... ." For "he remembered perfectly well that he would have had a bad conscience only if he had not done what he had been ordered to do—to ship millions of men, women, and children to their death with great zeal and the most meticulous care."

Extermination as Pseudoscience

As if to leave individual judgment in even greater perplexity, science—or, to be precise, pseudoscience (otherwise known as ideology)—was summoned to lend its pseudoauthority to the policies of extermination. In the late nineteenth century, in a wholesale resort to the persuasive power of sheer metaphor, social Darwinists had taught that nations in history, like species in evolution, were subject to the law of survival of the fittest. As early as 1848, Friedrich Engels had distinguished between "historical nations" (they included Germany, England, and France), which were destined to flourish, and "ahistorical nations" (they included most of the Balkan peoples), which were destined for history's scrap heap. His interest in these ideas is one illustration of the intellectual roots that the Marxist theory of classes shared with racial theories of evolution. In Stalin's Russia, classes—some doomed, some destined to rule—played the role that races played in Hitler's Germany.

Hitler's Final Solution of the Jewish "problem" was in his mind only one part of a vast scheme of ethnic expulsion, resettlement, extermination, and racial engineering, in which he planned to eradicate Poland and Ukraine, among other nations. For example, of forty-five million inhabitants in Western Russia, according to a memo prepared by the Ministry for Occupied Eastern Territories, thirty-one million were to be expatriated or killed. "Drop a few bombs on their cities, and the job will be done," Hitler suggested.

The extent to which Hitler, caught up in the grandiose theories of racial pseudoscience, had transcended mere nationalism is shown by his often-stated readiness to sacrifice even the German people if they showed themselves cowardly or weak. No nationalist could have said, as Hitler did in 1941, when still at the height of his power, that if the Germans were "no longer so strong and ready for sacrifice that they will stake their own blood on their existence, they deserve to be annihilated by another, stronger power." In that event, he added, "I would not shed a tear for the German people." He made good his promise when, facing defeat in 1945, he ordered the destruction of the entire infrastructure of German society, including its industry, buildings, and food stocks. But then had he not warned the world, as if in fulfillment of Conrad's vision of Kurtz devouring all the earth with all its mankind, that "we may perish, perhaps. But we shall take the world with us. Muspili, universal conflagration"? Hitler's willingness to accept—and even to carry out—the destruction of Germany (and the whole world into the bargain) was an early warning of the ease, later illustrated on a much greater scale in the nuclear policy of "mutual assured destruction" during the Cold War, with which those who adopt policies of annihilation can overshoot the mark and wind up involving themselves in suicidal plans. Unfortunately, once the scruples that inhibit the extermination of millions of "others" have been discarded, there are very few left with which to protect "ourselves."

Extermination as Radical Evil

THE NEW POLICIES—of which the extermination of human populations was the objective, states or whole societies were the authors, the instruments of modern science were the means, and for which the concepts of pseudoscience were the rationalization—prompted new thinking about the nature of evil. They precipitated what might be called a crisis in the meaning of evil, by which I mean a crisis in all of the human capacities whereby, once evils have occurred, the world tries, as best it can, to respond to them—to incorporate them into memory and the historical record, to understand them, to take appropriate action against their recurrence. The crimes of the twentieth century seemed to make a mockery of these powers. In *The Origins of Totalitarianism*, Arendt, making use of a phrase of Immanuel Kant, named the new phenomenon "radical evil." According to Kant, ordinary evil occurred when the will, driven by some fear or lured by some temptation away from the principles of equity and justice, committed a selfish act. Radical evil occurred when the will, even when unafraid or unswayed by temptation, somehow inspired itself to commit evil. Whereas ordinary evil, being dependent on the happenstance of external threats or temptations, was by its nature occasional, radical evil, being ever-present in the will, might infect any or all of a person's actions. If we extend this idea from the individual to the state, we arrive at the distinction between a state that commits a crime in violation of its own good laws and a state whose laws ordain and enforce evil. Obviously, the latter is more dangerous, for it has corrupted one of the main defenses we sometimes have against evil—the state and its laws. This nullification of the human power of response brings a new feeling of bafflement and helplessness. For outbreaks of radical evil, Arendt explained, do not only destroy their victims, often in stupefying numbers, but "dispossess *us* of all power" (italics mine), for they "transcend the realm of human affairs," and "we can neither punish nor forgive such offenses."

The problem for the most elementary of responses, memory—a problem deliberately created by totalitarian regimes, which have sought to erase their crimes from the historical record—was simply to rescue the facts from their intended oblivion. Against these efforts were eventually pitted heroic acts of witness—by an Aleksandr Solzhenitsyn, a Nadezhda Mandelstam, a Primo Levi. The problem for feeling was the exhaustion that empathy must encounter in the face of suffering on such a scale. And the problem for thought was nothingness—the sheer absence created by the extinction of communities. The problem for law, in addition to the corruption of the perpetrators' own laws, was the likely destruction of the victims' legal system, if one ever existed. What remained were third parties who might seek to judge the wrongdoers by newly created laws, as was done in the Nuremberg trials. (This problem was solved after the fact for the Jews by the foundation of the state of Israel, which put Eichmann on trial.) The twentieth century's policies of extermination were radical in one more sense. "Radical" evil, as the Latin origins of the word suggest, is evil that goes to the root. The root, though, of what? The answer must be: that which extermination afflicts and destroys; namely, life. The root of life, the spring from which life arises—as distinct from life itself—is birth, which is the power that enables communities composed of mortal beings to regenerate and preserve themselves in history. And it is this power, precisely, that acts of extermination annul.

After witnessing the trial of Eichmann, a "papier-maché Mephistopheles" if there ever was one, Arendt backed away from the phrase "radical evil." "Only the good has depth and can be radical," she wrote in a letter to her friend Gershom Scholem. Evil, she now believed, "is never 'radical,' only extreme." It was this very shallowness, she concluded, that produced the frustration of the mind faced with the new crimes. "It is 'thought-defying,'" she explained, "because thought tries to reach some depth, to go to the roots, and the moment it concerns itself with evil, it is frustrated because there is nothing." (This relationship between evil and nothingness, though it has been most clearly manifested in history only in this century, was signposted in Christian theology, in which, as St Augustine maintains, being, taken as a whole, is good, and its absence is called evil.)

In truth, though, "there is nothing" in two senses where radical evil is concerned. First, there is nothing (perhaps just "a little loose dirt") in the souls of bureaucrats such as Eichmann, for when the state of which they are a part goes berserk, they can, merely by thoughtlessly doing their jobs (*quitting* would take some imagination), participate in gargantuan evils. Second, as Arendt had pointed out earlier, the erasure of a community from the face of the earth leaves a kind of "nothing" behind; namely, the "hole of oblivion" in the human order where that community had once existed. Perhaps banal evildoers, as Conrad knew, are capable of

31

committing evil that is radical (or "extreme," if you prefer), as if the emptiness of their minds and souls prefigures the emptiness in the world that they and the policies they serve leave behind. What is "thought-defying" after the fact is, appropriately, done thoughtlessly to begin with.

The Second August: Nuclear Extermination

IN HER REFLECTIONS ON RADICAL EVIL, Arendt was addressing policies of extermination that had been adopted before the advent of nuclear weapons, but it is plain that what she had to say applies in almost every particular to nuclear policies and nuclear danger. In other words, although Hiroshima came as a great surprise and shock to the world, it did not arrive without a historical context and historical precedents. On the contrary, it was the supreme expression of forces that had been developing ever since Conrad had Kurtz write, "Exterminate all the brutes." Behind Hiroshima stood not only the obvious precedent of area bombing but all of the twentieth century's policies of extermination. These amounted, by the end of the Second World War, to what might be called a legacy of extermination, and in August of 1945 the United States fell heir to it. The hallmarks of the legacy were all present. The nuclear threat was a threat of extermination—extermination, this time, not only of nations and peoples but of the human species. The root of life that now would be severed would be the root of all human life, birth itself, and would shut all future human beings out of existence. The evil was a systemic evil: the system posing the threat, once the "balance of terror" was established, went beyond any single state to incorporate the greatest powers of the world, which, in the system of mutual assured destruction, became jointly complicit in the project. The threat was supported by pseudoscience, spun this time from game theory and other forms of futurology manufactured in think tanks and academic institutions that subserved power. Nuclear "strategy"—regarded by many as a contradiction in terms—became the very epicenter of banality. Nuclear arms increased the capacity of human beings to destroy one another to its absolute limit, beyond which any further improvements would merely be "overkill." The arsenals threatened radical evil, in the fullest and most exact sense of that term: they brought radical evil to perfection. The powers of human response to evil would be entirely destroyed by the evil deed itself. Policies of extermination again spilled over into suicidal policies. The "coldest reason" again was invoked to rationalize genocide. The conscience of the individual was again thrown into crisis by the policies of the state. The deeds in question again were, as Arendt had said, "thought-defying." The "nothingness" that now awaited was absolute, the crisis of meaning full-blown. The atomic bomb that burst over Hiroshima burned for a moment as bright as the sun, but at its heart was a darkness that was eternal. The twentieth century had, so to speak, arrived at the heart of the heart of darkness.

The advent of the nuclear age, however, brought with it

another major change in the development of the century's policies of extermination. At a stroke, it removed them from their totalitarian residence and planted them at the core of liberal civilization, which is to say at the core of the national security policy of the powerful democratic nation about to assume leadership of the non-Communist world—the United States. The new location brought with it a new moral and practical riddle of the first order. Instruments of the most radical evil imaginable—the extinction of the human species— had appeared, but they were first placed in the hands of a liberal republic. The fact that, more or less by an accident of history, the bomb was born in New Mexico, USA, in 1945, rather than, say, Heidelberg, Germany, in 1944 (no sheer impossibility of science or history rules out our imagining the latter possibility), lent it a triple warrant of virtue that it otherwise would have lacked.

In the first place, the bomb gained luster from its new residence. Without becoming jingoistic about the United States or overlooking the dark passages in its history, including slavery and the near-extinction of Native Americans, it must be said that the United States was no Nazi Germany or Stalinist Russia. History had in a sense played a trick on the world, as it so often does. If history had been logical, it would have given the bomb to Hitler, whose policies (including his suicidal inclinations) so clearly pointed in the direction of extermination on the new scale. It's easy to imagine what civilized people would have said if Hitler had been the first to use nuclear weapons—perhaps against Moscow or London.

They very likely would have said that nuclear war was a natural culmination of *Vernichtungskrieg* and an ideology that sanctioned the extermination of peoples, and that with nuclear weapons Hitler was enabled to do quickly and efficiently what he had already been doing slowly and clumsily with gas chambers. The United States, on the other hand, had shown no recent inclination for policies of extermination, as was demonstrated shortly by its mild, liberal, extremely successful occupation policies in Germany and Japan. In the second place, the bomb arrived just in time to hurry along the end of the most destructive war in history. It made its appearance as a war-ending, war-winning device. The totalitarian and the liberal regimes had arrived at their policies of extermination along very different historical paths. Whereas Hitler and Stalin destroyed peoples, classes, and cities for reasons that even today defy rational explanation, the United States destroyed Hiroshima and Nagasaki for the perfectly clear and comprehensible purposes of ending the war quickly and getting the upper hand over the Soviet Union in the embryonic Cold War. (To point this out is not to justify these acts; it is only to observe that the goals of policy were conventional and rational.) In the third place, the almost immediate outbreak of the Cold War with the totalitarian Soviet Union created a justification for continuing to build nuclear arsenals, lending the bomb still another warrant of virtue. It assumed the role of guardian of the free world.

To this triple validation of policies of nuclear extermination, accorded by the accident of timing and place, a fourth, of later origin, must be added. Although it was true that with the growth of the arsenals the depth and range of terror were soon increased to their earthly maximum, it also happened that none was ever used after Nagasaki. Instead, they were held suspended, like the sword of Damocles cited by President John Kennedy, over a completely jeopardized yet undevastated world. It was as if, in the nuclear arsenals of the Cold War, the destruction and mass killing of the entire first half of the twentieth century had been distilled into a poison of fantastic potency but then this poison, instead of being administered to a doomed world, had been held in reserve, being employed only to produce terror. To the question whether Western civilization had put behind it the legacy of extermination that it had been developing for half a century, the nuclear policymakers of the Cold War in effect gave an equivocal answer. Their answer was, No, for we have plans for extermination that beggar Hitler's and Stalin's, but our sincere wish is never to be provoked into actually committing the deed. Certainly, the legacy of extermination had not been renounced. Rather, it had been hugely developed and assigned a more important role in world affairs than ever before. Now the world's greatest power as well as its adversary relied upon it for basic security. On the other hand, the very fearsomeness of the new threat was invoked to prevent its being carried out. And not only did the bomb prevent its own nuclear war, the theorists said; it prevented the worst of the conventional wars: no conventional third world war broke out. In the meantime, however, an estimated forty million people, most of them civilians, were killed in local wars—a fact suggesting that major war was as much displaced as deterred.

Whether a third world war was headed off because of nuclear deterrence or for some other reason is a question not easily resolved. It is a historical fact, however, that in the minds of most policymakers as well as millions of citizens nuclear deterrence worked. The bomb, already seen as a war-winner and a freedom-defender, now was granted the additional title of peacemaker. (The MX missile was given this very name, and the Strategic Air Command adopted the motto "Peace Is Our Profession.") Here was a bargain with the devil to make Faust green with envy. Victory, freedom, peace: was there anything else for which the world might petition an open-handed Lucifer?

And yet none of these benefits altered in the slightest particular the irreducible facts of what nuclear weapons were, what they could do, and what they were meant to do "if deterrence failed." One bomb of the appropriate megatonnage would still obliterate any city; ten bombs, ten cities. Hitler had killed an estimated six million Jews; Stalin had sent an estimated twenty million of his fellow Soviet citizens to their deaths. A few dozen well-placed nuclear bombs could outdo these totals by an order of magnitude. But at the height of the Cold War, there were not a few dozen nuclear bombs; there were almost 70,000, with thousands poised on hair-trigger alert. A policy of extermination did not cease being that because the goals it supported were laudable. Described soberly and without the slightest hyperbole, it was a policy of retaliatory genocide.

For most people most of the time, these perils remained all but unimaginable. But every now and then the reality of the policy was borne in on someone. That happened, for instance, to Robert McNamara shortly after he became secretary of defense in 1961, when he received a briefing on the Single Integrated Operational Plan at the headquarters of the Strategic Air Command. In the event of a Soviet conventional attack on Europe—or merely the plausible likelihood of such an attack—the United States' Plan 1-A, which was its only true option for major nuclear war, McNamara learned, was to annihilate every Communist country from East Germany to China. There were no operational means, he further learned, by which, if the president desired, he could spare one or more of these countries. Albania, then engaged in bitter polemics with Moscow, was to be obliterated merely because a Soviet radar facility was stationed on its soil. The plan was for oblig-atory multiple acts of genocide. In *The Wizards of Armageddon*, Fred Kaplan reports that "McNamara was horrified." He set about trying to create other options. Today McNamara favors the abolition of nuclear weapons because, in his carefully chosen words, they threaten "the destruction of nations." In sum, Hiroshima had created a gulf between ends and means. Never had evil been more radical; never had the good that was hoped from it been greater. The means were an evil that exceeded the capacity of the human being to imagine them; the ends were all the splendors of liberal civilization and peace.

Thus, through the invention, production, and deployment of nuclear arsenals, was the tradition of extermination glimpsed in prospect by Conrad in colonized Africa, pioneered and developed under totalitarian government and in total war, conjoined to the liberal tradition, which had prided itself on opposing such practices, but had been knocked off course at the beginning of the real twentieth century by the First World War. In a political as well as a moral sense, however, the union was tentative. During the Cold War years, the Western nuclear powers (the United States, England, and France) did indeed learn the art of *Living with Nuclear Weapons*, in the title of the Harvard-sponsored book of 1983, but they had not taken the marriage vows. Reliance on nuclear arms was widely considered an extraordinary, provisional response to an extraordinary, provisional emergency: the threat, as many people in the West believed, to the freedom of the entire world by the Soviet Union, which, of course, soon developed nuclear arsenals of its own. The Soviet threat shaped the West's embrace of nuclear terror in two fundamental ways. First, it was placed in the moral scales opposite the nuclear threat, rendering the latter acceptable. The mere physical existence of humankind, many people believed, was worth risking for the sake of its moral and spiritual existence, represented by the survival of freedom. Second, most people were persuaded that the secretive nature of the Soviet regime ruled out effective inspection of radical nuclear arms control agreements, thus making full nuclear disarmament impossible. In 1946, when the United States put forward the Baruch Plan, which proposed the abolition of nuclear arms, the Soviet Union, now working at full tilt to develop its own bomb, turned it down. Historians still argue whether it was reasonable for the United States, already in possession of the bomb, to expect the Soviet Union, which did not yet possess the bomb, to close down its nuclear program as part of a global agreement to abolish nuclear weapons. However that may be, there is no doubt that the Soviet rejection of the Baruch Plan played an important role in the United States' understanding of its own moral and historical responsibility for the nuclear arms race that followed. The United States, Americans believed from 1946 on, had proved itself ready to eliminate nuclear weapons, but the Soviet Union stood in the way. The Soviet threat, in American eyes, thus both justified nuclear arms and placed an insuperable practical obstacle in the way of their abolition. As long as this appeared to be the case, the United States could regard itself as a reluctant threatener of nuclear destruction, merely forced into this unwelcome role by the character of the regimes it felt obliged to oppose.

The Future of Extermination: The Third and the Fourth Augusts

THE THIRD OF OUR AUGUSTS, in which the failed coup in Moscow brought on the collapse of the Soviet Union, dissolved this equation. The age of totalitarianism, which had opened in October of 1917, was over. The balancing factor in the moral equation that for almost fifty years had justified nuclear arsenals had fallen away. Would total war survive the loss of its linguistic and historical brother? Could the one exist without the goad of the other? Should nuclear weapons survive the end of the "short twentieth century," not to speak of the "end of history"? And if they did, had the century (the "real" one) or history really "ended"? This question, which has hung over the decade between the end of the proposed short twentieth century and its calendrical end, has acquired even greater urgency as we move into the next century and millennium.

At the beginning of this essay, I recalled the old Greek idea that because the end of a story can force us to rewrite its earlier chapters, we cannot know what the story is until it is over. No single narrative can or should attempt to encompass the history of an epoch, which contains a limitless variety of entwined tales; yet, as the concept of a real twentieth century suggests, the very choice of the dates that mark off one era from another means that certain stories lay special claim to our attention. It's already clear that it will be impossible to write the political history of the twentieth century without reference to the many-chaptered story of the century's policies of extermination, some of whose main chapter headings will surely be the three Augusts we have mentioned. The final shape of that story, however, will not be known until the arrival of that future date—some future August day, perhaps— on which the ultimate fortunes of the arms that were born in 1945 are decided. Interpretations of the real twentieth century now require not so much smarter interpreters as the world's decision whether, in the wake of the Cold War, it will reject nuclear weapons or once again embrace them. Let us, then, perform a thought experiment in which we try to imagine how the twentieth century will appear in retrospect, in light of two possible next chapters of the nuclear story. In the first, we will imagine that the next chapter is the last— that the world decides to eliminate nuclear weapons. In the second, we will imagine that the Cold War legacy of nuclear arms has been accepted and has led to their proliferation. Our glance, in the two cases, is not chiefly forward, to the world that lies ahead, but backward upon the century that has just ended.

In the event that abolition is embraced, we will find, I suggest, that what the American government said and the American public believed from 1946, when the Soviet Union rejected the Baruch Plan, until 1991, when the Soviet Union collapsed, was essentially true: that the policymakers were as dismayed by nuclear danger as ordinary people were; that in their minds the reason for enduring the risk of human extinction really had been the threat to freedom around the world posed by the Soviet Union; that the government would indeed have preferred to abolish nuclear weapons in 1946 but had been prevented by the Soviet Union; and that this was truly why, when the Soviet Union collapsed, the United States seized the opportunity to lead the world to nuclear abolition. We will, further, take seriously the often-repeated argument that "arms control" was an invaluable temporary holding action for reducing nuclear danger until political conditions were ripe for full nuclear disarmament. We will take even more seriously the arguments of those who held that it was not nuclear arms that fueled the political differences of the Cold War but the political differences of the Cold War that fueled the nuclear arms race, and who therefore argued against arms control. And then we will show how, precisely because the anti-Communism of the time had been authentic, Communism's end naturally opened the way to abolition of the arms that had protected us against Communism. We will be unsurprised to record that many of the Cold War's fiercest hawks had become abolitionists. And we will note with satisfaction how the example of these former hawks was emulated by hawks in other nations, including India, Pakistan, and Israel, who therefore agreed to relinquish their countries' nuclear weapons as part of the general settlement.

Even the evolution of high nuclear strategy, historians may go on to relate, will then seem to have been a slow education in the realities of the nuclear age, especially after the shock of the Cuban Missile Crisis in 1962, which left such a deep impression of the horror of nuclear war in the minds of later abolitionists, such as Robert McNamara. It will be the gratifying task of analysts to record how, even on the political right, the most militant believers in armed force slowly came around to an understanding that, in the words of Ronald Reagan, the most conservative president of the era, "nuclear war can never be won and must never be fought," and they will trace the path from that understanding to his discussion of nuclear abolition at the Reykjavik summit meeting of 1986 with the Soviet leader Mikhail Gorbachev.

Paralleling this slow evolution in thought, we will see, was the equally slow development in practice of the so-called tradition of nonuse, which gradually taught statesmen that even when they possessed a nuclear monopoly they could extract no military or political benefit from it and so did not use nuclear weapons after Nagasaki. In this story, acts of nuclear restraint—by the United States in Vietnam, by the Soviet Union in Afghanistan, by China in its border war with Vietnam in 1979—will have the place that battles have in bloodier narratives. The Cold War thus will be partially redeemed in our eyes as a vast laboratory in which, at the price of a few hair-raising close calls, the world learned through patient reflection and oblique experience that nuclear weapons were as futile as they were abhorrent and that they could and should be eliminated.

The lessons will go deeper still. When the last nuclear plutonium pit has been liquidated (or, more likely, adulterated and buried away in some deep cavern), we will see that the ground for nuclear disarmament had been prepared, on the one hand, by the peace movement in the West, and, on the other, by the movement against Soviet power by dissidents in the Soviet empire (two movements that at the time failed, on the whole, to grasp the common drift of their activity). The astounding success of the resistance movement in the East will emerge as the first stage in a global movement against not only Soviet terror but all terror—against not only totalitarianism but its close relative, total war—whose last stage will be the elimination of nuclear arms, thereby truly ending the spiral of violence that began in 1914.

The rise and fall of totalitarianism from start to finish will wear an altered aspect. It will turn out to have been a ghastly, protracted detour from the progress (the word itself might even gain new credit) and enlightenment offered by liberal civilization, which, although capsized in 1914 by the First World War, will have righted itself in 1991, bringing on an era of prosperity and peace. Then liberal civilization itself, freed of its complicity in the policies of extermination it adopted in 1945, will rest at last on a sure foundation. The political history of the twentieth century will thus be the story not only of the rise of policies of extermination in all their variety but also of the human recoil against them, leading, first, to the renewed rejection of totalitarianism and embrace of democracy in the 1990s and then, in the years following, to the abolition of nuclear weapons along with other weapons of mass destruction.

In the second thought experiment—in which we suppose that the nuclear powers have renewed their embrace of their nuclear arsenals in the post-Cold War period, setting the example for several other powers, and so installing nuclear weapons as a deep- and many-rooted structural feature of life in the twenty-first century—the political and military history of the twentieth century will have to be written very differently. To begin with, we will not be able to take so seriously the West's stated justifications for building nuclear arsenals. How will we continue to believe that the democratic nations endured the risk of human annihilation for the sake of human freedom when, with the threat to freedom gone, the threat of annihilation is preserved? How will we continue to say that the totalitarianism of the Soviet Union was the great obstacle to full disarmament when, with the Soviet Union collapsed and inviting full inspection and proposing full disarmament, the United States refused? Having discovered that the end of Communism left our will to possess nuclear arms intact, the old claim that in the Cold War we chose to risk being "dead" rather than going "Red" will ring hollow. The entire fifty-year confrontation between totalitarianism and democracy will shrink in importance as an explanatory factor. Our attention will be drawn instead to the ease with which the United States shifted its nuclear planning in 1945 from Germany to Japan, and then from Japan to the Soviet Union, and we will see this flexibility as a precedent for the much more drastic and shocking shift of targeting at the end of the Cold War from the Soviet Union to ... well, what? A few feeble "rogue" states, the mere possibility that Russia will again become an enemy of the United States?

We'll hardly be surprised to see that several nations outside the original nuclear "club" have followed the American example. As for arms control, it will be understood as just one of the means by which public anxiety about the nuclear danger was put to sleep. Our policy of nonproliferation will seem to have been half-hearted, since it will have been shown that we preferred to permit the whole world to acquire nuclear arms than to give up our own.

The process of education that occurred during the Cold War will seem to be the opposite of what it would have seemed had we abolished nuclear weapons: one not of deepening understanding of the horror and futility of the arsenals but of simply getting used to them in preparation for accepting them fully and without reservation as a normal instrument of national policy, of learning to "stop worrying and love the bomb," in the words of the subtitle to the movie *Dr Strangelove*, which will have lost their ironic connotations.

A graver suspicion will be confirmed: that the United States and its nuclear allies did not build nuclear weapons chiefly in order to face extraordinary danger, whether from Germany, Japan, or the Soviet Union, but for more deep-seated, unarticulated reasons growing out of its own, freely chosen conceptions of national security. Nuclear arsenals will seem to have been less a response to any particular external threat, totalitarian or otherwise, than an intrinsic element of the dominant liberal civilization itself—an evil that first grew and still grows from within that civilization rather than being imposed from without. And then we will have to remember that the seminal event of the real twentieth century, the First World War, sprang in all its pointless slaughter and destructive fury from the midst of that same liberal civilization, and we will have to ask what it is in the makeup of liberalism that pushes it again and again, even at the moment of its greatest triumphs, into an abyss of its own making.

Our understanding of the historical place of totalitarianism will likewise change. Instead of seeming a protracted bloody hiatus between the eclipse of liberal civilization of 1914 and its restoration in 1991, totalitarianism will appear to have been a harsh and effective tutor to liberalism, which was its apt pupil. The degree of moral separation from the tradition of extermination that was maintained during the Cold War will have disappeared. If we look at nuclear arms as a lethal virus that spreads by contagion around the world, then totalitarianism in this picture of events becomes a sort of filthy syringe with which the dominant liberal civilization managed to inject the illness into its bloodstream, where it remained even after, in 1991, the syringe was thrown away. Liberalism will itself have unequivocally embraced extermination.

AT STAKE IS THE VERY CHARACTER of the victorious civilization that in the twentieth century buried its two greatest totalitarian antagonists and now bids to set the tone and direction of international life in the century ahead. Will it shake off the twentieth century's legacy of terror or, by embracing nuclear weapons even in the absence of totalitarian threat, incorporate that legacy into itself? Will we find that protecting civilization is unimaginable without threatening extermination? If so, a critical watershed will have been crossed, and we will have passed, by default, from a period in which an extraordinary peril, such as the Soviet threat, seemed needed to justify the extraordinary peril of nuclear arms to a period in which the quotidian fears, jealousies, ambitions, and hatreds that are always with us are found to be justification enough. At that moment, a nuclear arsenal will cease to be felt as Conrad's "dishonoring necessity" and become a fully legitimized voluntary component of the state: a permanent sub-basement, or catacomb, on which the fairer upper floors of civilization—the freedom, the democracy, the prosperity—rest. But if this happens, can liberalism itself survive, or will it in the long run find itself sucked, as in 1914, into a vortex of its own making that it cannot stop? Nuclear arsenals do not exist in isolation from the rest of politics, and no single policy, whether regarding these arms or anything else, can decide the character of the century that has just begun. Nor will a decision to abolish nuclear weapons even put an end to the legacy of extermination that disfigured the century that has just ended. The deeds of Pol Pot in Cambodia and of the former Hutu government in Rwanda have made it clear that genocide remains attractive and achievable for many governments in many parts of the world. No nuclear weapons or other weapons of mass destruction are needed to bring it off; Kalashnikovs, or even machetes or hoes, will do. What seems clear, however, is that if the triumphantly restored liberal order of the 1990s cannot renounce the threat of extermination of peoples as a condition for its own survival, then it will forfeit any chance that it can successfully oppose a resurgence of barbarism anywhere else in the twenty-first century. We will be unable to say that any year—whether 1991 or 2000 or 2050—has undone 1914 until we have also undone

1945. More than any other decision before us, this one will decide who we are, who we are to be, and who, when the last line of the story of the real twentieth century is truly written, we will have been.

The Pitiless Crowbar of Events

IT OFTEN HAPPENS THAT HISTORY places before the world a problem whose solution lies outside the bounds of contemporary political acceptability. Such was the case, for example, in the 1930s, when the rise of Hitler posed a threat to the European democracies which they lacked the resolve to face. To check Nazi aggression, most historians now agree, the democracies would have had to oppose it early and resolutely, as Winston Churchill advocated. But Churchill's prescriptions were beyond the pale of mainstream political thinking at the time, and he was forced "into the wilderness," as he famously put it. Not until the late 1930s did his ideas win political acceptance, and by then the price of stopping Hitler was the Second World War. The American war in Vietnam in the 1960s offers another example. In retrospect, it seems clear that among the many outcomes under discussion at the time, only two were really possible. One was war without end—the open, unlimited occupation of Vietnam by American forces. The other was withdrawal and defeat. But the political costs of either—on the one hand, of frankly imposing American rule on that country for an indefinite period; on the other, of "losing" Vietnam—were considered prohibitive. Deception and self-deception abounded on all sides. Those who opposed the war counseled withdrawal, but usually without admitting that this meant defeat. Those who supported the war pretended that victory was near—that light was dawning at the end of the proverbial tunnel. Only temporizing, middling policies—first, surreptitious escalation, then "Vietnamization"—which postponed the hard choice were within political bounds. The price was paid by the people of Vietnam and the United States.

A contrast is often drawn between idealistic and realistic policies. But the choices posed by Hitler's rise and the Vietnam War were different. They were between political realism—bound hand and foot by a conventional wisdom out of touch with events—and the reality of those events, which we might call circumstantial reality. The nuclear predicament in the post-Cold War period presents the United States and the world with a choice of this kind. Once again, political reality and circumstantial reality—what Aleksandr Solzhenitsyn called the "pitiless crowbar of events"—are in collision. The real alternatives—the ones that can actually occur—are at present found politically unacceptable, while the politically acceptable choices are all unreal.

These real alternatives, I shall argue, are, on the one hand, the unrestricted proliferation of nuclear weapons—leading to what the late nuclear theorist Albert Wohlstetter some time ago called a "nuclear-armed crowd" and what Harvard's Graham Allison has more recently called "nuclear anarchy"—and, on the other, the abolition of nuclear weapons by international agreement. The current American policy is to try to stop proliferation while simultaneously continuing to hold on to its own nuclear arsenal indefinitely. But these objectives are contradictory. The policy based on them is the equivalent—in the context of the nuclear dilemma as it exists at the opening of the twenty-first century—of appeasement in the 1930s and surreptitious escalation and Vietnamization in the late 1960s and early 1970s. It is a policy that conceals and defers the real decisions that need to be made. To govern is to choose. The current policy is a way of avoiding choice—a policy without traction in the world as it really is. Meanwhile, as in the earlier dilemmas, both the danger and the cost of dealing with it mount. For in the absence of a decision, events are drifting toward one of the real possible outcomes, namely, uncontrolled proliferation. In politics as in physics, entropy is a recipe for anarchy.

The Crisis of Arms Control

THE RISE IN NUCLEAR DANGER is already apparent in an across-the-board crisis that has developed in the last several years in the regime of nuclear arms control. The fabric of nuclear arms control is woven of four main strands, each the product of decades of negotiation. These were not conceived as parts of a grand design, yet over time they came to possess a certain coherence. The first strand is the Moscow–Washington negotiations to reduce the twin mountains of offensive nuclear weapons built up during the Cold War. Its accomplishments are the Strategic Arms Limitation Treaty (SALT), the Strategic Arms Reductions Treaties (START I and II). The second strand, which is closely entwined with the first, is the attempt to rein in defensive antinuclear systems. Its centerpiece is the Anti-Ballistic Missile (ABM) Treaty of 1972, in which the United States and the Soviet Union each agreed to field no more than one limited-range antinuclear missile system. Defensive limits are essential for offensive limits because a defensive buildup can upset any negotiated offensive balance. The third strand is the nuclear Nonproliferation Treaty (NPT), perhaps the most impressive and successful arms control treaty ever negotiated and the foundation-stone of any hope for nuclear sanity in the post-Cold War world. Under its provisions, two classes of nations were created—nations without nuclear weapons that agreed to forgo them, and nations that possessed them and were permitted, for a time, to go on possessing them. Today, 182 nations have ratified the NPT as non-nuclear powers, in return for which they have been given access to certain technology for nuclear energy, while five countries—the United States, Russia, China, the United Kingdom, and

France—belong to the NPT as nuclear powers. Four countries remain outside the treaty. Three of them—Israel, India, and Pakistan—have nuclear weapons, and one—Cuba—does not. The NPT does not, however, envision a permanent two-tier system of nuclear haves and have-nots. The nuclear powers are committed under the treaty's Article VI to "pursue negotiations in good faith on effective measures relating to cessation of the nuclear arms race at an early date and to nuclear disarmament, and on a treaty on general and complete disarmament under strict and effective international control." (Nuclear abolitionists like to emphasize the commitment to full nuclear disarmament, while their opponents like to emphasize the commitment to general and complete disarmament, since this makes the commitment in the nuclear sphere seem distant and unrealistic.) At the NPT review conference in 2000, the nuclear powers reaffirmed their commitments under Article VI in unusually clear language, stating their "unequivocal ... commitment" to the elimination of nuclear weapons. The fourth strand is the test ban negotiations—the grandfather of arms control measures, dating from the Eisenhower administration. Like the NPT, to which they are a crucial adjunct, the test ban talks are global. The Atmospheric Test Ban was signed and ratified in 1963. Its successor, the Comprehensive Test Ban Treaty (CTBT), would slow arms races since testing is considered necessary for many kinds of nuclear arms innovations. Companion efforts are the negotiations to ban the production of fissionable materials, the negotiations to tighten restrictions on the spread of missile technology, and the calls to take nuclear weapons off of alert status.

When the Cold War ended, the prospects for a steady strengthening of all four of these main strands of nuclear arms control looked better than at any time since Bernard Baruch had presented the Acheson-Lillienthal plan for the abolition of nuclear weapons to the United Nations in 1946. The global conflict between the Soviet Union and the Western democracies had seemed to be the main political engine propelling the nuclear arms race for four decades, and the collapse of the Soviet Union in 1991 promised a sharp decline in nuclear danger—the more so as no new global political struggle arose to take the Cold War's place. The mere relaxation of the struggle under Mikhail Gorbachev had given new impetus to START. In the Intermediate-range Nuclear Forces (INF) Treaty signed in 1987, all intermediate-range missiles were banned from the European theater, and under the 1991 START I agreement, strategic warheads were to be reduced to about 7,000 on each side. The START II agreement, which would reduce strategic warheads to 3,000–3,500 on each side, was signed in 1992, and the outlook for early ratification by both sides appeared favorable. The number of countries that had signed the NPT was steadily rising. A positive synergy among the different strands of negotiation seemed to be at work. Success in START and the CTBT promised to secure and strengthen the NPT bargain; a comprehensive test ban would help put a lid on proliferation; and an end to proliferation would encourage the nuclear powers to relinquish their arsenals. The convention banning biological weapons and the negotiations to found a convention banning chemical weapons (ratified by the Senate in 1998) suggested that the world was turning slowly but surely against weapons of mass destruction in general. Above all, the direction seemed right. Taken in their entirety, the world's nuclear arsenals seemed to be caught in a tightening net of treaties and agreements that, if they did not end nuclear danger altogether, would certainly reduce it radically. Nuclear weapons began to look like a thing of the past, and they all but disappeared from public consciousness.

As the new century begins, this hopeful direction of events has clearly reversed. The net of restrictions is rending, and nuclear danger is growing again. India conducted five tests in May of 1998, and Pakistan responded with seven, producing the world's first nuclear confrontation entirely unrelated to the Cold War. In the summer of 1999, an official commission in India, borrowing a leaf from the American playbook of the 1960s, recommended the creation and deployment of a deterrent arsenal based on a triad of forces delivering nuclear bombs from air, land, and sea. North Korea has engaged in on-again, off-again efforts to build nuclear weapons and missiles for their delivery. Saddam Hussein of Iraq, who was forced after the Gulf War of 1991 to endure the presence of UN weapons inspectors, has thrown them out. In 2000, the CIA reported that it was unable to assure Americans that Iran did not already have the wherewithal for building nuclear weapons. If either Iraq or Iran, or both, build nuclear weapons, the Middle East will join South Asia as a region in which a new nuclear arms race has arisen. (In considering proliferation, it is as important to consider the number of nuclear confrontations as to consider the number of nuclear powers. For example, when India declared itself a nuclear power, it placed itself explicitly in competition with China as well as Pakistan, adding two new hostile nuclear relationships to the world.) If this happens, Egypt may not be able to resist the temptation to nuclearize, and that could place the survival of the NPT as a whole at risk. The weapons programs in North Korea, Iraq, and Iran alarmed the United States, which now seeks to deploy an antinuclear national missile defense (NMD) as soon as technically feasible, placing the ABM treaty in jeopardy. The United States has asked Russia to amend the treaty to permit the deployment of NMD, but Russia has refused, on the ground that NMD would destabilize the offensive nuclear arms balance. The threat to the ABM treaty in turn threatens START II, whose implementation has been conditioned by Russia on the ABM treaty's integrity. A deployment of antimissile defenses in Taiwan or Japan, which the United States has discussed with those countries, could lead China to build up its offensive arms. Even the United States' closest allies, the principal members of NATO, are alarmed by the unilateral character of the American decision to deploy defenses when ready. They fear not only that the missile deployment will revive arms races with Russia and China but that the United States, feeling safe behind its shield, will leave Europe to face the renewed danger alone.

Meanwhile, they also fear that it will be the stalking horse for the weoponization of space. The danger increases that not merely governments but terrorist groups may obtain and use one or more nuclear weapons. Finally, in 1999, the American Senate voted down the CTBT.

The full extent of the jeopardy of arms control does not appear, however, until the interrelationships between these reverses are considered. A global drama, in which decisions regarding nuclear arms in any part of the world touches off cascades of consequences throughout the world, is unfolding. Does North Korea fires a ballistic missile over Japan and into the Pacific Ocean, as it did in 1998? Forthwith, the Senate votes to deploy NMD, even though it has not yet been shown to be technically feasible, and the administration announces that it will not be stopped from deployment by objections from Russia, which then draws back from implementing START II. (The US–Russia negotiations are further complicated by severe budgetary constraints in Russia, which may force her to reduce her strategic nuclear arsenal with or without agreements.) These reverses, of course, place new stress on the NPT, whose indefinite renewal in 1995 and 2000 was explicitly conditioned on progress in nuclear disarmament and ratification of the CTBT. Meanwhile, Japan, also alarmed by the North Korean missile test, agrees to share in the expense of developing a missile defense system, leading China to announce that if Japan (or Taiwan) should deploy such defenses, it might have to engage in an offensive buildup— something it may be in a better position to do thanks to its reported theft of American nuclear secrets pertaining to warhead miniaturization, which is a prerequisite for mounting several warheads on a single missile. That threat, of course, alarms India, which is at work on long-range missiles, and also buttresses the American decision to build national missile defense, and so forth. In short, a single missile test by a small, poverty-stricken nation touches off a string of consequences that tends to destabilize almost every aspect of the global nuclear arms control regime. Does Saddam Hussein drive out the UN inspection team that was overseeing the destruction of his programs of weapons of mass destruction? Before long, the United States Senate, alarmed by this and other breakdowns of nonproliferation, rejects the Comprehensive Test Ban, which in turn of course further reduces the pressure on other nations to hold fast in their renunciation of nuclear arms. Promptly, Pakistan does likewise. The US then imposes sanctions on both, but, before long, all but abandons them in favor of "engagement." Meanwhile, China discovers in the Indian build-up, which includes development of the Agni long-range missile capable of striking China, one more reason to modernize its nuclear forces. That threat, of course, alarms India, which is at work on long-range missiles, and buttresses the American decision to build NMD—and so forth.

Complex as these interactions are, they are governed by two extremely simple rules. Any development anywhere of nuclear weapons or their delivery vehicles creates pressure to do likewise throughout what is now a seamless global web of actions and reactions. No longer does an act of nuclear escalation, or the breakdown of a restraint, affect only a nearby adversary or two; its repercussions are felt around the world. Conversely, any reversal in nuclear armament or act of restraint encourages such acts elsewhere. The separation that existed during the Cold War between the bipolar nuclear balance on the one hand and proliferation on the other has been erased. The nations that had nuclear weapons during the Cold War and still have them, the nations that have developed them since, the nations that now are seeking to develop them, and the nations that renounced them during the Cold War and still renounce them find themselves on a single, indivisible playing field. Over them all hangs a momentous question: Shall the world as a whole go nuclear or shall it abolish nuclear arms?

THE STARTLING FACT IS THAT nuclear arms control is faring worse in a world without the Soviet Union than it did in the last days of the Cold War. Then, nuclear danger seemed to be declining. Now, it is on the rise. Then, nuclear arms control agreements were progressing. Now, they are at a stalemate or in danger of unraveling. How has this come about? Why has the end of the global conflict in whose name the great nuclear arsenals were built proved worse for nuclear disarmament than the conflict itself?

Several new adverse forces are at work. One is simply the ever-increasing availability of nuclear technology. By convention, the word "proliferation" refers to the actual acquisition of nuclear weapons. However, there is a sort of proliferation that falls short of this but is still highly significant. This is the proliferation of the basic scientific and technical capabilities on which the construction of nuclear arms is based. By nuclear capacity, I mean a country's ability, once it had made the decision, to produce nuclear weapons within a definite time. Sweden, for example, possesses a nuclear capacity in this sense, though it has no will to build nuclear bombs. Libya, on the other hand, has the will but not the capacity. That this sort of unrealized capacity would proliferate far beyond the number of countries that actually possess nuclear arms was inherent in the nature of nuclear weapons—which are based, of course, on scientific knowledge, which by nature tends to spread. In the early 1940s, for example, only one nation possessed unrealized capacity in this sense: the United States. That is to say, although it had not yet built a bomb, there was every reason to believe that its decision to do so would bear fruit. Today, many dozens of nations have such a capacity. The State Department puts their current number at forty-four and, in negotiating the now-rejected CTBT, required that it not come into force until all forty-four of them had ratified it. Nuclear technology is old technology. We are in the fifty-sixth year of the nuclear age. The secret of the bomb is out; it has been published in magazines. The same holds true for missile technology and chemical and biological weapons technology.

If we think of the NPT as a dam holding back nuclear proliferation, then the spread of nuclear capacity is like water collecting behind the dam. That tide can only rise, increasing the pressure. Within a few decades, most of the nations on earth probably will possess this unrealized capacity. A conclusion follows. If the spread of nuclear weapons is to be prevented over the long run, it cannot come through restrictions on nations' capacity. Instead, it must come by influencing their will, which entails the use of diplomatic and political means—the very means whose breakdown we are now witnessing. The world's safety ultimately depends not on the number of nations that want to build nuclear weapons but cannot, but on the number that can but decide not to.

A second new adverse element is the rise of antinuclear defensive technology. Antinuclear defenses have long been the wild card of nuclear policy, generating almost nonstop intellectual confusion and popular misunderstanding. Most people's visceral response to the idea of defenses in general is positive. The first duty of government is to preserve its citizens' lives, and defenses promise this. The doctrine of nuclear deterrence stood this commonsense appraisal on its head. Under that doctrine, safety depends on the absolute and unchallenged capacity of each side to annihilate the other's population—a capacity that, when recognized by all, is meant to prevent nuclear war from breaking out in the first place. By eroding this vulnerability, defenses destabilize deterrence. Furthermore, they fuel offensive-arms buildups, since a nation whose offensive power is eroded by defenses is likely to try to restore it by building up its offenses. That was why the first achievement of the Strategic Arms Limitation talks was the treaty banning all but one antiballistic missile system on each side. However sound this reasoning may have been—at least as an adjunct to the deterrence doctrine—the general public probably never grasped it. That may be why President Reagan's proposal for a Strategic Defense Initiative in the 1980s, although technically infeasible, enjoyed such wide popular support, and why national missile defense enjoys much support today.

The demise of the Soviet Union added fresh layers of confusion to this already bewildering situation. After the extraordinary expenditure since the early 1980s of some sixty billion dollars, national missile defense, in one form or another, may have drawn closer to technical realization, though none as yet has been demonstrated to be technically workable. Its goal, now, is to defend not against Moscow but against the handful of missiles that might be fired by a North Korea or an Iran or some other "rogue" state. Russia, however, regards the system as a threat to its "deterrent" power to annihilate the United States, and is protesting. Russia, far inferior to the United States both technically and financially, has no capacity to match the United States in building defenses. For antinuclear defenses are not, like nuclear bombs, old technology; they are brand new. (Indeed they are so new that they cannot properly be said to exist yet, and recent antimissile tests have been embarrassing failures.) Only one nation in the world—the United States—has the technical and financial capacity to even attempt to develop them in the foreseeable future. If, however, the United States does prove capable of building them, it will be in the position it was in with respect to nuclear weapons in 1943 or 1944—a potential monopoly position—and monopolies, almost by nature, destabilize military balances. Two caveats, however, are necessary. First, it is much more likely today that the defensive technology will still be unavailable in, say, four years, than it was likely in 1941 that the nuclear bomb would be a failure. That is, it's not yet clear that the whole development will not fall of its own weight. The second caveat is that in a radically altered context, defenses, if they are ever proven workable, would not be a disruptive element. In a world on its way to the abolition of nuclear weapons, in which no offensive buildup threatened, defenses could play a reassuring, positive role. Nations that had surrendered nuclear weapons would wish to have insurance against cheating by other nations, and antinuclear defenses, in this context, could help to provide it. When it comes to judging missile defense, context is all. In the absence of negotiated agreements that are pushing offensive nuclear weapons in the direction of zero, missile defense is a supreme folly. As an accompaniment to such agreements, it would make sense.

As important as both the spread of nuclear capacity or the invention of antinuclear defenses is a third adverse element: the decision by the nuclear powers to retain their Cold War nuclear arsenals even in the absence of the Cold War. If I carry a rifle on my shoulder during a war, it means one thing. If I continue to carry the rifle after the war has ended, it means something very different. When the Cold

War ended, the United States merely continued with the policy of nuclear deterrence of the Soviet Union/Russia, accompanied by negotiated reductions. Yet this continuation—this doing nothing—constituted one of the most important decisions of the nuclear age. It quietly set a standard for the post-Cold War period.

The negotiated nuclear reductions have now approached the levels specified in START I, which was negotiated mostly with the now-defunct Soviet Union, and implementation of START II is uncertain. Under President Clinton, the United States, though paying occasional lip service to full nuclear disarmament, insisted in its negotiations for a START III agreement on a lower limit of 2,500 nuclear weapons. Since no START IV has yet been discussed, the figure of 2,500 nuclear weapons represents the lowest negotiated level to which the United States has, so far, been willing to reduce its arsenal. At the same time, Clinton officials declared their intention to hold on to that arsenal indefinitely. President George W. Bush has expressed a willingness to go somewhat lower—perhaps to 1,500 warheads. But he, too, sees a role for offensive nuclear arsenals for the indefinite future. He proposes to add missile defenses to nuclear offense, not replace the latter with the former. In sum, as a matter of actual post-Cold War policy, the United States has consistently declared its intention to remain in a condition of mutual deterrence with Russia—to preserve the capacity of each side to annihilate the other. As Undersecretary of Defense Walter Slocombe explained, "A key conclusion of the administration's national security strategy is

[that] the United States will retain strategic nuclear forces sufficient to deter any future hostile foreign leadership with access to strategic nuclear forces from action against our vital interests and to convince it that seeking nuclear advantage would be futile."

DETERRENCE IS, OF COURSE, an old policy—a carryover from the Cold War. The argument put forward by the United States has been that because deterrence worked during the Cold War, it will still work today, and should not be abandoned. However, a nuclear arsenal built in a particular historic era to oppose a great and feared enemy possessing a like arsenal is something very different from one lacking any such purpose. Its moral, political, and military meaning are different, and its influence upon the world is different.

Whatever one thought about nuclear arms during the Cold War, it did not necessarily follow that because Moscow and Washington had them, everyone else should, too. The double standard provisionally built into the NPT, although obviously inequitable, could be understood. Once the Soviet Union disappeared, however, the foundations of the argument shifted. The Cold War was a special circumstance irrefutably different from any other struggle on earth. Now it appears that the Western nuclear powers believe that no special circumstance is needed to justify nuclear arms. The United States is less threatened militarily than any other nation, but it insists on retaining nuclear arsenals and has switched its first-use policy from its old Cold War rival to what some policymakers called the "generic" target of merely potential dangers that might arise somewhere in the world.

This shift in rationale has been accompanied by a shift in the arsenal's global influence. The American nuclear arsenal is often referred to simply as "our deterrent." But does anyone today seriously maintain that Russia has any thought whatsoever of launching a nuclear strike against the United States and is stopped only by a fear of US retaliation? On the other hand, can anyone doubt that these arsenals, both Russian and American, are a significant goad to proliferation—that they serve, in the words of Indian Foreign Minister Jaswant Singh, as a "nuclear paradigm" emulated by other powers?

Proliferance

IN THESE CIRCUMSTANCES, there is much more reason to call the American arsenal a "proliferant" than to call it a deterrent. This is not mere word-juggling. A central lesson of deterrence theory is that the psychological effects of nuclear arms are as important as the physical ones. According to the theory, deterrence "works" when the leaderships on both sides of a nuclear standoff so deeply fear the other side's retaliation that they do not dare to strike in the first place. If the weapons are ever used, deterrence has by definition failed. What we may call "proliferance," too, is a psychological effect of nuclear weapons. Proliferance occurs when a country, fearful of a neighbor's nuclear arsenals (and in the age of the intercontinental ballistic missile, who is not, for these purposes, a neighbor?), builds one in response. The difference between deterrence and proliferance is that whereas deterrence stops nations that possess nuclear arsenals from using them, proliferance inspires nations that lack them to get them. In a sense, therefore, the two effects arrive at a common destination: the possession—but not, it is hoped, the use—of nuclear weapons.

Any number of American politicians have stated that nuclear proliferation is the greatest threat to the security of the United States today. In the post-Cold War world, the effects of proliferance are much easier to demonstrate than those of deterrence. Proliferance led India—looking over the Himalayas to China, and beyond China to Russia and the United States—to turn itself into a nuclear power, and proliferance goaded Pakistan to promptly conduct its own nuclear tests. This influence acts both by example (the "nuclear paradigm" cited by Singh) and, even more powerfully, through the direct influence of the terror that is the chief product of nuclear arsenals.

Indeed, the proliferant influence of nuclear terror has been in operation since the earliest days of the nuclear age. The clear lesson of history is that nuclear arsenals breed nuclear arsenals. Even the United States—the first nation to build the bomb—did so, in a sense, reactively. Franklin Roosevelt and his advisers were worried that Hitler would get the bomb first. (If there has ever been a good reason for building nuclear weapons, preventing Hitler from having a monopoly on them in the midst of a world war was it.) The Soviet Union then built the bomb in response to the United States; China built it in response to both the United States and Russia; India built it in response to China; and Pakistan built it in response to India. (The cases of the United Kingdom and France, which already enjoyed some protection from the US nuclear umbrella, are less clear. Sheer national prestige appears to have been as important as any immediate security risks. Another, murkier case is Israel, which, like the United States in 1945, built its arsenal preemptively but also sought to counter conventional threats from its Arab enemies and deter them from ever dreaming of overrunning it.) Every nuclear arsenal is linked to every other nuclear arsenal in the world by these powerful ties of terror and response. And when the list of nuclear powers grows, the country in question—Iraq? Iran? North Korea? Egypt?—will probably have been inspired by the fear of some nuclear-armed foe. Deterrence is, in fact, the codification and institutionalization of this reactive cycle. Indeed, deterrence teaches that the way to avoid destruction by a rival is to possess nuclear weapons yourself. If this is not an invitation to proliferation, what would be?

Whereas in the Cold War, deterrence was the dominant effect, now proliferance is. Consider the increasing danger of nuclear terrorism. The continued possession by many nations of nuclear arms makes the diversion of nuclear materials or weapons into the hands of terrorist groups more likely. But terrorists, having no nation to lose, cannot be "deterred" by the threat of retaliation. In their case, the proliferant effect of nuclear arsenals is all, the deterrent effect nil. Conversely, the only policy that can seriously hope sharply to reduce (although not entirely eliminate) the danger of nuclear terrorism is abolition, because abolition alone can impose comprehensive global prohibitions on nuclear weapon technology.

The Evolution of Strategy

IN THIS SCENE OF GROWING NUCLEAR DANGER, no single actor, of course, is solely to blame. It is the essence of the new situation that the number of actors on the nuclear stage is growing. India, for example, bears a clear responsibility for nuclearizing South Asia with its May 1998 tests. But by signaling that the earth would remain nuclearized indefinitely even after the Cold War, Washington, Moscow, and Beijing also plainly incurred responsibility. If in the early 1990s the existing nuclear powers had committed themselves to the elimination of nuclear weapons and had by 1998 traveled some of the distance to that goal, it is hard to believe that South Asia would be engaged in a nuclear arms race today.

If, however, we invert the question and, instead of asking who is to blame for the crisis of arms control, ask which country has the greatest power to tackle the crisis, our attention must turn to the United States. Whether the situation can be retrieved at all remains an open question. But without American leadership, any effort must fail. The question of why the United States plans to hold on to its nuclear arsenal indefinitely is, accordingly, highly important. The answer must be sought at many levels—the moral, the psychological, and the cultural, as well as the political and the military—yet because of the dominant influence of the strategists in preserving the continuity of policy as the Cold War ended, the importance of nuclear strategic doctrine cannot be overlooked.

Four stages in the development of strategic thinking about nuclear abolition can be distinguished. In the first, American policy sought to head off a nuclear arms race by negotiating the abolition of nuclear weapons. In 1946, President Truman's representative for nuclear disarmament to the United Nations, Bernard Baruch, proposed that all nuclear weapons be eliminated and all nuclear technology placed under an international authority. In retrospect, the plan never had much chance. The Soviet Union was well into its own project to build the bomb (thanks in good measure to its outstanding spying on the American effort), and Stalin, according to the historian David Holloway, had no wish to barter away the Soviet Union's capacity to match the United States achievement. Former National Security Adviser McGeorge Bundy was probably right when, after examining the abolition proposals of that time, he concluded, "The bitter truth is ... that what we have just reviewed was not at any time a serious negotiation on either side."

In the second stage of the evolution of nuclear policy—

during the late 1950s and the early 1960s, after both powers had developed not only atomic bombs but hydrogen bombs as well—the earlier obstacles to full nuclear disarmament were, increasingly, publicly acknowledged as insurmountable. It was no longer enough, even politically, to make fine-sounding proposals for abolition that everyone knew must fail. So if nuclear disarmament was impossible, nuclear arsenals would have to be accepted for at least as long as the struggle with the Soviet Union lasted. The strategic form that that acceptance took was the doctrine of nuclear deterrence, with its teaching that the way to avoid nuclear war is to strike a nuclear balance.

In this new nuclear dispensation, there was still a role for nuclear disarmament. Its goals, however, would be different from what they had been in the time of Baruch. Instead of aiming for abolition, negotiations would seek to "stabilize" the nuclear stalemate. Accepting the inevitability of nuclear possession, these negotiations sought to diminish the possibility of use in two ways. First, they would mutually restrict the development of "first-strike" forces, which otherwise might tempt one side or the other to launch a nuclear war. Second, they would place a numerical, mutually agreed-upon cap on offensive nuclear weapons.

The negotiations based on these principles were called arms control, as distinct from nuclear disarmament. The shift was presented as a victory for realism, in which the surrender of the unachievable goal of abolition prepared the ground for the more modest and achievable goals of limiting and stabilizing the nuclear balance of terror. In practice, however, the modest goals proved almost as elusive as abolition had been. For one thing, the temptation to build first-strike forces regularly got the better of the hope for stability. Each side habitually saw itself as lagging behind. Cries of alarm and appeals to catch up—to close a "bomber gap," a "missile gap," a "throw-weight gap," a "window of vulnerability"—sounded through the halls of Congress as well as the hidden precincts of the Politburo. Nuclear terror, it turned out, was harder to control than theory had predicted. The hope for stability coexisted uneasily at best with the readiness for prompt mutual annihilation, and the very terror that was the mothers' milk of deterrence spawned nightmares that tended constantly to upset the whole arrangement. In the words of Yale's Paul Bracken, "Once the two sides understood the mechanism of deterrence, there would appear to have been little reason to keep piling up additional weapons. But that is exactly what happened: just as deterrence stabilized in the late 1960s, each side began a huge building program." Not until Gorbachev came to power and the Cold War began to wind down did significant reductions occur.

As the doctrine of deterrence became entrenched in official circles, attitudes toward nuclear disarmament underwent a subtle but deep transition. During the first two decades of the Cold War, the most intractable obstacles to abolition, in American eyes, stemmed from the totalitarian character of the Soviet Union, which both posed the global threat that justified nuclear arms and, owing to its extreme secretiveness, ruled out the kind of inspections essential to a reliable nuclear disarmament agreement. Over time, however, the particular reference to the Soviet Union as the obstacle to abolition began to give way to considerations of a more general character. Let us call the arguments based on the nature of the Soviet Union the limited theory of the impossibility of nuclear disarmament. In the new explanation, which we might call the general theory of the impossibility of nuclear disarmament, it was not particular problems caused by Soviet totalitarianism that were cited, but a set of difficulties seen as intrinsic to the nuclear dilemma, whatever regimes might be involved. Nations in general, the argument now ran, would be able to cheat on any abolition agreement; they would have good reason to cheat; they would cheat; and then they would use their sudden nuclear monopoly to bully the world.

In this more generalized view, the very fact that nuclear weapons had been invented was reason enough to believe that they could not be eliminated as long as lambs declined to lie down with lions. For even if the nuclear hardware were destroyed, the know-how would remain in people's minds, and someone would build them again. These views were expressed, to give one prominent example, in *Living with Nuclear Weapons*, which posed the question, "Why not abolish nuclear weapons?" and answered simply, "Because we cannot," explaining that "mankind's nuclear innocence, once lost, cannot be regained." In these circumstances—now regarded as immutable—abolition was seen not so much as difficult to achieve but as actually undesirable. A world free of nuclear weapons was intrinsically a less safe, less stable place than a world armed with nuclear weapons. In the words of *Living with Nuclear Weapons*, "If the political pre-conditions of trust and consensus are missing, complete disarmament is inherently unstable. In a disarmed world, the first nation to acquire a few arms would be able to influence events to a much greater extent than it could in a heavily armed world. Nuclear weapons greatly magnify this effect."

As this general theory of the impossibility of nuclear disarmament won official acceptance, a change in the valuation of nuclear weapons occurred. The deeper, less qualified embrace of deterrence (and of the nuclear arsenals the doctrine justified) opened the way to the idea that nuclear weapons, instead of being a necessary evil, were a positive benefit to the world—not so much a problem as a solution. They provided, thanks to the policy of deterrence, the only imaginable solution to themselves: they prevented nuclear war. Moreover, they prevented even conventional war—no mean achievement, considering what two world wars had done to the globe in the twentieth century.

There matters stood when the Cold War ended, opening a third stage in the development of American strategy. If the limited doctrine of the impossibility of nuclear disarmament had prevailed in the conventional wisdom, the policymakers might have reasoned as follows: We built up nuclear arsenals to contain the Soviet Union, whose secretive character stood in the way of nuclear disarmament, but now, with the Soviet Union gone, should we not consider the abolition of these weapons? If in 1946 the Soviet regime had been like the one in Moscow today, wouldn't Baruch's plan have had every chance of acceptance? Shouldn't something like it be possible today?

Unfortunately, what prevailed in the conventional wisdom was not the limited theory of the impossibility of nuclear disarmament but the general theory, and this has dictated a very nearly opposite response to the one sketched above. Nuclear deterrence, the policymakers said, worked during the Cold War; abolition, owing to the intrinsic nature of the nuclear dilemma, remained impossible; therefore the sensible course was to hold on to nuclear arsenals (albeit at reduced levels, in recognition of the improved political climate). Such was the conclusion of the "bottom-up" review of nuclear policy carried out in the early 1990s by the Clinton administration. Instead of saying to themselves, "During the protracted emergency that was the Cold War, we made a calculated gamble with the survival of the human race in the name of its freedom and were lucky enough to have survived to tell the story," the policymakers in effect said, "During the Cold War, we perfected a confidence-inspiring system for the management of nuclear weapons that should serve as our model for any future contingency." If deterrence, road-tested during the great US–Soviet conflict, was a proven success, then why give it up now? Didn't "the long peace" of the Cold War demonstrate that the world was better off with nuclear weapons than without them? In Undersecretary of Defense Slocombe's words, "It is a remarkable fact that for almost half a century, the US and its allies faced the USSR and its coerced auxiliaries in the division over ideology, power, culture, and the very definition of man, the state, and the world, and did so armed to the greatest extent huge sacrifice would afford, and yet did not fight a large-scale war. No one can say for sure why that success was achieved for long enough for communism to collapse of its own internal weakness. But can anyone really doubt that nuclear weapons had a role?"

Thus, at just the moment that a revolution in the international sphere seemed to call for a full-scale reappraisal of nuclear policy, the previous policy was reaffirmed with fewer reservations than ever before. Others embraced the positive role of nuclear weapons in even stronger terms. In the words of the nuclear theorist James May, "Nuclear weapons are not all that is needed to make war obsolete, but they have no real substitute." Because they "cheaply and predictably destroy whatever both sides are fighting for" and "destroy the battlefield as well as the enemy," they "are essential" for maintenance of global peace.

American thinking had come full circle. Preventing war, of course, had been the great unrealized goal of both Woodrow Wilson's beloved League of Nations and the United Nations. The new view, which might be called nuclear Wilsonianism, was that nuclear weapons could accomplish what these ambitious global institutions had not—the abolition of war (or, at least, of world war). The general theory of the impossibility of nuclear disarmament and nuclear Wilsonianism are complementary ideas. If you believe that it is impossible to get rid of nuclear weapons, then it is comforting to conclude that they are a boon anyway. Thus, in brief, did the United States, in the forty-six years between Hiroshima and the end of the Cold War, make the passage from abolitionism to a profound and complacent belief in the virtue of nuclear arms.

The post-Cold War nuclear policies of the United States have been easy to misunderstand. Both President Clinton and his predecessor were given to claiming that nuclear danger was a thing of the past. Both presidents also were committed to the policy of gradual reductions. Clinton continued to pay lip service to abolition required by Article VI of the NPT, but as a matter of actual policy, the United States has remained committed to retaining arsenals of thousands of warheads indefinitely. In the early 1990s, the disastrous consequences of this decision were hidden. The non-Russian republics that succeeded the Soviet Union were persuaded to surrender the nuclear weapons that had wound up on their soil, and South Africa's apartheid regime, anticipating majority rule, dismantled its nuclear-weapons program. France began a series of tests but curtailed them in the face of intense public condemnation. Not until the latter half of the decade did the damage become apparent. Deterrence had always been racked by the clashing requirements of both fostering terror and suppressing terror—of doing the first, indeed, to accomplish the second. In the late 1990s, this contradiction began to be played out for the first time on a global scale. The nuclear powers wanted to preserve the terror inspired by their own arsenals while suppressing the creation of arsenals in other countries. A policy of deterrence—whatever its other virtues may or may not have been—had to collide head on with a policy of nonproliferation, and the collision was not long in coming. History confirmed what common sense suggested: possession is incompatible with nonproliferation.

It was in these conditions that the third stage of American strategic thinking—in which deterrence won previously unequalled support and policymakers sought to reconcile it with a policy of nonproliferation—has begun to break apart, and a fourth stage has begun to loom. In this stage, the decision between possession (justified by deterrence) and nonproliferation will have to be made. The fissures dividing the two courses are already deep and wide. They appeared, for instance, in the world's reaction to India's nuclear tests. The United States and a few other countries promptly announced sanctions. But their resolve was weak, the sanctions were soon badly eroded, and Clinton, the leader of the drive for sanctions, soon made the first state visit to India by an American president in nearly a quarter-century. The recent history of relations with Iraq tells the same story. The United States sought to prevent Iraq from acquiring nuclear weapons—first by requiring Iraq to accept UN weapons inspectors and then by the direct use of air strikes. Iraq remained defiant, and now the international community has no reliable instruments for the achievement of its goal. The lesson is clear: Countries that possess nuclear weapons and mean to keep them are in an inherently weak position when they face countries determined to develop these same arms. The possessor nations not only cannot control the debate; they can scarcely get into the conversation.

Nuclear Wilsonianism

IN RESPONSE TO THE CRISIS of this fourth stage, some have frankly decided to resolve the contradiction in favor of proliferation. The political scientist Kenneth Waltz, for example, has argued in detail that it is a mistake to suppose that "new nuclear states will be less responsible and capable of self-control than old ones have been." Hence, he writes, "the gradual spread of nuclear weapons is more to be welcomed than feared." A world "with more nuclear states," he says, will have a more "promising future." And John Mearsheimer of the University of Chicago has called for "managed proliferation" and would welcome acquisition of the bomb by Germany, Japan, and one or more Eastern European countries. In the third stage of the development of nuclear strategy, deterrence was embraced, but only for a few major powers. Just as we can distinguish between a limited and a general theory of impossibility of nuclear disarmament, so we can distinguish between a limited nuclear Wilsonianism and a general nuclear Wilsonianism. The former school holds that nuclear weapons were a benefit—but only for ourselves and a few privileged friends and adversaries. The latter school, to which Waltz and Mearsheimer belong, holds that nuclear weapons are good for all who feel the need for them. A policy shift from limited nuclear Wilsonianism to general nuclear Wilsonianism would parallel the early shift from Baruch's policy of abolition to the policy of deterrence. Just as, in the earlier period, the American government, despairing of abolition, embraced the more modest goal of arms control, so now the government, in despair of repairing the broken policy of nonproliferation, would embrace global nuclearization. Giving up on a goal whose achievement it sees as impossible— nonproliferation—Washington would aim at the more modest but supposedly achievable goal of superintending a stable transition to a nuclearized world. At that point, the United States' embrace of nuclear weapons, having proceeded step by imperceptible step from 1946 down to the present, would have reached its logical destination. Living with nuclear weapons would then mean living with nuclear weapons on an equal basis with all other nations that wished to have them. This position has the merit, at least, of being attainable. An international order "with more nuclear states" can certainly be achieved and is, in fact, the destination toward which the world is drifting. Doing nothing will be sufficient to bring it about.

Those, however, who find the uncontrolled spread of nuclear weapons (together, almost certainly, with other weapons of mass destruction) terrifying and wish to persevere in the more active and difficult policy of nonproliferation will have to accept that it is fundamentally inconsistent with nuclear possession—and then embrace nuclear abolition. A policy that seeks to marry possession with nonproliferation lacks coherence—in the first place morally, but also militarily, diplomatically, and legally. It is a policy divided against itself. Its moving parts work against each other. Its deeds rise up to knock down its words. For the adverse factors that are breaking down nuclear arms control agreements form a vicious circle. Possession by the current nuclear powers breeds proliferation by new powers; proliferation by new powers breeds defenses in the old ones and undercuts the nuclear test ban; defenses upset the balance of nuclear terror and stalemate arms control; the stalemate of arms control confirms the nuclear powers in their possession of nuclear arsenals; confirmed possession breeds proliferation; and so on.

There are, it is true, countervailing tendencies. In many parts of the world, a steady undertow of nuclear sanity has impeded and slowed what otherwise might already have been a global scramble to obtain nuclear arms. The entire continent of South America, for example, is, in accord with the treaty of Tlatelolco, free of nuclear weapons. Brazil and Argentina—two fully nuclear-capable nations that were the last to join that treaty—proceeded quite far down the path to nuclear armament before turning back. The Cold War and its nuclear balance of terror held no attraction as a model in their eyes. They saw greater safety in the continent-wide abolition of nuclear arms. Africa and the South Pacific have made the same decision. The norm in the family of nations is to be nuclear weapon free, not nuclear armed.

Another broad tendency of the post-Cold War period—

democratization—might seem to offer help in reducing nuclear danger. Over the long run, the benefits may appear, but the record so far does not, unfortunately, sustain these hopes. On the evidence, democracy offers no immunity to the nuclear temptation. The world's first nuclear power was, of course, a democracy. Today, six of the world's eight nuclear powers— the United States, the United Kingdom, France, Russia, India, and Israel—are democracies. The democratization of Russia, as noted, did not inspire its democratic adversary, the United States, to seek to liquidate their balance of nuclear terror. In South Asia, democratic India led the way to the nuclearization of the subcontinent.

The second trend, economic globalization, seen by some as a key to peace, likewise has proved, at best, unreliable as a preventer of conflict. The high-water mark of globalization prior to our own time was the first decade and a half of this century—the prelude, as it turned out, to the First World War. The war system (of which nuclear weapons now form a part that is paradoxical, since they render victory and defeat impossible), has always possessed a remarkable degree of autonomy from domestic political systems and the global economic system. The formulas according to which balances of military power and the decisions to go to war are weighed are often eerily devoid of political and economic variables, which they rigorously exclude. This is especially true of the icy, value-free calculations of nuclear strategy, as the failure of the end of the Cold War to liberate the United States and Russia from their mutual nuclear suicide pact make clear.

Indeed, the greatest challenge of the second nuclear age can be defined as one of finding a way of bringing strategic reality into line with a revolutionized political reality. The greatest risk, correspondingly, is that the adjustment will be the reverse—that our politics will take the cue from strategy, and we will find political conflicts to justify our strategies.

Modest successes in one strand or another of nuclear arms control are still possible. Perhaps the Senate will reverse itself and pass the CTBT. Conceivably, Russia, yielding to financial need and US pressure, will accept some modification of the ABM treaty and implement START II. Yet it is getting harder by the day to imagine, given the tight connections between possession and proliferation, that the deterioration and even collapse of the fabric of nuclear arms control can be stopped absent a commitment to abolition. Nor, of course, can we afford to forget that the bare existence of the world's present nuclear arsenals poses the ever present danger of unimaginable catastrophe. Amid the legitimate concern regarding proliferation, it is easy to forget that nuclear peril flows from the nations that possess nuclear weapons, not from those that don't.

The Commitment

BUT WOULD EVEN A COMMITMENT by the nuclear powers to abolition serve to stop proliferation? Or has the world, perhaps without realizing it, proceeded so far down the path of nuclearization that a reversal is impossible, as the nuclear Wilsonians argue?

Even if the will were present, the practical obstacles would be immense. Basic security policies of half a century would have to undergo authentic "bottom-up" reviews in all the great powers. The conventional balances among them would have to be readjusted all over the world. There are few areas of actual or potential regional conflict—for example, East Asia, the Middle East, South Asia—in which the consequences would not be profound. The technical and diplomatic arrangements necessary to undergird abolition would be even more complex than those surrounding current arms negotiations. The inspections regime alone would have to be a masterpiece of science, diplomacy, and statecraft.

We must distinguish, however, between the achievement of the goal—destruction of the world's very last nuclear warhead—and the commitment to the goal. To reverse proliferation and START immediately to radically reduce nuclear danger, the destruction of the last warhead is not necessary. But the commitment by the nuclear powers to do so is. Figures of 2,500 and 1,500 nuclear weapons are already on the Russian–American negotiating table. The stages below these figures should, after suitable study, be delineated. A moment should be identified at which the lesser nuclear powers would be expected to join in the negotiations and begin to draw down their own arsenals. Qualitative steps, beginning with taking nuclear arsenals off their states of alert, would be planned. The expectations that the nuclear powers—once thoroughly embarked on their historic course—had of other nations, including those otherwise inclined to proliferate, would be specified. For example, from the outset, a sort of global freeze might go into effect, under which all countries with nuclear weapons would commit themselves to a process leading to abolition, and countries without nuclear weapons would be required to persevere in their vow not to acquire them. Increasingly severe transparency, inspections, and provisions to control nuclear weapon materials such as enriched uranium and plutonium could be negotiated promptly. The countries that had embarked on nuclear disarmament would agree on steps to take if proliferation was discovered.

Only by imagining this scene of comprehensively transformed expectations does the power of a policy of committing the world to nuclear abolition emerge—not as a remote vision but as an active force from the moment the commitment is made. Great nuclear powers that had committed themselves to nuclear abolition and taken serious steps toward that goal would have a far different attitude toward proliferators than those who plan to depend indefinitely on nuclear weapons for their ultimate security. They would possess a degree of will to enforce non-proliferation that the UN Security Council quite lacks at present. Under the above new conditions, a non-nuclear nation seeking openly to build a nuclear arsenal would arouse the anger and retaliation of the world. Consider again the case of Iraq. Saddam Hussein's strategy has been to kick out the UN inspectors at his pleasure and then play one great power off against another—for instance, Russia and France against the United States and the United Kingdom—as they attempt to reintroduce controls. Such tactics would be at an end if all of these countries had made the commitment to eliminate their nuclear arsenals. Nuclear powers that had jointly agreed to abolish their arsenals and were in the midst of so doing would be planning to rely on that agreement for their security to the same extent that they now rely on their nuclear arsenals. Would they let Saddam have what they were renouncing? They would possess an implacable will, based on the most elemental national interest, to stop proliferation, and they would possess the wherewithal to do it—including, certainly, the resolve and means to defeat and overthrow the offending regime. Curiously, today, it is just because the nuclear powers rely for their security on their own nuclear arsenals that they lack the will to eliminate Saddam's nuclear, chemical, and biological weapons programs.

Is the argument circular? Does it say that countries would have the will to stop proliferation if only they had the will to stop proliferation? Not at all. A real commitment to abolition would alter every equation, including those governing non-proliferation policy. The resolve to proceed to a world without nuclear weapons would be a dominant fact in the life of the world, from which dramatic consequences would flow long before abolition was achieved.

How, though, can the commitment by the United States and the other nuclear powers be signaled, and why should nations that lack nuclear arsenals but think they might eventually need them believe that commitment? Every now and then, a US official will say that the United States wishes to eliminate all nuclear weapons. At the nonproliferation review conference in 2000, the United States joined the other nuclear powers in making an "unequivocal commitment" to eliminate nuclear arms. Statements of this kind scarcely assure the world that the destination is in sight. Nor, of course, should they. A policy is not a dream. A policy is a plan of action that you believe can happen and that you intend to make happen. A president who intends to commit the United States to a policy of negotiating the abolition of nuclear weapons would not announce the fact in answer to a question at a press conference or in the peroration to some speech on an unrelated subject. Abolition is not a goal at which the world will arrive (to paraphrase the old saying about Britain's acquisition of its empire) through a fit of absence of mind. (Only proliferation can be achieved through absent-mindedness.) For such a commitment to be real—credible, to adapt a key word from nuclear strategy—a number of things would have to happen. A president who meant to embark on this path would choose, among others, secretaries of state and defense who publicly agreed with the abolition policy, and would battle to win their confirmation in the Senate. The president would give a solemn address to the nation— the first of many on the subject—announcing the initiative. The president would then launch an interagency review— or perhaps, first, a presidential commission—to study the feasibility and the precise features, in all their immense complexity, of a nuclear weapon-free world. The president would then consult with the United States' allies and approach the two next-greatest nuclear powers, Russia and China, and would, at the same time, seek bipartisan support, without which the initiative could never succeed and probably should not be launched. Nuclear abolition, as people used to say about revolution, is not a tea party, and anything less than a full-scale effort backed by the nation as a whole would be stillborn.

The path to a solution of the nuclear dilemma passes first through domestic politics. The public must give its permission and support. As it happens, in the presidential campaign, George W. Bush of Texas took the initiative with a bold if vague proposal. He has made the welcome statement that "our mutual security need no longer depend on a nuclear balance of terror." Today's large arsenals, he has said, "are the expensive relics of dead conflicts. And they do nothing to make us more secure." He would cut them to an unspecified "lowest possible number." He would also dealert as many nuclear forces as possible. At the same time, though, he would deploy missile defenses far more ambitious than even those favored by the Clinton administration. The problem with Bush's program is that his plans for reductions may collide with his plans for missile defense. He will not be able to get to his low number if missile defenses stoke nuclear buildups in Russia and China. Meanwhile, proliferation remains uncontrolled, and the slide towards nuclear anarchy continues. The way to make sense of this position is to enfold all of these proposals as steps toward the goal commitment to abolition. If Bush's "lowest possible number" is zero for all nations, his defenses will no longer be destabilizing. Whether possessed by the United States alone or, as Reagan suggested, shared with Russia and other nations, missile defenses could help safeguard a world free of nuclear weapons against secret or open nuclear rearmament.

But even a president's intentions alone would not suffice. The nation and the world would have to respond positively. A full-scale debate in the news media, universities, and civil society would have to ensue. Is safety to be found in nuclear arms or in their elimination? Can inspection of an abolition agreement be adequate? What should be the disposition of conventional forces—American and other? Would defense spending rise or fall? Can antinuclear defenses safeguard an abolition agreement? What will be the result of their deployment if offenses are uncontrolled? What should be done if a country violates the agreement? These and many other questions of similar importance have not been answered. They have not as yet, in any national debate worthy of the name, even been asked.

Introduction

xii   Hannah Arendt, *Totalitarianism* (HBJ, New York, 1973).

The Unfinished Twentieth Century

5   Francis Fukuyama, *The End of History and the Last Man* (The Free Press, New York, 1992).

8   "I saw the chance ...," Jonathan Schell "The Nuclear Threat is Not Over Yet," *Newsday*, 12 November 1992.
    "our children are growing up ...," President's Thanksgiving Day proclamation, *New York Times*, 27 November 1997.

9   "nuclear paradigm ... nuclear apartheid," *Foreign Affairs*, Vol. 77, No. 5, September 1998, p.41.

11   Paul Nitze, *New York Times*, 28 October 1999.

12   Joseph Conrad, *Youth/ Heart of Darkness/ The End of the Tether* (Penguin, London, 1995).

13   "It was like a weary pilgrimage ...," p.62.
      "dying slowly ... depair," p.65.
      "splendid leader ... extremist," p.141.
      "All Europe contributed to the making of Kurtz," p.109.

14   "Kurtz discoursed. A voice! a voice! ... emptiness," p.135.
      "The voice was gone ..." p.137.
      "At this hour ...," Joachim Fest, *Hitler* (Harvest, New York,
      1973), p.515.

15   "In the empty immensity of earth ...," *Heart of Darkness*,
      p.61.
      "I let him run on ...," p.78.
      "I resented bitterly ...," p.123.

16   Friedrich Reck-Malleczewen, *Friedrich Percyvaal, Diary of a
      Man in Despair* (Collier Books, New York, 1970), p.27.
      "There was nothing either above or below him ...," *Heart of
      Darkness*, p.132.
      "Exterminate all the brutes," p.110.

17   "I had a vision of him on the stretcher ...," p.142.
      Jessica Reifer, "Evil and the Frustration of Thought:
      Reflections on the Extinction of Mankind," unpublished
      manuscript.

18   George F. Kennan, *The Decline of Bismarck's European Order*
      (Princeton, Princeton, NJ, 1979), p.3.
      Martin Malia, *The Soviet Tragedy* (Free Press, New York,
      1994), p.82.
      Victor Chernov, in Malia, p.81.

19   "if at the beginning of the war ...," Richard Rhodes, *The
      Making of the Atmomic Bomb* (Simon and Schuster, New
      York, 1995), p.176.
      "Even today ... over flowing heart", in Fest, p.64.

20   Roosevelt–Sachs exchange, in Rhodes, p.314.

22   Latvian Latsis, in Fest, p.91.

23   Most Secret Operation Order No. 173, in Rhodes, p.471.
      "the center ... catastrophe," in Fest, p.649.

24   "I suppose that some people ...," in Rhodes, p.471.
      "national catastophe ... to the Finns," Alexander Dalinn,
      German Rule in Russia, 1941–45 (Macmillan, London; Simon
      and Schuster, New York, 1957), p.76.

26   Arendt, *Eichmann in Jerusalem* (Penguin, New York, 1964),
      p.146.

27   "Drop a few bombs ...," in Fest, p.685.

27–8 "no longer so strong ... for the German people," in Fest,
      p.655.

28   "may we perish ... conflagration," in Fest, p.208.

29–30 Hannah Arendt, *The Human Condition* (University of
      Chicago Press, Chicago, 1958), p.241.

31   Larry May and Jerome Kahn (eds), *Hannah Arendt, Twenty
      Years Later* (MIT Press, Cambridge, 1997), p.131.

38   Fred Kaplan, *The Wizards of Armageddon* (Simon and
      Schuster, New York, 1983), p.271.
      "the destruction of nations," in Jonathan Schell, *The Gift of
      Time* (Metropolitan Books, New York, 1998), p.50.

39   Harvard Study Group: Albert Carnesale, Paul Doty, Stanley
      Hoffmann, Samuel P. Huntington, Joseph S. Ny, Jr., Scott
      D. Sagan, *Living With Nuclear Weopons* (Harvard University
      Press, Cambridge, 1983).

43   Ronald Reagan, news conference, transcribed by the *New
      York Times*, 23 October 1987. He made the same statement
      for years, famously at the Geneva Summit in 1985.

The Pitiless Crowbar of Events

56   Aleksandr Solzhenitsyn, speech, "A World Split Apart,"
      Harvard on 8 June 1978. See www.columbia.edu/cu/
      augustine/arch/solzhenitsyn/harvard/1978.

57   Graham Allison, *Avoiding Nuclear-anarchy: Containing the
      Threat of Loose Russian Nuclear Weapons and Nuclear
      Materials* (MIT Press, Cambridge, 1996).

70–1 Hon. Walter B. Slocomb, Undersecretary of Defense, for
      Policy at the Subcommittee on International Security,
      Proliferation, and Federal Servies, Committee on
      Governmental Affairs, US Senate, 12 February 1997.

76   McGeorge Bundy, *Danger and Survival* (Random House,
      New York, 1988), p.166.

78   Paul Bracken, *Fire in the East* (Harper Collins, New York,
      1999), p.105.

79   "Because we cannot ... be regained," Harvard Study Group,
      p.5.

80   "If the political pre-conditions ... magnify this effect," p.190.

82   Slocomb, US Senate.
      James May, "Fearsome Security," *Brookings Review*,
      Summer, 1995.

85   "new nuclear states ... promising future," Scott Sagan and
      Kenneth Waltz, *The Spread of Nuclear Weapons* (Norton,
      New York, 1997), p.44.
      "managed proliferation," John Mearsheimer, "Managed
      Proliferation," *The Atlantic Monthly*, August, 1990.

94   George W. Bush for President website:
      http://www.georgewbush.com/speeches/natlsec.asp.

Also by Jonathan Schell

The Village of Ben Suc
The Military Half
The Time of Illusion
The Fate of the Earth
The Abolition
History in Sherman Park
Observing the Nixon Years
Writing in Time
The Real War
The Gift of Time